President Reagan

CONGRESSIONAL QUARTERLY INC.
1414 22ND STREET, N.W.
WASHINGTON, D.C. 20037

Congressional Quarterly Inc.

Congressional Quarterly Inc., an editorial research service and publishing company, serves clients in the fields of news, education, business and government. It combines specific coverage of Congress, government and politics by Congressional Quarterly with the more general subject range of an affiliated service, Editorial Research Reports.

Congressional Quarterly was founded in 1945 by Henrietta and Nelson Poynter. Its basic periodical publication was and still is the CQ *Weekly Report*, mailed to clients every Saturday. A cumulative index is published quarterly.

CQ also publishes a variety of books. The CQ *Almanac*, a compendium of legislation for one session of Congress, is published every spring. *Congress and the Nation* is published every four years as a record of government for one presidential term. Other books include paperbacks on public affairs and textbooks for college political science classes.

The public affairs books are designed as timely reports to keep journalists, scholars and the public abreast of developing issues, events and trends.

They include such recent titles as *Health Policy* and the second editions of *Energy Policy* and *Defense Policy*. College textbooks, prepared by outside scholars and published under the CQ Press imprint, include such recent titles as *The Supreme Court; Congress Reconsidered, Second Edition;* and *Energy, Politics and Public Policy*.

CQ Direct Research is a consulting service that performs contract research and maintains a reference library and query desk for clients.

Editorial Research Reports covers subjects beyond the specialized scope of Congressional Quarterly. It publishes reference material on foreign affairs, business, education, cultural affairs, national security, science and other topics of news interest. Service to clients includes a 6,000-word report four times a month, bound and indexed semi-annually. Editorial Research Reports publishes paperback books in its fields of coverage. Founded in 1923, the service merged with Congressional Quarterly in 1956.

Library of Congress Cataloging in Publication Data

Main entry under title:

President Reagan.

Bibliography: p.
Includes index.
1. Reagan, Ronald. 2. Bush, George, 1924- . 3. Cabinet officers—United States—Biography. 4. Presidents—United States—Election—1980. 5. United States—Politics and government—1981- . 6. United States—Politics and government—1977-1981. I. Congressional Quarterly, inc.

E877.P73   973.927'092'4   81-2283
ISBN 0-87187-172-6   AACR2

TABLE OF CONTENTS

Editor: Nancy Lammers
Supervisory Editor: John L. Moore
Contributors: Irwin B. Arieff, Christopher Buchanan, Nadine Cohodas, Rhodes Cook, Reid Dulberger, Gail Gregg, Kathy Koch, Larry Light, Alan Murray, John Noukas, Andy Plattner, Judy Sarasohn, Dale Tate, Pat Towell, Elizabeth Wehr, Michael D. Wormser
Design: Mary McNeil
Cover: Richard Pottern
Cover Photograph: Tony Lopez/*St. Petersburg Times*
Indexer: Nancy Nawor Blanpied
Production Manager: I. D. Fuller
Assistant Production Manager: Maceo Mayo

Editor's Note. President Reagan offers the reader a thorough introduction to the 40th president of the United States — the man, his philosophy and his record. The opening chapter discusses Reagan's early legislative initiatives, especially his proposals for spending and tax cuts, and his prospects for getting them through Congress. Other chapters examine the likely impact of Reagan judicial appointments on the court system and recap the 1980 presidential election. Profiles are provided of both Reagan and Vice President George Bush, as well as of Cabinet members and key White House aides. *President Reagan*, like other CQ public affairs books, is designed as a timely report to keep journalists, scholars and the public abreast of developing issues, events and trends. The latter part of the book contains the transcripts of Reagan's recent major speeches and his debate with Jimmy Carter, a chronology of the election and a collection of the president's statements on various issues. There is also a selected bibliography.

Introduction

The day that Ronald Reagan became the 40th president of the United States, the federal government was spending at an annual rate $2,600 for every man, woman and child in the United States. The *Federal Register* was publishing some 98,000 pages annually of new regulations that touched, in some way, on the lives of every citizen. Americans were paying 12.5 percent more for goods and services than they had a year earlier.

In Reagan's conservative philosophy, the growth of federal spending and regulation under two decades of Democratic rule had spurred inflation, slowed productivity and caused such serious dislocations as the near-bankrupt condition of Detroit's automobile industry. In his third bid for the presidency, the 69-year-old Reagan appeared to have convinced a majority of Americans that it was time for something very different.

"In this present crisis, government is not the solution to our problem," Reagan said in his Jan. 20 inaugural address. Sounding the dominant theme of his campaign, Reagan declared that government itself was "the problem."

A Mandate for Change?

The 1980 election gave Reagan and his party the opportunity of a lifetime. Republicans won both the White House and a majority in the Senate. It was the first time the party enjoyed majority status on Capitol Hill since 1953-55, when Republicans held narrow margins in both houses of Congress. The combined presence of 192 Republicans and more than 30 avowedly conservative Democrats in the House gave Reagan an ideological majority in that body sufficient for a strong and popular president.

But the central question was whether 1981 was, in fact, the beginning of a new political era as in 1932, or a more ephemeral change. The 1952 Republican congressional majority lasted only two years.

Reagan and his associates viewed their 1980 electoral victory as a national mandate for conservatism. Political scientists questioned, however, whether the November vote was more for Reagan than it was against his predecessor, Jimmy Carter.

Throughout the Carter presidency, White House officials and Cabinet secretaries had boasted that Carter had met head-on every difficult issue — "every miserable issue conceivable," in the words of his vice president, Walter F. Mondale. With only mixed success, Carter tried to force congressional decisions on such controversial issues as energy pricing and production, and balancing the budget. Carter's moralistic, sometimes fitful style irritated members of Congress. He told Americans there were no easy answers to the nation's problems.

Perhaps the most politically damaging event in Carter's presidency was ending at the moment that Reagan became president. Fifty-two U. S. diplomatic and military personnel were flying out of Iran after having been held hostage by anti-American militants there for more than 14 months. Many commentators felt that without that crisis Carter would have had a much better chance of winning a second term. Their release began Reagan's presidency on a high note.

Reagan's message to the public was far more reassuring than Carter's. "There is nothing wrong with America that — together — we can't fix," he told Congress.

The national high continued in the first month of the presidency as Reagan aides orchestrated a sweeping reorientation of federal economic policy. Early polls showed that Americans were pleased with their new president's performance, but also that their expectations might be unrealistically high. A *Washington Post*/ABC News poll the last week of February showed that most people thought they would be significantly better off after Reagan had been in office for a year.

First Steps on the Economy

Reagan's transition operation had been criticized for employing more people, and costing more money, than ever before. By Inauguration Day the transition leaders were very far from realizing their early promises of filling top-level policy positions throughout the government. But their stress in the transition period on policy development had more effect. On economic matters, the Reagan administration did "hit the ground running," as presidential counselor Edwin Meese III had promised.

Reagan's first official acts as president were to cancel all federal hiring, retroactive to the Nov. 4 election, and to freeze pending regulations until they could be reviewed. On Feb. 18 the president brought to Congress an ambitious plan to slow the growth of government and return billions of dollars in taxes to workers and businesses.

1

Four years earlier, Carter also had reworked his predecessor's budget, adding a $19 billion "economic stimulus" package and trimming some costs. But Reagan's proposed reductions in Carter's budget were both larger and broader. And his tax proposals were based on the controversial "supply-side" economic theory, which assumed that substantial tax cuts would induce people to save that extra money instead of spending it and worsening inflation. The increased savings, it was thought, would be invested, thus heightening productivity, creating new jobs and lowering prices.

It was a risky strategy. Reagan's vice president, George Bush, had characterized the theory on which it was based as "voodoo economics" when he ran against Reagan for the Republican nomination in 1980. Republicans worried privately that the president had committed too much to untested economic theories. The administration upped the ante by deliberately fanning, in public speeches and private briefings, high hopes for the president's economic plan.

The risk, of course, was that the plan would not work, or that it would fail to show results quickly enough to keep the nation's optimistic expectations from going sour. Administration economists admitted, off the record, that a "weak" economy in 1981 could become their "Achilles' heel."

Energy and food costs — two of the most visible forms of consumer spending — were expected to rise sharply by midyear, if not before. The administration's economic predictions assumed rapidly declining interest rates, but a week after the Feb. 18 message the Federal Reserve System announced new restrictions on the supply of money. Such restrictions usually caused interest rates to rise because borrowers had to compete for a shrinking supply of money.

A second uncertainty was whether Americans would really lower their demands on the federal government. The Post/ABC poll showed that most Americans backed Reagan's budget cuts by 3 to 1, but the poll also showed that these same people overwhelmingly disapproved of cuts in a range of specific programs.

Nevertheless, Reagan's aggressive young budget director, David A. Stockman, was credited with extraordinary powers for having crafted a $41 billion budget-cut plan for 83 major programs in such a short time. The administration's swift action kept interest groups and potential opponents in Congress off balance. The depth of the nation's economic problems was expected to be a brake on opponents reluctant to appear to be spoilers.

Other Issues

Reagan's opposition to abortion and his other conservative stands on social issues that appealed to his supporters on the far right were not much in evidence during his first weeks in office. Though Reagan spokesmen said otherwise, it appeared that the president had sidelined such politically explosive issues, so as not to deflect attention from his economic program.

In foreign affairs, the Reagan administration issued stern warnings to the Soviet Union to refrain from interfering in the internal political troubles of Poland and El Salvador. Despite campaign promises to lift Carter's unpopular embargo on most sales of U.S. grain to the Soviet Union, Reagan did not immediately do so. Farm leaders were told that the president expected the Soviet Union to make certain concessions, such as showing an interest in renegotiating the Carter administration's arms limitation (SALT) agreement, which the Senate had never ratified.

Substantially downgrading Carter's emphasis on human rights, the Reagan administration instead stressed that it would back those nations that struggled against "international terrorism" instigated by communists. Military aid was greatly increased to the rightist government of El Salvador, under siege from guerrilla forces that Reagan officials maintained were being supplied by Cuba.

—Elizabeth Wehr
March 1981

Reagan and Congress

Five days after his first inauguration, on March 9, 1933, Franklin D. Roosevelt sent a major banking bill to Congress and had it back at the White House for his signature by dinner time the same day.

Though none could wish for the economic disasters that made the legislators grasp so eagerly at that measure, presidents since Roosevelt must have envied the ease with which he moved bills through a largely uncritical Congress in his first term.

It wasn't likely to be that easy for Ronald Reagan.

The Capitol, which loomed behind the nation's 40th president as he took the oath of office Jan. 20, housed the biggest potential obstacle between Reagan and his vision of a leaner, less ambitious federal government.

Like any president, Reagan faced the job of moving difficult legislation through a difficult institution. But unlike his Democratic predecessor, Jimmy Carter, Reagan had a second task: to establish a new majority coalition in Congress. He needed that coalition to pass his bills and to solidify the gains Republicans made in the 1980 elections.

No Easy Task

Although Reagan began his term with the customary pledges of bipartisan cooperation, his task was not likely to be easy. "When you're rearranging national priorities for the first time in 40 years, you've got problems," remarked Sen. Paul Laxalt, R-Nev., Reagan's close friend whom the new president asked to serve as his "eyes and ears" on Capitol Hill. *(Laxalt profile, p. 6)*

Reagan clearly had advantages over his predecessor. More than one Carter loyalist expressed the belief that the former president "softened up" Congress by forcing members to deal with such issues as balancing the budget and energy pricing and production. "The president took on every miserable issue conceivable," says former Vice President Walter F. Mondale.

Reagan's assets, evident well before the inauguration, included an active network of congressional contacts, a team of seasoned lobbyists led by Washington veteran Max L. Friedersdorf and the easy "insider" style of the president and his top aides.

Members of both parties expressed delight with Reagan's festive dinners for Washington political and business leaders during the transition; his decision to retain Mike

Mansfield, former Democratic Senate majority leader, as ambassador to Japan; and his aides' early contacts with key members of Congress and their staffs.

Reagan also expected to count on powerful party loyalty among Republicans, who have not enjoyed majority status in Congress since 1953-55, when they narrowly held both chambers. In 1981 the GOP had a 53-46 majority in the Senate. And, although Democrats held the majority in the House, Republicans claimed a "working conservative majority" there.

"I sense a tremendous desire to present a united front," Friedersdorf told a National Press Club breakfast Jan. 5, 1981. "I don't think they're going to blow it."

Nature of the Problems

One of Reagan's biggest advantages as he began his term was the sense of both parties in Congress that the nation's problems had reached a very serious level indeed. It was anticipated that a key factor favoring Reagan's success likely would be his stress on economic, regulatory and military issues, which have the broadest political appeal. Many Republican goals in these areas were "not dramatically hostile to Democratic sympathies," said Thomas S. Foley, D-Wash., House majority whip.

On the other hand, abortion, busing and school prayer — the divisive social issues so important to Reagan's most conservative supporters — looked as if they had been moved to the bottom of the GOP congressional agenda. "We're not on any political kamikaze trips," said Laxalt.

Prominent Republicans, such as Robert Dole, R-Kan., chairman of the Senate Finance Committee, publicly advised Reagan to "not get off on these single issues" until economic problems are in hand "because we can dissipate a lot of political strength."

Many Democrats noted that if they appear too obstructionistic, Reagan and the Republicans could, in the 1982 elections, accuse them of wrecking the nation's chances for economic recovery. "We don't want to look like spoilers, and we really don't want to *be* spoilers either," Foley stressed.

To hope the Republicans fail badly and the nation's economic situation worsens "is a very crabbed and perverse sort of politics," he said. Success, Foley added, would "help anybody in office." That sentiment was reinforced by

House Speaker Thomas P. O'Neill Jr., D-Mass., who declared shortly after the election that "America comes first; party comes second."

Carter's Difficulties

Before he had been in office six months, President Carter had set congressional teeth on edge with a series of miscalculations from which his reputation never fully recovered.

The record showed that he had wrung important legislation from Congress. Yet to the end of his term members, including many from his own party, continued to complain of real or imagined defects in his congressional relations. He started by bombarding the lawmakers with more legislation than they could handle expeditiously.

And many members believed Carter continued to run "against Washington" — and them — even after his election. Few forgot his threats to go around them and appeal to their constituents directly through national television if Congress balked at his bills.

One area in which Carter trod upon congressional sensibilities was his early campaign against what he considered wasteful dams and other water projects. In 1977 he devised a "hit list" of projects he opposed. Four of the projects on the final list of 23 were in Louisiana, home state of Russell B. Long, then the powerful Democratic chairman of the Senate Finance Committee.

Some complaints about Carter's style seemed merely humorous — such as O'Neill's public grousing about a sparse coffee-and-Danish breakfast for congressional leaders early in Carter's term. ("There were lumberjack breakfasts at the White House after that — bacon, sausages, eggs, grits, potatoes, you name it," according to Foley. And, contrary to rumor, no bills for the food were sent to members.)

There were more serious complaints, though, of poor coordination between departmental and White House lobbyists and unanticipated reversals of presidential policy, such as Carter's abandonment of his $50 tax rebate plan or the change in his views on natural gas deregulation.

From the viewpoint of members of Congress, Carter's worst problem was probably that he did not seek their advice early enough or often enough. "The last time I counted, there were a hundred prima donnas in the Senate," Dole remarked. The senator said he did not mean to be critical of his colleagues but wanted only to emphasize that "we were elected, too. We believe our ears are fairly close to the ground."

Complicated Issues

By drafting his massive energy package and other bills with little congressional input, the president deprived himself of important political expertise and good will.

But Dan Tate, Carter's chief Senate lobbyist, believed that his boss's reputation suffered because of the inherent complexities of the issues Carter chose to confront. Tate conceded that the authors of the 1977 energy package "played their cards pretty close to the vest." But he maintained that "energy is so controversial that a maximum degree of consultation" would not have erased the difficulties for Carter's plan.

Foley said he found issues these days enormously more complicated than when he came to Congress in 1965. He noted that the civil rights issue then facing the legislators was whether the right to vote should be federally guaranteed for blacks and Hispanics. In the 1980s members have been called on to deal with more ambiguous policies such as affirmative action and racial quotas.

Institutional Difficulties

Institutional changes of the last decade, such as the decline of the rigid seniority system and slackening party loyalty, also made Carter's relations with Congress more uncertain. "There is no such thing as cutting a deal before a bill and having it go through like a dose of salts," said Tate.

In 1981 nearly half the members of both the House and Senate had been there four years or less. The fast turnover has resulted in "a decline in institutional memory" and "reduced specialization" among members, said Thomas Mann, co-director of the American Enterprise Institute Congress Project and assistant director of the American Political Science Association. And, "because every person who gets elected to Congress wants to hit the floor . . . ready to legislate," there are more floor amendments, resulting in "sloppy legislation," Mann told an AEI conference in December 1980.

Foley suggested that rebuilding party loyalty could mitigate some of those problems. But he saw no possibility of going back "to the days when Lyndon Johnson ran the Senate and Sam Rayburn ran the House, and they went down and saw President Eisenhower. The three of them came to a tripartite agreement, and that was the end of that."

In addition, special interest groups had become a chronic complication. "Those people have a direct pipeline to Congress," said one prominent Democrat. "They didn't fold up their tents and steal away Nov. 5."

Reagan's Assets

Reagan likely faced all of these challenges as well as the special problems of a party more experienced in opposition than coalition-building. Several conservative junior House Republicans were well-known in the 96th Congress for their distaste for their leadership's compromises with Democrats and their demands for ideological purity.

In the Senate during confirmation hearings on Reagan's Cabinet choices, there were indications of divisions to come. A few very conservative Republicans, such as Sens. Charles E. Grassley and Roger W. Jepsen of Iowa, pointedly reminded Cabinet designees of Reagan campaign promises to balance the budget and end the Russian grain embargo. And conservative Republicans Jesse Helms and John East of North Carolina voted against Caspar W. Weinberger for secretary of defense, arguing that his views were not sufficiently hard-line. *(Cabinet appointments, p. 39)*

The task before Republicans likely would be to prevent those internal divisions from widening, while drawing enough Democrats into their camp to pass legislation. In that regard Laxalt, scheduled to sit in on both congressional leadership and White House policy sessions, was expected to be a unique asset for Reagan.

It was generally understood that Laxalt was assigned to the task of "keeping the Right from tearing things apart early on," as one Reagan administration official put it. Laxalt agreed with a suggestion that building a new coalition would be a major Republican goal.

White House Lobbying Staff

Max L. Friedersdorf, who left the chairmanship of the Federal Election Commission to head the White House legislative liaison staff, described himself as "the ham in the sandwich" between Capitol Hill and President Reagan. He was well equipped to fill that role, having served in a similar capacity for Presidents Nixon and Ford and having worked for Republicans on the Hill. To supplement his own wide acquaintanceship with members of Congress, he hired experienced staff members with many Hill contacts and the sure knowledge of how to "tell a member what he needs to know in a minute," as one congressional aide remarked. *(Friedersdorf biography, p. 70)*

Following are short biographies of the other congressional liaison staff members:

Hired as chief Senate lobbyist was **Powell Moore**, who began working in Washington in 1964 as an aide to former Sen. Richard B. Russell, D-Ga. (1933-71). He worked in the Nixon administration as deputy director of public information at the Department of Justice and as a White House lobbyist in 1973-75.

Moore's staff was made up of:

Pamela J. Turner, 36, who spent the previous five years as top aide to Sen. John Tower, R-Texas. Before that she worked eight years in a similar post with former Sen. Edward J. Gurney, R-Fla. (House 1963-69; Senate 1969-74).

David Swanson, 38, a Senate Energy Committee staff member from 1978 to 1981. From 1974 to 1977 he served as an aide to former Rep. John B. Anderson, R-Ill. (1961-81).

William J. Gribbin, 37, an analyst from 1977 to 1981 for the Senate Republican Policy Committee, where he specialized in health, welfare and Social Security. He also was an aide to former Sen. James L. Buckley, Cons. R-N.Y. (1971-77).

Named chief House lobbyist was **Kenneth M. Duberstein**, 36, former director of business-government relations for the Committee for Economic Development, a Washington-based think tank. Duberstein also worked for former Sen. Jacob K. Javits, R-N.Y. (House, 1947-54; Senate, 1957-81), and as director of congressional relations for the General Services Administration and the Department of Labor under Nixon and Ford.

Members of his staff were:

Nancy Risque, 34, a former lobbyist for Standard Oil of Ohio.

David Wright, 31, administrative assistant from 1977 to 1981 to Rep. William C. Wampler, R-Va., and previously an aide at the House Agriculture Committee.

John Dressendorfer, 40, chief lobbyist from 1974 to 1981 for the Uniformed Services University of the Health Sciences in Bethesda, Md., with prior experience in lobbying for the Navy and for the deputy secretary of defense.

M. B. Oglesby, 38, from 1979 to 1981 a staff member of the House Commerce Committee specializing in transportation. From 1977 to 1979 he was deputy and acting director of the Washington office of the state of Illinois.

Serving as the lobbying office's "inside man," tracking White House developments, was **Paul Russo**, 37. Russo directed congressional relations for the Reagan for President Committee and was special assistant to Gov. Reagan in 1973-75. Russo also had worked for Rep. Thomas B. Evans Jr., R-Del.

Two liaison staff members who went with Friedersdorf from the Federal Election Commission to the White House were legislative counsel **Sherrie Cooksey**, 27, former minority counsel for the Senate Rules Committee, and administrative assistant **Nancy Kennedy**, 41.

California Experience

The lessons Reagan learned as governor of California for eight years were expected to help him avoid the pitfalls Carter encountered during his first term as president.

Ed Salzman, editor of the political monthly *California Journal*, said Reagan had to scale down or reverse initiatives that were unacceptable to the state Legislature, and his manner became less confrontational. "He stopped referring to legislators as 'those bastards,' and discovered the grand art of compromise," Salzman said.

Though Reagan and Carter both were forced by political realities to change course on significant issues, Reagan came away with a reputation for pragmatism, while Carter often was labeled indecisive. Part of the reason for the difference was that during all but two years of his eight as governor, Reagan was dealing with a Democratic legislature. Expectations were lower than those for Carter and the Democratic Congress.

Carter also tended to present his proposals in moralistic terms, making public retreat more difficult. In 1977, for example, he called the energy crisis the "moral equivalent of war."

Reagan seemed to weather reverses more comfortably. As an illustration of his pleasant style, Salzman recalled that Reagan once vowed his feet were "set in concrete on withholding" state income taxes from payrolls. Later, when Reagan retreated on the issue, he joked that "the sound you hear is the concrete cracking."

Rep. Anthony C. Beilenson, D-Calif., was a prime author of the landmark 1971 California welfare reform bill passed during Reagan's term as governor. The liberal Beilenson did not share Reagan's philosophy, and he believed that the governor was "not terribly interested" in the sort of details that can make major differences in how a program works.

However, he found Reagan a "quick study" when the governor sat in on general discussions of the final compromise bill, and he warmly praised Reagan's top aides, including White House Counselor Edwin Meese III, who worked with California legislators on the measure. "Very straight, very bright, very hard-working," Beilenson said of the Reagan staff. Salzman predicted that President Reagan would find Congress "more partisan, stiffer" than the California Legislature.

Seeking Congressional Support

Reagan began courting Congress extraordinarily early. In 1977 he organized a political action committee called Citizens for the Republic to finance Republican candidates for state and national offices. During the 1980 campaign Reagan backers in Congress created a network of congressional advisory committees to develop policy positions for him and to advise him of key concerns of constituents before his campaign stops.

During the fall of 1980, to dramatize their connections, Reagan and congressional Republicans staged a "media event" on the steps of the Capitol, where they declared their support for a broadly worded "compact" of principles.

Reagan's courtship of Congress intensified after he won the election, when the opinions of Dole and Sens. John Tower, Texas, Strom Thurmond, S.C., and other Republican members heavily influenced Reagan's Cabinet choices. According to transition insiders, Dole handpicked Agriculture Secretary John R. Block and influenced the choice of Donald T. Regan for Treasury secretary.

Republican members also were invited to advise departmental transition teams. Reagan aides promised regular bipartisan leadership meetings with the president. And Reagan himself "met privately with a number of senators . . . Democrats and Republicans . . . touching all the right keys," Dole said. Among others, Reagan met with Long and Sen. Ernest F. Hollings, D-S.C., ranking minority member of the Senate Budget Committee.

Courting Dole

Dole's cooperation likely would be essential to Reagan's economic program, and the president clearly was not planning to make the same mistakes that Carter made with Long.

As Dole observed, his Finance Committee had jurisdiction over "about half" of the entitlement programs that "everyone" wanted to control. Such programs, which included Medicare, Medicaid and Social Security, "entitled" to benefits everyone who met the statutory eligibility standards. The programs accounted for about 60 percent of the federal budget.

The food stamp program, another target of budget-trimmers, was under the jurisdiction of a second Dole-chaired panel, the Senate Agriculture Subcommittee on Nutrition.

Elizabeth Hanford Dole, the senator's wife, won a senior White House post as presidential assistant for public liaison. The position, filled by Anne Wexler in the Carter administration, had been a politically oriented one, and Mrs. Dole was charged with building support for the president's policies among ethnic, women's and other groups.

Elizabeth Dole, a highly respected attorney and former Federal Trade Commissioner, was clearly qualified for the job in her own right. But, just as clearly, each Dole benefited from the other's position.

Reagan Style

Congress had an early taste of Reagan's congressional liaison style during the lame-duck session of the 96th Congress. Tom C. Korologos, a veteran of the Nixon and Ford congressional liaison offices and a prominent Washington lobbyist, won high marks for professionalism as he made known the positions of the president-elect.

Much of the "ticklish" job his transition unit performed, Korologos said, consisted of fending off congressional requests for Reagan positions on legislation to avoid the appearance of usurping President Carter's prerogatives. For issues that could not be avoided, such as an appropriations rider to end the grain embargo and a congressional pay raise, Korologos sought a "Reagan" position at the daily 7 a.m. conference of Meese, Reagan's domestic affairs adviser Martin Anderson and Edwin L. Harper, deputy director-designate for the Office of Management and Budget.

In other notable ways, the Reagan administration also did things differently from Carter from the start. Officials said they did not plan to load up Congress with more legislation than it could digest — as Carter did in his ambitious first year.

And while Carter placed an inexperienced Georgia friend, Frank B. Moore, in the critical position of White House legislative liaison, Reagan chose Friedersdorf, a knowledgeable Washingtonian who was a congressional lobbyist for Presidents Ford and Nixon. Friedersdorf, in turn, turned largely to Capitol Hill for his staff of associates.

Similarly, Reagan relied on old friends in Congress to help smooth the way for his programs. In that endeavor, no one took on a heavier burden than Sen. Paul Laxalt.

LAXALT: REAGAN'S MAN ON CAPITOL HILL

Just 65 minutes after his plane touched down at Andrews Air Force Base Nov. 17, 1980, for his first post-election visit to Washington, President-elect Reagan already was sequestered in a lengthy private meeting with Laxalt.

The next morning, as Reagan walked out the door of his downtown Washington quarters for a series of meetings with congressional leaders, Laxalt was by his side. As Reagan wended his way from office to office in the Capitol building, Vice President-elect George Bush followed a respectable 10 paces behind his future boss.

But Laxalt never was more than an arm's length away from Reagan.

Laxalt's performance as Reagan's Washington tour guide underlined the close relationship the Nevada Republican had developed over the years with the new president and the key role he likely would play in the Reagan administration.

"He will be the strongest outside influence on Reagan of anybody," Reagan aide Michael K. Deaver predicted to reporters Nov. 18. "The governor respects him and they have a friendship that goes back as far as any in politics for the governor. He will rely on Paul's advice."

Laxalt was expected to be included in the uppermost circle of Reagan policy advisers, a group of about six or seven individuals whom campaign officials likened to a super-Cabinet.

It was widely predicted the group would run the government just as a board of directors runs a corporation, with Reagan acting as the chairman and chief executive officer.

Reagan's 'Eyes and Ears'

While this group was expected to include counselor to the president, Edwin Meese III, and the top Reagan Cabinet officers as well as Laxalt, it was not expected to include any other member of Congress.

In a post-election interview, Laxalt said he saw his job as being Reagan's "eyes and ears in the Senate." But the job, he said, would entail more than liaison between the president and Congress; he also would serve as a sort of two-way conduit between the legislative and executive branches. Laxalt would advise the president. After a policy or program proposal had been formulated, he would help the administration present it to Congress. Then, after the proposal had been submitted, he would help ease its way toward enactment.

"I've been Gov. Reagan's man in the Senate for the past five years anyway, so there's really nothing new about that," he said. But he acknowledged that the position he and Reagan envisioned was "rather unique and probably unprecedented" in Senate history. Although he would not be part of the formal Senate GOP leadership, he expected to work along with the party's elected leaders in promoting President Reagan's programs, he said.

"I didn't want to go into the Cabinet," Laxalt said, explaining how he and Reagan formulated his role. "Nor did I want any other job in the administration. I wanted to remain here in the Senate.

"Being a part of the leadership was a problem," he said. "So I float."

Stepping on Toes?

One of the most ticklish aspects of Laxalt's new job was structuring it so that he wouldn't step on the toes of the Senate's regular Republican leaders — Majority Leader Howard H. Baker Jr., Tenn., and Majority Whip Ted Stevens, Alaska.

Both Laxalt and Baker maintained their jobs would not overlap, yet in previous Congresses their functions were performed by a single individual — the majority leader.

Despite the generally conservative voting records of both Baker and Stevens, the Senate's Republican right wing had in the past portrayed Baker, especially, as too eager to accommodate the party's more moderate members. In contrast, Laxalt had chosen to hew strictly to the conservative line and to oppose accommodating the moderates.

The political differences between Baker and Laxalt, however slight to an outsider, led to something of a rivalry between them. In January 1978, for example, Laxalt warned that any Republican senator who backed ratification of the Panama Canal treaties "wouldn't have a snowball's chance in hell" of securing the Republican Party's presidential nomination. Although he didn't specifi-

cally name Baker, the remark clearly was aimed at convincing Baker to oppose the treaties' ratification.

Laxalt went on to lead the Republican opposition to the canal treaties. Baker, on the other hand, voted for them. The treaties were ratified in the spring of 1978 by the razor-thin margin of one vote. When Baker subsequently declared his presidential candidacy, the conservatives — including Laxalt — hounded him over his Panama vote until his campaign foundered.

Later, when the Reagan campaign was looking for a moderate GOP vice presidential candidate to "balance" the Republican ticket, Baker seemed a natural choice. But the conservatives once again mounted a campaign to discredit him by challenging his conservative credentials. As a result, Reagan was obliged to turn to Bush instead of Baker to avoid losing his most loyal supporters.

At about the same time, Senate conservatives quietly were urging Laxalt to challenge Baker for the majority leader spot. But when Baker asked Laxalt if he planned to run, Laxalt again promised Baker his vote.

After Reagan's Nov. 4 victory — and after Republican senators found they would be a majority in the Senate instead of a minority — Baker once more telephoned Laxalt to ask whether he would oppose him in the leadership contest. Once more, Laxalt told him he would not and promised him his vote.

Baker then asked Laxalt if he would nominate him for majority leader. Laxalt agreed. Later that day, when Reagan was asked at a press conference whether he would be happy with Baker as majority leader, the president-elect looked to Laxalt, standing behind him, before responding that Baker had his confidence.

'No Sharp Divisions'

According to Laxalt, no tension existed between the two men during their years working together in the Senate, apart from some friendly political ones.

"We really haven't been rivals," Laxalt said. "I've never had any designs on the leadership post. I've been asked by conservatives to run. But I've declined." His decision to nominate Baker, he said, "really seals the bargain" for cooperation between the two men.

In any case, there were "no sharp divisions" between him and Baker ideologically, he maintained. Apart from conflicting votes on the Panama Canal treaties, District of Columbia voting rights, establishment of a new Department of Energy and creation of a new Education Department, Laxalt said, "I suppose our respective voting records wouldn't be that different."

Laxalt maintained there was "no way" in which his role in the Reagan administration would conflict with that of Baker or Stevens. "I don't consider it to be any muscle position or power-broker position. What I want to do is help the Hill and the president straighten this country out."

"There is no way I can assume any role in being point man on a particular piece of legislation," he continued. "This should be left to the elected leaders. But if I see a trouble spot, I imagine I could play a role there. I also hope the leaders will call on me from time to time, if they need me."

Baker told the Associated Press Nov. 10 he "welcomed" the Laxalt appointment. "It is an essential role and an appropriate role," he said. "I'll have my hands full here trying to lead a Republican majority in the Senate. I think for him to help us interface with the Republican administration is very, very useful."

"We are looking forward to the Laxalt appointment," Sen. Stevens told a reporter following a Nov. 18 meeting between Reagan and Senate Republicans. "We told the president-elect we are delighted to have a man in the Senate who has this kind of relationship with him."

A Question of Leverage

When asked to comment on how he thought the arrangement would work out, the Senate majority leader of the 96th Congress, Robert C. Byrd, D-W.Va., smirked before responding: "I'll just leave that to the historians and the political pundits." Byrd was elected in December 1980 to lead the Democratic opposition as the Senate minority leader for the 97th Congress.

"He [Laxalt] has a good personality," commented Alan Cranston, D-Calif., the minority whip. "He's got a personality that fits into that kind of a role. The fact that he's nominating Sen. Baker and can keep the conservatives behind him should help the situation. Of course, that gives him a lot of leverage with Baker as well, doesn't it?"

With the Republicans in control of the Senate, the ability to keep the party's conservative and more moderate factions united behind the president's legislative program would be the key to enactment of Republican legislative goals. In the likely event that Laxalt and Baker found themselves on opposite sides of the fence on some key issue, Laxalt's ability to control the conservatives' votes could thus give him the means to keep Baker under his control.

Laxalt's colleagues suspected the primary weapon in his political arsenal would be his good nature. By all accounts, he had gained the respect and admiration of individuals from all segments of the political spectrum.

"He is a folksy, genial, open guy," commented a liberal Democrat who asked not to be identified. "He's a charmer. I consider him a guy I probably disagree with more than anyone else in the Senate. Yet I get along with him just great. He's as political as the next guy. He's just better able to gloss it over."

"He's probably the Senate's most popular man," commented Margo Carlisle, executive director of the Senate Steering Committee, a group of senators concerned with conservative causes. "He's a man who's both palatable and principled."

On touchy issues such as the Panama Canal treaties, common situs picketing legislation and labor law reform, she said, "he has taken very controversial positions, but if anything, he gains friends during the fight.... He doesn't let himself get irritated or angry. He doesn't lose his temper. He doesn't do anything to make enemies, because his sense of perspective is good. He just realizes that there's no reason to develop enmities over small things, that friendship is just as important."

Longtime Friends

Laxalt's friendship with Reagan began in 1964 when the two men campaigned for Barry Goldwater for president. Laxalt went on to chair Reagan's presidential campaign in both 1976 and 1980. The two men have much in common. Both are former governors of Western states. Both are well-spoken, personally charming and handsome individuals. Both are unabashed conservatives.

Ironically, Laxalt — but for Reagan's apparent willingness to accept his advisers' judgment over his own — might

Reagan meets with Sens. Baker, left, and Laxalt.

have been the vice president rather than the junior senator from Nevada. Laxalt was Reagan's No. 1 choice for the vice presidency, but other advisers insisted he needed geographical and political "balance" if he wanted to win more than the West. As a result, Bush — slightly more moderate than Laxalt and a man who was born in Massachusetts, raised in Connecticut and transplanted to Texas — was named to the ticket.

Precisely because he had been considered more moderate than both Laxalt and Reagan, it was suspected that hard-line conservatives were hoping Bush would not assume that he automatically would become Reagan's heir-apparent. If Reagan himself chose not to run in 1984, conservatives likely would push Laxalt to step in to prevent the nomination from going to Bush. Some political observers predicted Laxalt might choose to challenge Baker for majority leader in 1982 and use the post as a springboard for a presidential race two years later.

For his part, Laxalt denied any ambition for higher office. In 1982 as well as in 1984, he said, "I see myself right here in the Senate."

First Basque-American Senator

The son of an immigrant Basque shepherd who came to the United States at age 16 from France, Laxalt was born in Reno, Nev., on Aug. 2, 1922. He spent many of his early summers on the sheep range with his father. His official biography notes that he became "the nation's first Basque-American senator."

His first foray into politics occurred in 1950 when he was elected to a four-year term as Ormsby County, Nev., district attorney. He then practiced law in Carson City, the state capital, until elected Nevada lieutenant governor in 1962.

He made his first bid for the Senate in 1964, running for the seat occupied by incumbent Howard W. Cannon, D-Nev. (1959-81). He lost that race by just 48 votes but went on to be elected governor in 1966. As governor of a state in which gambling is a mainstay of the economy, he created quite a stir in political circles with a proposal to require that casinos register as corporations, making it more difficult to hide the identity of the true owners.

After the legislature obliged and changed the law, Laxalt invited the late Howard Hughes, then head of the

Hughes Tool Co., to invest in the state's gambling industry. Hughes subsequently bought seven casinos, and the two men soon developed a mutually beneficial working relationship.

In February 1970, for example, Hughes agreed to purchase $6 million in state bonds at only 7 percent interest — the maximum interest rate allowed by Nevada law at the time. Because state officials had feared the bonds would not sell at such a low rate, Hughes' move enabled Laxalt to avoid calling a special session of the state Legislature in order to raise the interest-rate ceiling.

Laxalt maintained that by encouraging legitimate investors such as Hughes, he had cleaned up the state's gambling operations. His relationship with the controversial Hughes was to haunt him, however, and was a factor in his 1970 decision to bow out of politics.

A Stint as Casino Operator

Although he received strong encouragement that year from President Nixon to run once more against Sen. Cannon, Laxalt instead began a new career as a businessman. He and a brother built and operated a 237-room hotel-casino in Carson City.

A few years in the casino business, however, did not live up to his expectations, and in 1974 he re-entered politics by running for the seat of retiring Sen. Alan H. Bible, D-Nev. (1954-74). Although he defeated Democrat Harry Reid by only 624 votes, he won in a year dominated by post-Watergate politics. Laxalt became the sole Republican that year to take a Senate seat previously held by a Democrat.

In November 1980 Laxalt won a comfortable re-election victory with 58 percent of the vote. His margin of victory, however, lagged behind that of Reagan, who amassed 64 percent of the vote statewide.

Laxalt's re-election and closeness to Reagan placed him in a strategic position to help win support in Congress for the new president's legislative initiatives.

ECONOMIC PLAN
TOPS PRIORITY LIST

Reagan had made clear during the campaign that the economy would be his first priority if he were elected. Once in office, he moved quickly to make good on that promise.

He appealed to Congress Feb. 18 to give America a new economic beginning by adopting his ambitious plan to scale back the growth of government and return billions of dollars of taxes to workers and businesses.

In a prime-time televised address to a joint session of the Senate and House, Reagan warned that the nation was facing a "day of reckoning." He urged immediate approval of his sweeping economic proposals. *(Text of address, p. 115)*

"If we don't do this, inflation and a growing tax burden will put an end to everything we believe in and to our dreams for the future," he said. But he stressed that the nation's economic problems easily could be cured if Congress accepted his program as its own.

"We are in control here," he said. "There is nothing wrong with America that — together — we can't fix."

Later he reminded the lawmakers that "the people are watching and waiting. They don't demand miracles. They do expect us to act. Let us act together."

The actions Reagan proposed would cut President Carter's fiscal 1982 spending request, as adjusted for new economic assumptions, by $41.4 billion and slash personal income and business taxes by $53.9 billion. Combined with a "predictable and stable" monetary policy and a reduction in the recent "explosion" of regulations, Reagan claimed, these budget and tax reductions would cause the economy to flourish and prices to plummet.

Although the administration did not plan to release full budget details to Congress until March 10, Reagan said he would recommend that spending in fiscal 1982 total $695.5 billion; tax receipts, $650.5 billion; and the deficit, $45 billion.

Reagan maintained that his program was "evenhanded" and could be accomplished "without harm to government's legitimate purpose or to our responsibility to all who need our benevolence." He promised to retain "social safety net" programs for the truly needy and recommended a funding increase in only one department: Defense.

The president's economic plan represented a dramatic departure from what he called "business as usual." It assumed that if the "cycle of negative expectations" about inflation could be broken through a commitment to reduced government, Americans would save more of their earnings.

Such a growth in savings — spurred on by tax cuts — would free as much as $44 billion in new funds for investment. That, in turn, would improve productivity, provide more jobs and bring down prices, according to Reagan.

Many economists questioned that supposition, however, and warned that large-scale tax cuts could trigger an increase in spending rather than savings. That would push inflation even higher.

Some Republicans privately worried that the president was risking all on untested economic theories. They feared the GOP would be blamed if the economy did not respond as he predicted.

In assembling his "program for economic recovery," Reagan was forced to back off from several promises he made during his campaign for the presidency. The tax cut he proposed did not provide for automatic adjustment of tax rates to offset inflation and it was set to go into effect July 1, 1981, rather than be retroactive to the first of the year.

He was unable to make the 2 percent cut in the fiscal 1981 budget that he had promised for so long. He made only a small dent in reducing the "waste, fraud and abuse" he had railed against in speeches for five years. Finally, the president again postponed his goal of balancing the budget. He had begun his campaign by promising to eliminate the federal deficit in fiscal 1982. That date was revised to 1983 just before the election. His new plan set fiscal 1984 as the target.

The Congressional Mood

The president won a standing ovation for his appeal that the White House and Capitol Hill work in tandem to enact the package of budget and tax cuts that he claimed would constitute "America's new beginning."

The reaction from the cheering lawmakers — especially the Republicans — was so enthusiastic that Reagan departed from his prepared text and joked, "I should have

President Reagan acknowledges members' applause during his economic address to Congress.

arranged to quit right here." Just how long Congress' zeal would last was open to question, however. The package Reagan submitted contained by far the most ambitious budget scaleback ever proposed by any president.

Special interest groups, which got a preview of the economic plan through contraband copies of the administration's "black book" of spending cuts, already had begun campaigns to pressure lawmakers to spare their programs from the budget knife.

Many representatives and senators would be reluctant to curtail or eliminate the programs they designed and nurtured over the previous few decades.

Likewise, opposition already had surfaced to Reagan's proposed Kemp-Roth tax cut plan, which would provide for a 10 percent reduction in individual income tax rates for three years beginning July 1. *(Tax cut plan, p. 14)*

Democrats charged that an across-the-board income tax reduction would benefit the well-to-do more than poorer Americans. Many Republicans, including Senate Finance Chairman Dole, shared Democrats' concern that a personal tax cut of that magnitude would heighten inflation.

Reagan used his address to put a challenge to opponents of his package. "Have they an alternative which offers a greater chance of balancing the budget, reducing and eliminating inflation, stimulating the creation of jobs and reducing the tax burden?" he asked. "And if they haven't, are they suggesting we can continue on the present course without coming to a day of reckoning?"

Initial Reaction

The success of Reagan's program on Capitol Hill depended in good part on whether lawmakers viewed the massive spending cuts as equitable. Reagan argued in his address that the cuts he was recommending hit all programs equally — and most Republicans agreed.

But House Speaker Thomas P. O'Neill Jr., D-Mass., when asked whether he believed there were inequities in the package, retorted, "You bet there are." He added, "It is important that the sacrifices called for in the proposed budget are shared equally and that the benefits of the tax cut are not reaped primarily by the few."

Sen. Edward M. Kennedy, Mass., who challenged President Carter for the Democratic presidential nomination in 1980, warned that he was "not prepared to see the social progress of a generation swept aside in a few short weeks."

Senate Appropriations Chairman Mark O. Hatfield, R-Ore., pledged to "scrutinize all federal programs to ensure that everyone share in the sacrifices ahead. The military budget will not be exempted from this scrutiny."

Even larger roadblocks loomed to passage of the president's tax cut plan. House Ways and Means Chairman Dan Rostenkowski, D-Ill., said Reagan should be happy if he got "half" of what he was asking.

Senate Finance Chairman Dole said he assumed the tax plan was "going to be modified. . . . I listened to the speech and heard no applause [for the tax cut proposals] and I've been in the Senate 20 years."

Also crucial to success of the package was whether budget cuts would be enacted to offset the proposed tax reductions. Traditionally, lawmakers voted readily for tax cuts but shied away from reducing spending.

"The real test will be whether it can be kept together during the legislative journey," Senate Budget Committee

Chairman Pete V. Domenici, R-N.M., said during a television interview Feb. 15. "It is important that it not be cut up piecemeal by various congressional committees."

Finally, the president's program was subject to failure because lawmakers were reluctant to curtail pet projects or afraid to cut programs that benefited the people who elect them. As Treasury Secretary Donald T. Regan put it, "we'll have a struggle on quite a few" of the cuts because "practically everybody's ox is being gored."

The day after Reagan's speech, for example, two press releases from Orrin G. Hatch, R-Utah, appeared side by side in the Senate Press Gallery. "Hatch Pleased with Budget Plan," read the headline on one. "Budget Cuts Won't Slow Down Final Completion of C-U-P [Central Utah Project], Hatch Says," read the other.

That was fiscal conservative Hatch's way of assuring his constituents that funding for the Central Utah water project would not be cut in the fiscal 1982 budget.

House Budget Chairman James R. Jones, D-Okla., said he believed that although many of the proposed cuts will be contested, Congress would find other places to trim the budget. "We have a good chance of succeeding no matter what the special interests are saying," Jones said.

Senate Majority Leader Baker agreed. He said, "It may very well be that the mix of cuts will differ from the president's request, but I expect the magnitude of the cuts will be about the same."

But even as Baker was urging "swift" action on the president's proposals, House Speaker O'Neill was cautioning that "legislating in haste makes waste all along the line."

Details of Economic Plan

Accompanying Reagan's address Feb. 18 was a "white paper" detailing his tax and budget proposals and spelling out in urgent prose his free-market economic philosophy.

"We have forgotten some important lessons in America," the paper said. "High taxes are not the remedy for inflation. Excessively rapid monetary growth cannot lower interest rates. Well-intentioned government regulations do not contribute to economic vitality."

The most important cause of the nation's economic problems, the paper concluded, is "the government itself.... The federal government, through tax, spending, regulatory and monetary policies, has sacrificed long-term growth and price stability for ephemeral short-term goals."

At a press briefing Feb. 18, Council of Economic Advisers Chairman Murray L. Weidenbaum characterized Reagan's program as "fundamentally different" from those of the past. (*Economic advisers, box, pp. 12-13*)

Central to those new plans, according to the white paper, was the view that "decisions to work, save, spend and invest depend crucially on expectations regarding future government policies." Once an environment was created that ensured "efficient and stable incentives for work, savings and investment," the Reagan paper said, the economy would recover quickly.

Economic Assumptions

The paper predicted the Consumer Price Index (CPI) would average 11.1 percent in calendar 1981, 8.3 percent in 1982 and 6.2 percent in 1986. Unemployment would average 7.8 percent in 1981, 7.2 percent in 1982 and 6.6 percent in 1986. The total number of jobs would rise by 13 million — 3 million more than otherwise.

The gross national product (GNP) was projected to rise from an average rate of 1.1 percent in 1981 to 4.2 percent in 1982 and 5 percent the next year.

By contrast, Carter predicted an average 12.5 percent change in the CPI in 1981, an average unemployment rate of 7.8 percent and GNP growth of .9 percent. In 1982, he predicted, the CPI would climb 10.3 percent, unemployment would fall to 7.5 percent and the GNP would grow by 3.5 percent.

That forecast, which Carter presented Jan. 15, five days before leaving office, was in line with those of most private economists. The new administration said that its predictions differed because they assumed speedy enactment of the "recovery" program resulting in a quick rebound by the economy.

One House Budget aide described the Reagan economic assumptions as "made of green cheese imported from the moon." The staffer said the optimistic predictions made analysis of the budget figures difficult.

Spending Cuts

According to Office of Management and Budget chief David A. Stockman, the "leading edge" of the budget package was a "dramatic and sharp downward shift" in the growth of government, accomplished through outlay cuts of $4.4 billion in fiscal 1981 and $41.4 billion in fiscal 1982.

In addition, another $2 billion would be saved in fiscal 1982 by charging user fees for certain government services. Interest costs would be cut $5.7 billion by limiting borrowing through the Federal Financing Bank. That brought the total budget savings contained in the plan to $49.1 billion.

Stockman said the cuts Reagan was proposing would allow the government to grow by only 6 percent in fiscal 1982, rather than by the current rate of 16 percent. They would reduce budget outlays from the 1981 level of 23 percent of GNP to 21.8 percent in 1982 and 19 percent in 1986.

Although Reagan stressed that his proposed reductions were evenhanded, his budget would trigger a major shift in spending priorities: The percentage of outlays spent on military programs would jump from 24.1 percent in 1981, to 32.4 percent in 1984.

The "safety net" programs for the needy and elderly would grow from 24.5 percent to 40.6 percent of the budget during that period. Interest payments on the public debt would rise from 6.4 percent to 8.6 percent.

But spending for all other government programs would decline from 25.2 percent of the budget to 18.4 percent. In a jab at the Carter administration and previous Democratic-controlled Congresses, the administration white paper charged that, during the "fiscal open season" of recent years, "almost no demand for federal assistance from any sector of the economy, region of the nation, other unit of government or the non-profit sector was considered invalid."

The paper said Reagan rejected using a "meat-ax" approach to cut such "runaway" spending. Instead, it said that all programs were examined with "great care, judgment and sensitivity," using "a careful set of guidelines ... to identify lower-priority programs." The guidelines called for:

● Revising entitlement programs to eliminate unintended benefits.

Economic Officials Unite Behind . . .

The senior White House and Cabinet officials who were given the responsibility for carrying out President Reagan's economic program had broad experience in economic and financial matters. Although they had expressed differing opinions before Reagan took office on how to cure America's ailing economy, all of them put their differences over budget and tax cuts aside and got behind the president's ambitious policies.

Orthodox Republicans such as Treasury Secretary Donald T. Regan, who once opposed across-the-board personal income tax cuts, stumped for congressional acceptance of the Kemp-Roth plan calling for reductions in individual income tax rates of 30 percent over three years. Regan also modified his earlier insistence that any tax cut be linked to cuts in spending, a condition sought by most big businesses.

"This tax program cannot wait until budget outlays are reduced," he said after being confirmed by the Senate. In his confirmation hearings, Regan had warned that increasing the deficit to finance a tax cut would only heighten inflation.

Regan's conversion to the "supply side" theory that the budget was out of balance because of the economy — rather than the other way around — put him in agreement with the outspoken director of the Office of Management and Budget (OMB), David A. Stockman.

Stockman and other supply-siders, such as Rep. Jack F. Kemp, R-N.Y., co-author of the income tax cut plan, maintained that cutting business and individual income taxes would free more capital for investment and increase work incentives, thus curbing inflation and making the economy more productive.

However, another factor in the "united front" the Kemp-Roth plan received within the administraton may have been due to Reagan's unwavering insistence on cutting personal taxes. Reagan for years had promised that, if elected, he would slow the growth of government, reduce government regulation and return tax dollars to the people. And because he already had made up his mind on so many key economic issues, the charge to his economic team was focused on implementing, rather than designing, his budget and tax policies.

Regan: Chief Spokesman

Reagan designated Treasury Secretary Regan as his chief economic spokesman and head of his Economic Policy Council. Members of the council were expected to include Stockman, Council of Economic Advisers Chairman Murray L. Weidenbaum, Commerce Secretary Malcolm Baldrige and U.S. Trade Representative William E. Brock III. Weidenbaum, in particular, was expected to be a leading force in the drive to cut back on government regulation.

Although the Treasury secretary, a newcomer to government service, secured these two power bases, his authority over economic policy did not go unchallenged. The most aggressive competitor for influence over fiscal affairs was Stockman, the articulate former House Republican from Michigan who was known for his dogged determination to push his brand of economic conservatism.

The public spotlight turned on Stockman soon after his nomination when newspapers published his memo to Reagan warning that the nation faced an "economic Dunkirk" if emergency cuts in the budget, taxes and regulations were not adopted.

Consensus: How Strong?

How long the administration's unity on economic questions would last was not expected to become clear until the economic staff had gone through its first test with Congress on the tax cut-budget cutting package. Some observers questioned Regan's commitment to push for the Kemp-Roth plan if Congress balked and chose another method of tax reduction. And it was considered inevitable that infighting would occur over where budget cuts would be made.

The public got a preview of such battles when OMB plans for a major cutback in foreign aid spending were leaked to reporters. Secretary of State Alexander M. Haig Jr. called an emergency meeting with Stockman and convinced him to scale down much of the proposed reduction, according to administration sources.

OMB

A team of aggressive, fiscal conservatives and campaign loyalists quickly assumed the reins at OMB, which was charged with formulating the agency budgets. With Stockman as director — and an administration firmly committed to spending cuts — OMB was certain to play a more activist role than it had under President Carter. For reasons Domestic Adviser Martin C. Anderson described as "partly symbolic, partly operational," Reagan upgraded the agency's directorship to Cabinet status and designated the OMB deputy director as "assistant to the president" — the first time a deputy OMB director had been given such a title.

Although he said he planned to propose a program of stiff spending cuts for the next several years, Stockman appealed to Congress not to await enactment of a tax cut before trimming the budget.

Assisting Stockman were:
● Edwin L. Harper, OMB deputy director. Harper, 39, vice president of the Emerson Electric Co. of St. Louis, served on the spending control task force during the campaign and the economic policy team during the transition.

. . . Reagan Plan for Spending, Tax Cuts

● Glenn R. Schleede, executive associate director. Schleede was the senior vice president of the National Coal Association in Washington. A former associate director for energy and science for the Domestic Council under Nixon, Schleede also spent seven years at OMB.

Treasury

Secretary Regan became the stalwart administration soldier, sounding like a true believer in the Kemp-Roth individual tax cut plan. At a Jan. 7 press conference, Regan noted that he always had believed tax cuts would stimulate the economy and help balance the budget. He said he had been a supply-sider without really knowing it. Yet as late as July 1980 Regan testified before the House Ways and Means Committee against the Kemp-Roth plan and pushed instead for generous business tax relief. And it was Regan who convinced the president not to declare an "economic emergency," as Stockman advocated.

A test of Regan's convictions would be reflected in his relations with other Treasury officials. Many of the top positions at the department were filled with supply side diehards and confirmed monetarists. Monetarists maintain that the only way to achieve economic stability is for the Federal Reserve to hold the growth of the money supply to a steady rate.

New Treasury officials included:

● R. Timothy McNamar, deputy secretary. McNamar, who served as a recruiter for the Reagan transition, had been executive vice president of Beneficial Standard Corp., an insurance holding company, since 1977.

McNamar, a lawyer by training, served in two previous GOP administrations. During the Ford years, he was executive director of the Federal Trade Commission. In 1973 McNamar was an internal consultant to the Cost of Living Council and before that served as director of the Pay Board's Office of Case Management and Analysis.

● Norman B. Ture, under secretary for tax policy. Supply side advocates were pleased by Ture's appointment to a newly created tax policy position. Previously, oversight of tax policy had been handled by an assistant secretary.

An economist, Ture was known in Washington as an outspoken proponent of market-oriented, business-related tax cuts designed to promote capital formation and across-the-board individual income tax cuts. In the conservative Heritage Foundation's "Agenda for the Future," published at about the time Reagan took office, Ture argued that tax and economic policy within the department had to be "expanded and coordinated if Treasury and the administration are to play a prominent role in tax policy in the future."

Ture had headed his own economic consulting firm, Norman B. Ture Inc., since 1971 and was president of the Institute for Research on the Economics of Taxation since 1977. During the Nixon administration, he worked as a consultant to the Treasury Department under Deputy Secretary Charls E. Walker — one of Reagan's top tax advisers during the election campaign. Ture served on the board of Walker's American Council for Capital Formation, a lobbying group that pushed tax breaks for business.

● Beryl W. Sprinkel, under secretary for monetary affairs. Sprinkel, an economist, had been executive vice president of the Harris Trust and Savings Bank in Chicago since 1952. He also had been the publisher of the bank's economic and financial forecasting service, *Harris Economics.*

Sprinkel was known as a monetarist, and some Wall Street bond houses worried about how his focus on the money supply might affect Treasury's borrowing patterns. Although apparently at ease with Reagan's supply side economists, Sprinkel, in a 1979 interview with *U.S. News & World Report*, said he opposed major personal tax cuts because a "tax cut strictly on consumer incomes would further stimulate consumption and make our present problems even more serious."

● Paul Craig Roberts, assistant secretary for international economics. Roberts, a senior fellow at Georgetown University's Center for Strategic and International Studies and professor at Virginia's George Mason University, had served as a congressional aide to Kemp.

Roberts, who also was a monetarist, was an associate editor of the editorial page of *The Wall Street Journal* at the time of his appointment.

● John E. Chapoton, assistant secretary for tax policy. Chapoton, a lawyer with the Houston firm of Vinson & Elkins, was legislative counsel for the Treasury from 1969 to 1972. Chapoton had a reputation for being able to move legislation through Congress.

White House

Reagan's appointment of Martin Anderson as his assistant for policy development underscored the new administration's concern with the economy. The new domestic policy adviser had called the economy the "paramount" issue for Reagan. "I think there is a difference in attitude now," he said in a Jan. 4 television interview. "I remember when I came to Washington in 1969, people were saying similar things, that it was important to control federal spending, that we should do it. The difference now is that everyone I talk to says that it has to be done."

Also serving on the White House economic team was William E. Brock III, Reagan's U.S. trade representative.

• Reducing government subsidies to middle- and upper-income groups.

• Recovering costs that could be clearly allocated to users.

• Applying sound economic criteria to subsidy programs.

• Stretching out and redirecting capital construction programs.

• Imposing fiscal restraint on other programs.

• Consolidating categorical grant programs into block grants.

• Reducing the overhead and personnel costs of the federal government.

Stockman said the cuts in these categories were "the big ticket items" and that details of another $6 billion in reductions not included in the white paper would appear in the March 10 budget. The fiscal 1982 savings total of $49.1 billion included that sum, however.

Among the 83 programs targeted for cuts were:

• *Food Stamps.* Among other changes, eligibility would be limited to families whose annual income was less than 130 percent of the official poverty level for an outlay savings of $1.8 billion in fiscal 1982.

• *Social Security.* The special minimum monthly Social Security benefit would be eliminated, for a savings of $1 billion in fiscal 1982. Instead, most retirees would receive payments based on the amount they had paid into the system. Poorer pensioners still would benefit from other programs.

• *Public Housing.* The contribution by public housing tenants to the cost of their rentals would rise from the existing 25 percent to 30 percent over the next five years, for a savings of $232 million in fiscal 1982.

• *Trade Adjustment Assistance.* Aid paid to workers whose jobs were eliminated by foreign competition would be capped at the level of regular unemployment benefits and would be paid only after such benefits ran out, saving $1.2 billion in fiscal 1982.

• *Airport Users.* Increased taxes would be levied on air passengers, airplane fuel and air freight to raise $1.9 billion in new revenues in fiscal 1982 to support airport programs.

• *Dairy Price Supports.* The mandatory April 1 increase in dairy subsidies would be eliminated for a savings of $1.1 billion in fiscal 1982.

• *Mass Transit Grants.* Subsidies for construction of new subways would be curtailed or postponed for a savings of $270 million in fiscal 1982.

• *Federal Employment.* Civilian, non-defense federal employment would be reduced by 83,000 jobs in fiscal 1982, for a savings of $1.9 billion. And comparability pay standards for federal workers would be changed to match actual levels in private business, saving $5.3 billion in fiscal 1982.

• *Block Grants.* Thirty-eight health and social services grant programs and 45 education grants programs would be combined into single block grants to states and local governments, for a budget authority savings of $1.5 billion and an outlay savings of $100 million in fiscal 1982.

• *Export-Import Bank.* Lending authority would be cut by a third in fiscal 1982, saving $2 billion in budget authority and $400 million in outlays.

• *National Endowment for the Arts.* Endowment grants for cultural and scholastic activities would be cut in half for a total savings of $85 million in fiscal 1982.

Tax Cut Plan

Treasury Secretary Regan described the president's revenue proposals as a "two-pronged" attack on the increasing rate of taxes: Individual income tax rates would be reduced 10 percent for each of three years and depreciation write-offs for business investments would be speeded up, for a total cut of $53.9 billion in 1982.

Regan said the administration was pushing for across-the-board tax cuts to offset increases caused by inflation and as a means of stemming the growth in "unlegislated" federal spending increases.

President Reagan said in his address that the change in the depreciation allowances was recommended because the current system was "obsolete, needlessly complex and is economically counterproductive."

According to the white paper, the tax cuts for individuals would cost the government $6.4 billion in fiscal 1981 and $44.2 billion in 1982, rising to $162.4 billion in 1986.

The proposed tax breaks for businesses would result in $2.5 billion in lost revenues in fiscal 1981, $9.7 billion in 1982, hitting $59.3 billion in 1986.

Asked why the deficit was being permitted to rise to make up for the individual income tax cut, Treasury Secretary Regan said the administration expected the reduction to spur savings and thus "finance" the red ink by freeing new money for investment.

Prospects for Change

Early reactions from Capitol Hill indicated that lawmakers would make substantial changes in the part of the bill that called for cutting individual income tax rates by 10 percent a year for three years. This proposal mirrored the Kemp-Roth tax plan — the centerpiece of Reagan's economic plank during the presidential campaign.

The second feature of the Reagan tax package — speeding up the rate at which businesses could deduct the cost of purchasing new plants and equipment — appeared to have solid congressional support.

Reagan pledged to send to Congress at an "early date" a second tax parcel, including proposals to index income tax brackets; do away with the marriage penalty, which discriminates against working married couples; provide tuition tax credits; and revise inheritance taxation.

But many congressional observers agreed with Senate Finance Chairman Dole that members would not wait for the second round to offer their pet tax proposals. "If you were a hitchhiker you wouldn't wait for the second ride," Dole said.

"Unlike some past tax 'reforms,' this is not merely a shift of wealth between different sets of taxpayers," Reagan said in describing his controversial individual tax cut plan. "This proposal for an equal reduction in everyone's tax rates will expand our national prosperity, enlarge national incomes and increase opportunities for all Americans."

Concerted Lobbying on Reagan Economic Plan

President Reagan's first economic address to Congress was only part of a carefully orchestrated administration campaign to win passage of his controversial belt-tightening plans.

Under normal practice, the speech would have been the president's "State of the Union" message, but the Reagan White House decided to postpone comment on other issues until work on the budget and tax cut program was under way.

The address to a joint session of Congress was Reagan's second prime-time televised talk in two weeks. On Feb. 5, he took to the air to warn Americans of an "economic calamity of tremendous proportions" if his program were not adopted.

The White House hoped the earlier address, scheduled just before lawmakers left Washington for a week-long recess in their districts, would convince constituents to pressure their representatives to accept Reagan's prescription for the economy.

In an unusual move, the new president had visited the Capitol before the Feb. 5 speech to explain his program to Democratic and Republican leaders, and he invited them to White House briefings.

Treasury Secretary Donald T. Regan and Office of Management and Budget (OMB) Director David A. Stockman shuttled to Capitol Hill dozens of times to convince Republican committee leaders of the necessity of making painful spending cuts.

On Feb. 18, Reagan again met with congressional leaders and about two dozen committee and subcommittee chairmen and ranking minority members. And Stockman and Council of Economic Advisers (CEA) Chairman Murray L. Weidenbaum briefed the Republican and Democratic conferences of the House and Senate.

Outsiders Drawn In

Reagan also had help in promoting his economic program from a group of outside political loyalists who hired a Washington public relations firm to create television commercials calling for support of the president's program. They also organized a grassroots letter-writing campaign to convince representatives and senators to back the spending and tax cuts.

"We're trying to create a favorable climate of media coverage and popular approval. And we want to resist breaking the program apart," explained Joseph Baroody, whose public relations firm of Wagner & Baroody was hired to coordinate the private effort.

The administration also brought in an experienced hand to coordinate press coverage of Reagan's economic message. He was David Gergen, former director of communications under President Ford.

Gergen arranged a series of lunch and breakfast briefings by the administration's top economic officials for reporters and columnists with the wire services, television networks and major newspapers — those media assured of capturing the largest audiences. Other publications, such as periodicals, were banned.

After the speech, Regan, Stockman and Weidenbaum were dispatched for a number of television appearances and to stump for the program in speeches around the country.

Special interest groups and newspaper editors were invited to the White House for briefings on the program. The Republican National Committee supplied informational packets to thousands of state and local party officials.

In addition, Vice President George Bush wooed support from Brooklyn, N.Y., Republicans in a speech on the economic package Feb. 15, and on the following day, Senate Majority Leader Howard H. Baker Jr., R-Tenn., took the administration's case to the AFL-CIO's annual midwinter meeting in Bal Harbour, Fla.

Empty Offices Preferred

Reagan's effort to make the first "serious" cuts in the budget "in a good many years," as OMB's Stockman put it, was aided by the absence of high-level officials in most government departments.

The Reagan staff insisted it was having difficulty finding qualified people to fill the posts. But some observers maintained the administration had moved slowly on government hiring so that the budget could be drafted before newly appointed officials developed loyalties to their departments.

Edwin Meese III, counselor to Reagan, confirmed that the administration preferred an empty office to one occupied by an appointee of President Carter who might try to defend his turf against Stockman.

Reagan's campaign to curry support for his program on Capitol Hill stood in marked contrast to the attempts of his predecessor.

"Unlike the Carter administration, Reagan made contact in the first month, and a relationship already has been established," said one Democratic Senate aide.

But some Democratic leaders were not entirely enthusiastic about his efforts to win their backing. House Speaker Thomas P. O'Neill Jr., D-Mass., complained that Reagan did not provide him with any details of his economic program during his sessions with congressional leaders. "Only yesterday did the president make available any details of his proposed spending cuts," O'Neill told reporters Feb. 19.

Likewise, Senate Minority Leader Robert C. Byrd, D-W.Va., labeled his meetings with Reagan "window dressing."

But Capitol Hill skeptics quickly began pecking away at Reagan's plan. Even Senate Majority Leader Baker admitted that the tax bill would be the hardest part of the economic recovery plan to get through Congress. "I expect it would be unrealistic for the [tax] package to be unchanged," he said.

Senate Minority Leader Robert C. Byrd, W. Va., said he detected a "consensus emerging" among Senate Democrats who believed as he did that the Reagan tax cuts would be "inflationary, beneficial to the affluent and unfair to poor and middle-class Americans."

House Budget Chairman Jones said he thought the personal tax cut should be limited to one year and "targeted more toward savings and investment in productive assets."

House Ways and Means Chairman Rostenkowski predicted that the package would not emerge from his panel in the form that Reagan had proposed but would contain "some improvements" in its final form.

Individual Cuts

Reagan proposed to cut individual marginal tax rates by 10 percent a year for three years. The marginal tax rate is the rate at which one's top dollar of income is taxed. However, because of an anomaly in the tax law, individuals in the highest income brackets would not receive so large a percentage decrease in their rates as lower- and middle-income individuals.

In early 1981 the maximum marginal tax rate was 70 percent. But that rate affected only unearned or investment income, such as interest and dividends, because the tax code imposed a maximum rate of 50 percent on earned income, such as wages, salaries and fees.

Rep. Jack F. Kemp, R-N.Y., hoped the administration's tax cut would trim the maximum tax on earned income as well as the marginal tax rate. But the administration proposed only to reduce the marginal rate. Therefore, even if the administration's plan were fully implemented, the maximum tax rate that people paid on earned income still would be 50 percent. The minimum would drop from 14 to 10 percent.

Thus, a family with a taxable income of $60,000 or more per year would receive a proportionally smaller tax cut than a family earning $20,000. Eventually, however, the 50 percent marginal rate would apply only to families with incomes in excess of $215,400. Those earning less than that amount would pay less than 50 percent.

27.3 Percent Reduction

President Reagan told Congress, "Our proposal is for a 10 percent across-the-board cut every year for three years in the tax rates for all individual income taxpayers making a total cut of 30 percent." However, the total reduction in tax liabilities by 1984 actually would be 27.3 percent, according to the Treasury Department.

The 10 percent yearly rate cuts would become effective on July 1, 1981, when the withholding tables would be adjusted, and on July 1 in each of the two succeeding years. As a result, tax rates in calendar 1981 would be reduced only 5 percent on total 1981 income, since a taxpayer would only get half a year of the 10 percent rate reduction. But the reductions would grow to 15 percent in 1982, 25 percent in 1983 and 30 percent in 1984.

For a family of four with gross income in 1980 of $25,000, the Reagan tax cut would provide tax relief amounting to $153 in 1981. But by 1984, assuming its

earnings did not rise, its tax cut would amount to $809. If earnings increased to $30,300 in 1984, the tax break would be $1,112.

Side Effects

As a result of the personal rate cuts, once the top marginal rate dropped to 50 percent the distinction between earned income and unearned income would be eliminated. The administration hoped that this change, along with the fact that individuals would have more disposable income, would lead to more savings.

In fact, administration officials said that these tax cuts should result in a 2 percent increase in the rate of savings, which would amount to between $44 billion and $60 billion. These savings, they claimed, would help finance the deficit without the need to step up growth of the money supply. "That's what we're betting on, that's what we're counting on," said one official.

Another side effect of the rate reductions, according to the Treasury Department, would be a cut in the capital gains rate. Under existing law, 60 percent of net capital gains were excluded from an individual's income when computing taxes, leaving 40 percent included in income that was taxed at normal rates.

As a result of the president's proposal, however, the maximum tax rate on that 40 percent would be reduced from the existing 70 percent to 50 percent as individual tax cuts were phased in. Thus, the top capital gains rate would be reduced from a maximum of 28 percent to 26.4 percent in 1981, 24 percent in 1982, 21.2 percent in 1983 and finally to 20 percent in 1984 — that is, to 40 percent of the 50 percent marginal rate.

If these tax cuts were not enacted, the administration said in documents accompanying the president's speech, "federal taxes would consume a rapidly increasing share of the national income — rising to 23.4 percent of GNP [gross national product] after 1985." Under the president's program, the Treasury Department said, tax receipts would drop to 20.4 percent of GNP in 1982 and 19.3 percent by 1985.

Individual rate reductions would cost the Treasury $44.2 billion in fiscal 1982, rising to $162.4 billion in fiscal 1986.

Business Cuts

To do away with the depreciation system for business investments, Reagan proposed the "accelerated cost recovery system," which he said would "provide the new investment which is needed to create millions of new jobs between now and 1986 and to make America competitive once again in world markets."

The effect of the president's faster and simpler depreciation schedule would be to provide businesses with $9.7 billion for investment in fiscal 1982, rising to $44.2 billion in fiscal 1985. Those figures reflected the projected loss in revenues to the Treasury.

The plan was a slightly altered version of the "10-5-3" accelerated depreciation plan, which had great bipartisan support in both houses of Congress in 1980.

Details of Write-offs

While the proposed personal income tax reductions would not take effect until July 1, 1981, the business tax breaks would be retroactive to Jan. 1, 1981. However, the program would be phased in "progressively" over a five-year period for machinery and buildings acquired before 1985.

Under existing law, businesses that wanted to write off the cost of capital investments had to use a complicated system that placed plants and machinery in categories according to their "useful lives." Businesses were then allowed to deduct the cost of their investments over the useful life period. But the depreciation schedules were so stretched out that it could take up to 40 years to write off certain buildings and up to 28 years to depreciate some types of machinery.

The Reagan plan attempted to simplify the system and accelerate the rate at which these investments could be written off. Specifically, the program would replace the complex useful life provisions with "easily identified" classes, each having a standard schedule of deductions that could be taken over a fixed recovery period.

These proposed classes were:

● *Three-year property* — outlays for autos and light trucks, and machinery and equipment used in research and development activities. These assets could be written off in three years, as follows: 33 percent in the first year, 45 percent in the second and 22 percent in the third.

● *Five-year property* — outlays for machinery and equipment including public utility property. After a phase-in period, property in this class would be written off in five years: 20 percent in the year acquired and 32 percent, 24 percent, 16 percent and 8 percent in succeeding years.

● *Ten-year property* — outlays for factory buildings, retail stores and warehouses used by owners and public utility property. These could be written off over 10 years: 10 percent, 18 percent, 16 percent, 14 percent, 12 percent, 10 percent, 8 percent, 6 percent, 4 percent and 2 percent.

Finally, there would be two new depreciation categories — a 15-year and an 18-year category — for other types of real estate. These depreciation periods would be "audit proof" — that is, they would not require subsequent audit. The costs would be written off on a "straight-line basis," so that the same percentage of the original cost could be written off each year.

In addition to the changes in the depreciation schedules, the president's plan would allow increases in the investment tax credit to take effect at once as opposed to the depreciation reforms that would be phased in — 6 percent for investments in the three-year write-off category, an increase of 2-2/3 percent, and the full 10 percent investment tax credit for investments in the five-year category, as compared with the 6-1/2 percent credit currently used.

User Fees

In an effort to raise new revenues by "recovering clearly allocable costs from users," Reagan proposed to increase user fees in three areas. Taken together these taxes would generate $2 billion in revenue in fiscal 1982.

The largest revenue gain would come from increasing taxes on both commercial and general aviation. The plan would include: increasing the current 10 percent aviation fuel tax to 20 percent; increasing the passenger ticket tax from 5 percent to 9 percent; and levying a 5 percent air freight tax.

The second user fee, a so-called "yacht fee," would be charged for Coast Guard services such as the issuance of marine licenses and periodic safety inspections. Finally, the

administration proposed increasing the existing four-cents-a-gallon tax on barge fuel used in inland waterways to 30 cents a gallon in 1983.

Meets With House Chairmen

A month before he presented his economic plan to Congress, President Reagan began smoothing the way for its acceptance on the Hill. He met briefly Jan. 22 with four Democratic House committee chairmen whose cooperation would be essential for his economic package. The four were Ways and Means Chairman Rostenkowski, Budget Chairman Jones, Government Operations Chairman Jack Brooks, Texas, accompanied by that committee's ranking minority member, Frank Horton, R-N.Y., and Commerce Committee Chairman John D. Dingell, Mich.

Jones told reporters afterward that at that time he thought there was "still rather active debate within the administration" on the size and timing of tax cuts and where to make the budget cuts.

Immediately after taking office, Reagan also started using executive orders to implement his ideas for turning the economy around. While these did not require congressional action, they generated activity on Capitol Hill as affected groups sought legislative relief from the presidential actions.

HIRING FREEZE, OIL DECONTROL ORDERS ISSUED

Reagan's first official acts took place in the Capitol after his swearing in. He signed the order freezing the hiring of federal employees and officially submitted his Cabinet nominations to the Senate. In the ensuing weeks he followed up those actions with others blocking 11th-hour regulations the Carter administration had imposed, lifting federal price controls on oil and effectively ending Carter's wage-price control program.

Federal Employment

Reagan aides said the hiring freeze was stiffer than the partial hold on federal hiring that Carter had imposed on March 14, 1980.

Before the inauguration, Reagan's transition staff had taken the unusual step of notifying about a third of the White House operations staff, approximately 60 secretaries and other non-policy personnel, that they would lose their jobs. These positions normally are not treated as political jobs; some of the dismissed workers had been at the White House as long as 14 years.

The next day, Jan. 21, Reagan told his first Cabinet meeting that "through attrition, we can reduce the size of government very drastically." He also issued a memorandum directing his Cabinet to request resignations of top-level officials left over from the Carter administration.

The order affected about 200 government officials, including 15 departmental inspectors general, whose job was to eliminate fraud and abuse in federal programs. White House press secretary James S. Brady said later that the inspectors would be replaced by "meaner" individuals who would "ferret out" wasteful spending.

On Jan. 22 Reagan issued four thrift orders to department heads. White House officials said they would save an estimated $300 million in the fiscal year already under way. The Cabinet officials were told to cut travel obligations within their departments by 15 percent, to reduce spending for consulting services by 5 percent, to halt procurement of office furniture and equipment and to refrain from redecorating their offices.

In Carter's fiscal 1982 budget, submitted to Congress Jan. 15, $3.3 billion of the $4.8 billion budgeted for federal travel and transportation was slotted for the Department of Defense.

Also on Jan. 22, Reagan made a surprise visit to the White House press room to announce the appointment of Vice President George Bush as head of an interagency task force to "cut away the thicket of irrational and senseless regulation," as Reagan put it.

Oil Price Controls

Reagan abolished the oil price controls Jan. 28 by executive order. He said decontrol would stimulate both energy production and conservation and reduce the importation of foreign oil.

Although some Democrats were outraged by the action, Congress made no immediate move to reimpose the controls. Both House Speaker O'Neill and Senate Majority Leader Baker said that any congressional attempts to overturn Reagan's order would fail.

Reagan's action, which he promised during his election campaign, was greeted with delight by most Republicans. The oil industry, which expected billions of dollars in additional profits as a result, also was quite happy with the decontrol order. However, it was split over what federal programs, if any, should be established to protect small refiners whose hefty subsidy was wiped out by the decontrol order.

Decontrol allowed producers, refiners and retailers of crude oil, gasoline and propane — the only petroleum products that were still under controls — to set prices without restriction. It also eliminated the complicated procedures by which the government allocated gasoline in times of shortage, and ended, effective March 31, 1981, requirements that large oil companies sell crude oil to small refiners.

Reagan's order did not affect controls on natural gas prices, which were being phased out through the mid-1980s.

Crude oil prices had been controlled in one form or another since 1971, gasoline prices since 1973. Without Reagan's action, those controls had been scheduled to expire Sept. 30. President Carter began a phase-out of controls in 1979 to help win congressional approval of his energy programs. Only about 20-25 percent of domestically produced oil remained under controls when Reagan issued his order. He said domestic oil production had been stifled by industry fears that, for political reasons, controls would not be phased out. His immediate decontrol would erase those fears, he said.

Price Rise Seen

The price of oil produced in the United States, which had been averaging about $30 a barrel before decontrol, was expected to quickly rise to the world price of about $38 a barrel. Consumer groups estimated that gasoline prices would go up 8 to 12 cents a gallon. The House Energy and Commerce Committee staff estimated the increase would be about 9 cents a gallon.

Energy Secretary James B. Edwards told reporters Jan. 28 that he expected gasoline prices to go up by no more than 3 to 5 cents a gallon in the few weeks following decontrol. Noting that gasoline was selling below federal ceiling prices, he said competition would keep the price from going higher immediately.

Edwards predicted that prices for petroleum products at the end of 1981 would be no higher than they would have been with decontrol in the fall — just that they would reach a higher level sooner. He said it was better to decontrol oil prices now, when oil supplies were adequate, than to wait until fall, "when we do not know what the world oil supply situation will be."

Blaming the long gas lines of the 1970s on government regulation, Edward said the elimination of allocation procedures should provide more reliable supplies to drivers.

Decontrol also was expected to provide a "fringe benefit" of $3 billion to $4 billion in additional federal revenues through the windfall profits tax, according to Edwards. Before-tax additions to oil industry revenues resulting from immediate decontrol were estimated at $10 billion to $13 billion through Sept. 30, when controls would have expired.

Edwards said that higher prices resulting from decontrol would save up to 100,000 barrels of oil a day.

Democratic Objections

Many congressional Democrats vehemently disagreed with Edwards' contention that there would be a free market in world oil pricing after the decontrol of U.S. petroleum. They claimed that allowing U.S. oil prices to rise to the world level would enable the Organization of Oil Exporting Countries (OPEC) to set American oil prices.

"Anybody who believes there is a free market in oil is either very naive or very foolish," said Sen. J. Bennett Johnston, D-La. However, Johnston, a member of the Senate Energy Committee, supported decontrol.

Another committee member, Dale Bumpers, D-Ark., said immediate decontrol would do little to spur production and would provide enormous oil company profits — "all paid by people who can't afford it."

Henry M. Jackson, Wash., ranking Democrat on the Senate Energy Committee, said Reagan's decontrol of oil prices came at the expense of the American consumer and would not produce more oil. "Decontrolling oil prices removes an incentive for domestic producers to fight OPEC price increases," he said. "As OPEC prices rise, so will domestic prices. It places our total supply at the pricing whim of OPEC."

Ellen Berman, executive director of the Consumer Energy Council, called Reagan's decontrol order "nothing more than picking the pockets of consumers to further bloat oil company profits."

Two congressional liberals, Sen. Howard M. Metzenbaum, D-Ohio, and Rep. Toby Moffett, D-Conn., said they would lead efforts to block Reagan's action. However, they acknowledged it was an uphill battle for which they did not have the votes. They were not sure whether the immediate decontrol order should be fought in Congress or in the courts.

Metzenbaum said decontrol could force gasoline prices up as much as 17 cents a gallon and add a full percentage point to the inflation rate. "By the end of the year," Metzenbaum said, "$2-a-gallon gasoline could be a reality." Decontrol provided "a virtual gift" to the major oil companies of as much as $170 billion in the additional value of their oil reserves, he added.

House Energy and Commerce Committee Chairman Dingell criticized the immediate decontrol but, according to a spokesman, did not feel Congress was in any mood to reimpose controls.

James A. McClure, R-Idaho, chairman of the Senate Energy Committee, praised Reagan's action. He said decontrol would benefit the United States by increasing domestic production, encouraging the use of alternative fuels and providing more incentive for conservation. He also said removal of the government from the gasoline allocation process would avoid "artificial shortages" caused by regulation. "The free marketplace is still our very best allocation system," he said.

Both Edwards and McClure warned the major oil companies not to take undue advantage of decontrol. McClure said Congress would reconsider controls if the oil companies pull out of "essential regions, particularly rural and agricultural communities."

Regulations Blocked

In his first full week in office, Reagan also put a freeze on many new federal regulations — steps he had pledged during his campaign.

The president eliminated the major function of the Council on Wage and Price Stability (COWPS) — to monitor price and wage increases and to set voluntary guidelines for them. The agency had been a failure at fighting inflation, Reagan said.

In one of its earliest requests to Congress, the administration asked members to raise the nation's debt ceiling by $50 billion, to $985 billion. Reagan expressed regret at the action, indicating that government deficits were one of the causes of inflation. Congress cleared the measure Feb. 6, giving Reagan his first legislative victory. Many Republicans who supported the bill never before had voted for an increase in the debt limit.

At his first news conference, held Jan. 29, the president issued stern warnings to the Soviet Union, while declaring himself uninterested in "revenge" on Iran for its 444-day imprisonment of 52 Americans. He reiterated campaign promises to pare government spending and to abolish the Departments of Education and Energy.

He also used the news conference to announce his 60-day freeze on regulations and his decision on COWPS.

The regulation freeze directed the heads of the Environmental Protection Agency and all Cabinet-level departments, except State and Defense, to delay the effective date of new regulations and to refrain from issuing new ones for 60 days. Included in the freeze were more than 100 rules, dubbed "midnight regulations" by Reagan, issued in the waning days of the Carter administration.

Exempted were regulations: 1) with deadlines, set by statute or court order, that would fall within the 60-day period; 2) issued according to a formal rulemaking process spelled out in the Administrative Procedures Act (PL 89-554); 3) affecting military or foreign policy; 4) affecting agency organization, management or personnel and 5) issued by the Internal Revenue Service.

For COWPS, Reagan eliminated 135 positions of staff members who monitored wages and prices and who had developed the voluntary guidelines. Reagan said the move would save $1.5 million a year. About 35 COWPS employees whose principal duties were to review and analyze government regulations would continue that function for the Office of Management and Budget (OMB) and the presidential task force on regulation headed by Bush.

Reagan: Actor to President

When Ronald Reagan finished the prepared text of his acceptance speech for the Republican presidential nomination, he paused dramatically.

"I have thought of something that is not part of my speech," he said with a slight quaver in his voice, "and I'm worried over whether I should do it."

The delegates in the hall collectively held their breath. So did the nation's television audience. Then the former movie and television actor asked the delegates to join his "crusade" to "recapture our destiny" with a moment of silent prayer.

"God bless America," he said, after the pause.

The performance demonstrated why Reagan was the GOP's strongest candidate in two decades, one who was able — largely through his mastery of television — to win enough support from American voters to achieve a landslide victory over incumbent President Jimmy Carter.

The addition of this dramatic touch to his acceptance speech was another manifestation of Reagan's ability to merge the skills he gained during 28 years as an actor with those developed in 16 years as a politician.

Virtually all Reagan watchers agreed that, as *The New York Times* stated in 1979, "Reagan is still the most accomplished politician in the country in using television as a campaign medium." The political power of this skill was keenly noticed after each of the two presidential debates during 1980. Reagan's performance in the second debate, against Carter only days before the election, was credited with helping to turn an apparently close race into a last-minute landslide for Reagan. *(Debate text, p. 103)*

For an actor who never won much acclaim or any awards, Reagan's success on the political stage was impressive from the start. In his first try for elective office, in 1966, he ousted California Gov. Edmund G. "Pat" Brown by nearly a million votes — the largest plurality by which a sitting governor had been defeated in the nation's history.

Two years after he finished his second term in Sacramento, Reagan nearly denied his party's nomination to the incumbent president, Gerald R. Ford. And in 1980, when many predicted he was too old to wage a strong presidential campaign, Reagan ran an astonishingly successful one.

Same 'Island of Freedom'

Whether running for public office, hosting television's "General Electric Theater" or speaking on the banquet circuit, for more than a quarter century Reagan espoused a political line that changed very little in either content or style.

In his 1964 national political debut, when he was supporting Barry Goldwater's presidential candidacy, Reagan spoke of the United States as "the only island of freedom that is left in the whole world." Sixteen years later, just before asking for the silent prayer in his acceptance speech, Reagan again spoke of "the island of freedom," and called the United States "a refuge for all those people in the world who yearn to breathe freely."

Reagan believed that over the years the country gradually had shifted to his conservative position and that in 1980 he represented the political mainstream.

To bolster his conviction that most of the electorate had grown tired of "big government," Reagan pointed to numerous primary victories where he attracted a large percentage of ethnic, blue-collar voters whose traditional allegiance to the Democratic Party dates to the Depression.

In the fall of 1980 Reagan's general election strategy revolved around seeking out those disaffected blue-collar Democrats once again. He made many appearances in the Northern industrial states and quoted Democratic presidents — Franklin D. Roosevelt, John F. Kennedy and Harry S Truman.

But Reagan's ability to capture the GOP nomination, and then the White House, went beyond a shift in the mood of the voters. Unlike 1968 when he campaigned reluctantly and 1976 when he began late, Reagan was prepared in advance and clearly wanted to win in 1980.

1980 Campaign Issues

The cornerstone of Reagan's platform was his long-held belief that reducing the size of the federal government would go a long way toward solving most of the nation's troubles.

Trimming the federal government had long been at the core of most of Reagan's domestic policy proposals. During the primary campaign he called for elimination of the Energy and Education departments. But a later proposal, announced Sept. 9, 1980, was to "squeeze and trim" $195 billion from the federal budget by cutting "waste, extravagance, abuse and outright fraud," without eliminating any major federal programs.

Reagan said he would freeze federal hiring the day he entered office and would try to reduce spending levels so the budget could be balanced by 1983. He also supported a tax package that would reduce personal income tax rates by 30 percent over three years and allow businesses to write off the costs of machinery and equipment 40 percent faster than they did in 1980.

During the primary season, Reagan reiterated his 1976 idea of giving state and local governments responsibility for many programs then in federal hands. "The federal government has taken on functions it was never intended to perform and which it does not perform well," he said, officially opening his 1980 quest for the White House.

Defense, space exploration, veterans' affairs and the environment should remain under federal control, Reagan said. Just about everything else should be turned back to local governments.

But in announcing a scaled-down economic growth plan to the International Business Council in Chicago Sept. 9, 1980, Reagan backed away from such a massive overhaul of government programs. Instead, he talked about reducing government regulations and appointing a citizens' task force to seek ways to make government more efficient.

Foreign Policy, Defense

The views Reagan espoused during the campaign on foreign policy reflected a hard-line approach toward the Soviet Union that had deviated little since the 1950s. His

overriding fear of Soviet expansion was developed at that time and was a major factor in his conversion from a liberal Democrat to a conservative Republican.

Reagan made it clear he believed the United States should increase its military strength to combat the influence of what he calls "the Moscow-Havana axis." The Russians, he has said, have "never retreated from their Marxist dream of one communist world."

Reagan called for substantial annual increases in the defense budget. He stated the second Strategic Arms Limitation Treaty (SALT II) was "fatally flawed" and that he planned to renegotiate its terms only after the United States had built up its military arsenal.

In 1978 Reagan campaigned across the country in opposition to the Panama Canal treaties. In hundreds of speeches, he recited his anti-treaty litany: "We built it. We paid for it. It's ours, and we are going to keep it."

After the Soviet invasion of Afghanistan in December 1979, Reagan suggested that the United States blockade Cuba in retaliation.

Domestic Issues

On domestic issues, Reagan's campaign views reflected his own conservative philosophy. He opposed abortion, the Equal Rights Amendment (ERA) and decriminalization of marijuana and maintained that the courts had become too lenient. He had complained in the past of a "virus of permissiveness [that] spreads its deadly poison."

He opposed busing of schoolchildren to achieve racial integration. During the height of the civil rights struggles, Reagan opposed California's 1963 open housing law and the 1964 U.S. Civil Rights Act. But he denied allegations made during his 1966 gubernatorial campaign that he was racially biased.

Reagan supported capital punishment and opposed gun control laws, suggesting instead that mandatory jail sentences be imposed on those who use weapons in crimes.

Midwestern Upbringing

Reagan's conservative political outlook closely matches his lifestyle. He does not smoke and drinks only occasionally. Although he and his wife Nancy entertained frequently during their first few weeks in Washington, it was expected that their routine in the White House would settle down to one similar to the one they followed in their California days. There the Reagans preferred to spend their evenings at home, dressed in pajamas, watching television and then going to bed early.

The switch to the White House also forced a change in Reagan's reticence concerning his family life. His four children — two from his marriage to actress Jane Wyman, which ended in divorce, and two from his current marriage — became celebrities in their own right. From their backgrounds, the public could see that the Reagan children did not fit their father's image of an "all-American family." His oldest daughter, Maureen, is a twice-divorced actress and fervent supporter of the ERA. An adopted son, Michael, sells gasohol and racing boats and has been divorced once. Another daughter, Patricia, an actress who uses her mother's maiden name of Davis, composes rock music and spent some time living with a rock musician. And the youngest son, Ron, is a ballet dancer who is married and lives in New York City.

Reagan's own childhood, spent in several small towns in rural northern Illinois, also diverged from his much-touted image of the wholesome American family. He was the younger of two sons of an alcoholic Irish-Catholic father, who had trouble keeping a job, and a Protestant mother of Scottish descent, who loved the theater. Reagan painfully recalls the day he came home from school and found his father passed out, drunk, on the front porch.

When Reagan was nine, his family settled in Dixon, Ill., where his father tried to make a living selling shoes. It was there, while attending high school, that Reagan did his first acting.

After graduating from Eureka College, a small liberal arts school near his home, Reagan began working as a sports announcer for WOO, a Davenport, Iowa, radio station. Using the name "Dutch" Reagan, which his father had given him, his reputation increased when that station and its sister station, WHO in Des Moines, joined the NBC radio network. Doing the play-by-play of football and baseball games, Reagan became widely known throughout the Midwest.

While Reagan was in California in 1937 for baseball spring training, an agent from Warner Brothers signed him for his film debut — to play a radio announcer in "Love Is On The Air." The part marked the beginning of a 28-year acting career that included more than 50 films.

Few of his films received much attention; fewer still won Reagan much acclaim. His favorite and best-known roles were in "Knute Rockne — All American," in which he played George Gipp, a Notre Dame football player, and in "King's Row," in which he was a small-town playboy who had had both legs cut off by a vengeful doctor.

Reagan would probably prefer to forget his roles in such other films as "Bedtime for Bonzo," where he played a college professor who tried to raise a chimpanzee as a human, and "The Killers," — his last film — in which Reagan had his only villainous role.

Reagan's acting career was interrupted in 1942 by a three-year stint in the Army, where he made training films. After he was discharged, he turned his attention more to the political aspects of his profession, taking fewer and fewer film roles. In 1947 he was elected president of the Screen Actors Guild, one of the major labor unions representing Hollywood talent. During his six one-year terms in that post, he successfully negotiated several contracts.

But Reagan is remembered in the profession more for his support of the blacklist, which was created by Hollywood producers to deny work to actors and writers suspected of having communist ties. In October 1947 Reagan appeared before the House Un-American Activities Committee (HUAC) as a friendly witness in its investigation of communism in the movie industry.

Political Beginnings

Reagan's political beliefs underwent a radical shift in the late 1940s and early 1950s. In his 1965 autobiography, *Where's the Rest of Me?*, Reagan characterized himself during the late 1940s as "a near-hopeless hemophiliac liberal. I bled for 'causes.'" But many of those causes, Reagan believed, had been infiltrated by communists. He moved away from them and, in the 1950s, away from movies as well.

Instead, he took on a new role as a spokesman for the fundamentalist right, railing against big government, high taxes and encroaching communism.

The General Electric Co. gave him a pulpit from which to preach his developing conservative ideology. Reagan not only hosted television's "GE Theater" from 1954 until 1962, but was sent by the company on two- and three-month speaking tours. It was at small gatherings of G. E. employees and civic groups across the country that Reagan developed his set speech that remained virtually unchanged over nearly three decades.

When General Electric did not renew his contract in 1962, Reagan decided to devote his political energy to the Republican Party and changed his party registration.

He initially reflected the New Deal Democratic beliefs of his parents and had campaigned for the liberal Helen Gahagan Douglas when she ran against Richard M. Nixon for the U.S. Senate in 1950. But starting in 1952, when he supported Eisenhower for president, Reagan began siding with the candidates of the party he would join 10 years later.

It was his "island of freedom" speech made on national television in the fall of 1964 to raise funds for Barry Goldwater that assured Reagan's place as an articulate spokesman for the Republican Party's right wing. After that appeal, several California businessmen approached Reagan — then the host of television's "Death Valley Days" — with the suggestion he run for governor.

In a state where parties traditionally held little influence, it hardly mattered that Reagan had not "paid his dues" in the GOP. He easily captured the party's 1966 nomination for governor, winning 64.7 percent of the vote in a five-candidate race. In the fall campaign against Gov. Brown, the Democratic incumbent, he railed against welfare cheaters and campus dissidents.

Brown, like many of Reagan's later opponents, underestimated his appeal with the voters. In his 1970 book, *Reagan and Reality*, Brown wrote that he "thought the notion was absurd" that his administration could be toppled by the host of "Death Valley Days."

But when the votes were counted, Reagan was the winner by 993,739 votes. His total vote of 3,742,913 was more than any previous California gubernatorial candidate had received up until that time.

Almost immediately after his election Reagan assumed national political stature. In 1968 his name came up repeatedly as a possible presidential candidate. He made a few tentative campaign swings but did not shift from his favorite-son status to a full-fledged candidate until two days before the Republican convention balloting in Miami Beach.

California Governor

Reagan's eight years in the California governor's office gave him more experience in an elective executive office than many presidents have brought to the job.

It was a sobering experience for Reagan to discover the wide gulf between what he had preached and what he could get through the relatively unfriendly Legislature, which was in Democratic hands for all but two years of his tenure.

Reagan had very little interest in trying to deal with the Democratic Legislature. On the few issues where he demonstrated a keen interest — most particularly welfare reform, education, and holding down the size of state government — he eventually accomplished at least some of his goals.

Ronald Reagan and his family watch the Republican National Convention from the candidate's hotel room in Detroit, July 1980. From left are: son Michael and his wife Colleen, Reagan, son Ron, Nancy Reagan and daughter Patti. Daughter Maureen was absent.

The Record

Reagan used those achievements during the presidential campaign to illustrate his success as governor of the nation's most populous state. Critics noted, however, that on all three the record was not without blemishes.

Reagan's supporters have considered his overhauling of the state welfare system to be his most successful endeavor as governor. Welfare reform became a major issue after Reagan won a second term in 1970, when he defeated Democratic Assembly leader Jesse Unruh by a half-million votes.

Reagan was alarmed at the swift increase in the state's welfare rolls. In 1961 there were 620,000 people receiving welfare benefits in California. Ten years later, the figure was 2.4 million, or one of every nine Californians. Reagan proposed a 70-point welfare and Medi-Cal reform package. Medi-Cal is California's more liberal version of Medicaid, the federal program that pays for medical care for low-income persons.

After considerable wrangling with the Legislature and in the courts, a compromise was reached that achieved Reagan's primary goal. The welfare caseload began to drop while benefits for those who remained eligible increased by more than 40 percent.

Some detractors of Reagan's welfare efforts charged he took a meat-ax approach that cut benefits to the needy as well as to welfare cheaters.

Reagan's economic actions also met mixed reviews while he was in the governor's chair. Although he campaigned for the governorship on a platform to "squeeze and cut and trim until we reduce the cost of government," the state budget more than doubled during his eight years in office — from $4.6 billion to $10.2 billion.

But with the help of a state hiring freeze, similar to the one he ordered as soon as he took office as president, California's government bureaucracy did not increase sig-

nificantly under Reagan. The number of full-time state employees rose by fewer than 6,000 from the 102,000 he inherited from Brown.

Reagan came under attack for the large tax hikes that were imposed while he was in office. Reagan defended the $865 million increase in sales, income and business taxes, all imposed during his first year in office, by stating they were necessary to compensate for Brown's high spending policies in previous years.

Many of the state taxes that were increased later in Reagan's administration were designed to raise revenues so the state could relieve local governments of welfare and education costs. That action, in turn, allowed for lower homeowners' property taxes. Reagan boasted that $5.7 billion in direct tax relief was granted during his eight years as governor. During the same time, the portion of California's budget earmarked for aid to localities jumped $5 billion to $7.8 billion.

Reagan's third major interest as governor was the state's public higher education system, the largest in the country. When he entered office, student unrest, particularly at the Berkeley campus of the University of California, was mounting. Reagan had little tolerance for the "free speech movement" or the growing protest over the Vietnam War.

One of his first actions as governor was to urge the state Board of Regents to fire University of California President Clark Kerr, who Reagan felt was too lenient with student demonstrators. He had praise, on the other hand, for S. I. Hayakawa, whose hard-line actions against students at San Francisco State College helped catapult the semanticist and college president into the U.S. Senate in 1976.

During his first two years, Reagan cut university funding by 27 percent. But once the protest movement died down, the state university system began to receive sizable funding increases. By the end of Reagan's second term, financial support for all levels of education had more than doubled over what it had been when he assumed office.

Early Days in Washington

To help him run the country, Reagan brought to Washington numerous longtime advisers who dated back to his California days. The so-called "California mafia," the political entourage that surrounded Reagan through most of his political life, formed the nucleus of Reagan's successful presidential campaign, and a number of these men — Edwin Meese, William Casey, Lyn Nofziger and Michael Deaver, to name a few — accompanied him to Washington.

Judging from his first few weeks in the White House, Reagan also brought with him the decision-making process that he used in Sacramento. The Reagan statehouse, like the presidential campaign, was known for a "collegial" working environment in which Reagan listened to a variety of opinions culminating in a round-table discussion with his top advisers. Then he made the broad policy judgment and relied on his aides to carry out the details on their own.

Ed Salzman, editor of the *California Journal* and a veteran Reagan observer, remarked, "What [Reagan] did once in office didn't always match what he said on the dinner circuit. As governor, Reagan was a pragmatic compromiser."

As president, Salzman predicted, Reagan would run an efficient White House in which he would serve as the chairman of the board, in much the same way he operated in Sacramento.

Judson Clark of the California Research Institute agreed. "Reagan was essentially a presider, not an administrator," Clark said. "He generally didn't roll up his sleeves and get deeply involved." Instead, as governor, Reagan preferred to receive one-page summaries of issues from which he would make a decision.

Reagan's Background

Profession: Public official and former actor.
Born: Feb. 6, 1911, Tampico, Ill.
Home: Los Angeles.
Religion: Christian Church.
Education: Eureka (Ill.) College, B.A., 1932.
Professional career: Radio sports announcer, 1932-37; motion picture actor, 1937-54; president, Screen Actors Guild, 1947-52; host, General Electric Theater, 1954-62; host and actor, Death Valley Days, 1962-66; California governor, 1967-75; newspaper and radio commentator, 1975-80; candidate for Republican presidential nomination, 1968, 1976, 1980; U.S. president, 1981-__.
Military: U.S. Army, 1942-45.
Family: Wife Nancy; four children. (Married 1940-48 to Jane Wyman.)

In his first news conference as president, on Jan. 29, Reagan indicated that he would be using much the same approach in the Oval Office. In reply to question after question, Reagan said he would not have an answer until the Cabinet met the following week to thrash out the problem he was being asked about. To longtime Reagan watchers, that confirmed their predictions that Reagan's style as president would not differ greatly from his style as governor.

Handyman of American Politics

Vice President George Herbert Walker Bush has been called the handyman of American politics. He has served as a congressman from Texas, United Nations ambassador, Republican National Committee chairman, envoy to China and Central Intelligence Agency director.

Apart from this much-needed Washington know-how, Bush brought two other important commodities to the Reagan administration: relative youth — he turned 56 in June of 1980 — and a bridge to the Eastern Republican establishment.

Like Jimmy Carter, Ronald Reagan never had held a federal office before his election to the presidency; it was anticipated that Bush's extensive experience in Washington would partially offset Reagan's lack of experience there.

For a man with such an extensive political history, though, Bush has remained a difficult politician to label — not so much because he has a reputation for changing his mind as because his positions so often have been couched in careful, some say equivocal, language. Indeed, he has disdained ideological categories. "I avoid being labeled," he said in January 1979. "We Republicans — that is our death wish — we try to categorize some person, label them. I don't want to be labeled."

Bush became known as a centrist in politics during his brief career in the U.S. House (1967-71), where he avoided extreme positions, shunned rhetorical hyperbole and often put something in his speeches to appeal to almost everybody.

But his voting record was more clearly conservative. It had to be to please his affluent constituents in suburban Houston's conservative 7th District.

His Republican orthodoxy was most evident on issues involving the role of the federal government and on fiscal policy. He backed such proposals as the Human Investment Act, which was designed to combat poverty through tax incentives rather than categorical grant programs. Bush did display more moderate leanings, however, especially in the area of civil rights. He voted for the Open Housing Act of 1968.

"I do not want it on my conscience," he said at the time, "that I have voted against legislation that would permit a Negro, say a Negro serviceman returning from Vietnam, where he has been fighting for the ideals of his country, to buy or rent a home of his choosing if he has the money."

As a Senate candidate in 1970, however, he espoused more cautious views about legislation to encourage civil rights, saying no more legislation was needed at that time.

During his legislative career Bush showed particular interest in environmental, consumer and world population matters. *(See Bush on the Issues box, p. 30)*

'The Perfect Staff Man'

Bush once was called "the perfect staff man," and his ability to be a team player likely will help him in occupying the number-two position. During his own presidential campaign, Bush steadfastly refused to consider the traditionally uninfluential vice presidential spot.

"You can take General Sherman's old line about unavailability and cube it," he told the convention about his lack of interest in the vice presidential nomination.

But in January of 1981, as Bush was being inaugurated into the vice presidency, he speculated on what his own responsibilities would be in the Reagan administration. He told a *New York Times* reporter that "Only time will tell, and I have stopped short of asking for and he's [Reagan] stopped short of defining any specific duties."

Bush commented in the same interview on the closeness of the Carter-Mondale relationship. "My conclusion is that the Mondale model is a very good model," he said. In particular, Bush pointed to the confidence that Carter placed in Mondale.

Several indications that Reagan intended to give Bush access to him, at least initially, surfaced during the first weeks of the new administration. Bush was given an office with close proximity to the Oval Office in the west wing of the White House, and he was scheduled to confer with the president, along with the national security adviser, each morning.

In the policy area, Bush announced in late January that Reagan had appointed him chairman of the Presidential Task Force on Regulatory Relief. The membership of the committee — including Donald Regan, William French Smith, Malcolm Baldrige, Raymond Donovan, David Stockman, Martin Anderson, and Murray Weidenbaum — indicated that the reduction of federal regulation was a top priority of Reagan's economic policy.

According to many observers, Bush assembled one of the most talented 1980 election staffs by drawing from traditional Republican talent pools. Reagan has recognized this. He chose as White House chief of staff Bush's campaign chairman, James A. Baker III. Baker also headed Gerald Ford's 1976 general election organization.

David A. Keene, the 1976 Southern states coordinator for Reagan, functioned as political director for candidate Bush, and former Republican National Committee spokesman Peter E. Teeley served as press secretary. Teeley was named press secretary to Vice President Bush.

Differences With Reagan

Although a favorite of many moderates, Bush actually espoused views markedly in line with those of Reagan during his own campaign for the presidency in 1980. The chief difference exhibited was one of style: Bush improvised more than his adversary and seemed less doctrinaire.

Yet there were some substantive differences. Bush and Reagan parted company in several areas during the 1980 primary campaign.

Bush criticized Reagan's proposal to blockade Cuba in retaliation for the Soviet invasion of Afghanistan. Reagan opposed the Equal Rights Amendment to the Constitution, and Bush supported it. Reagan wanted an anti-abortion constitutional amendment. Bush, while against publicly funded abortions, did not.

Bush also said in the spring of 1980 that the Reagan proposal for a massive, three-year, 30 percent federal tax cut would be inflationary; he favored a smaller reduction.

But on July 17, the morning after the announcement of Bush's selection as Reagan's running mate, Bush papered over his disagreements with Reagan and stressed their similar stances on economic, foreign and defense policy.

"I emphasize the common ground," said Bush. "I'm not going to get nickled and dimed to death [over the differences]."

'Up for the '80s'

Bush's treatment of Reagan during the campaign may work to his advantage as he occupies the number-two slot with his former adversary. During the primaries, Bush confined all criticism of front-runner Reagan to a handful of specific issues, such as the Reagan position on tax reduction. Otherwise, the attempt to draw differences was subtle. Bush would speak of his extensive government experience and underscore the need for a seasoned hand in the White House without mentioning Reagan directly.

Similarly, he avoided overt references to Reagan's age. His technique instead was to have photographers take pictures of him jogging. "I'm up for the '80s," Bush would exuberantly proclaim, thus only obliquely suggesting that because he was more than 13 years Reagan's junior, he stood a better chance of living through the decade.

Patrician Background

Bush was born to a wealthy New England family and looks every bit the pin-striped Ivy Leaguer. He is a gentlemanly type with a buoyant style, and his conversation is replete with upbeat expressions such as "gosh" and "that's fantastic." Although transplanted from Connecticut to Texas, Bush's political roots are in the Eastern Republican

faction that once held sway over the party. The late Sen. Prescott Bush, R-Conn. (1952-63), was his father.

The product of a well-to-do upbringing, Bush graduated from Phillips Academy, an elite prep school in Andover, Mass. He served in World War II as a Navy pilot. He was 18 at the time, reportedly the youngest pilot in the Navy, and was shot down in the Pacific but rescued by an American submarine that raced a Japanese ship to reach him.

After the war he attended Yale University and after graduating Phi Beta Kappa in 1948 moved to Texas to enter the oil business. His first job was as a warehouse sweeper and he then became a supply salesman with Odessa's Dresser Industries, an oil supply firm his father directed.

Backed by family money, Bush in 1951 helped start the Bush-Overby Development Co. Two years later he co-founded Zapata Petroleum Corp., and in 1954 became president of Zapata Off-Shore Co. In 1980 he used this experience to boast that he was the only one in the GOP contest "to meet a payroll."

In Houston, Bush became active in local Republican affairs and became chairman of the Harris County party organization.

Start in Politics

In 1964 Bush took his first step in electoral politics when he ran for the Senate. He finished first with 44 percent of the vote in the initial Republican primary against three other candidates despite the stigma of being

George Bush on the Issues

During his 1980 campaign for the presidency, George Bush took traditionally conservative positions on most issues.

Domestic Economy

Bush proposed a $20 billion tax cut, half of which would go to individuals to encourage increased personal savings and to provide tax incentives for home purchases, and half to the business sector for investment tax credits and tax incentives to hire and train young workers. He said he would not allow federal spending to grow by more than 7 percent a year.

On CBS-TV's "Face the Nation" in October 1979, Bush said that if he were president he would propose a balanced federal budget for 1982. But he said he didn't want to achieve a balanced budget through higher taxes. Bush acknowledged that his goals of reducing taxes and balancing the budget would be reached partly by inflation, which would increase the total amount of taxes collected. But he maintained that inflation would be eased by his tax and budget program.

While Bush favored a balanced budget, he was opposed to a mandatory balanced-budget amendment to the Constitution. He also expressed opposition to a constitutional convention on the subject. He was opposed to wage and price controls,

Energy

As a presidential candidate, Bush supported decontrol of oil prices as well as a windfall profits tax on oil companies. He also favored expansion of nuclear power, although he said some reforms were needed to ensure public safety, such as improving the safety procedures of the Nuclear Regulatory Commission.

Bush also advocated increased tax credits for individuals who made energy-saving improvements in their homes. He was opposed to gasoline rationing except in the event of a wartime emergency.

Defense and Foreign Affairs

Bush advocated restoration of new weapons systems canceled or delayed by the Carter administration, including the neutron bomb.

"Over the past decade, the Soviets have engaged in a massive, unprecedented buildup in their military arms, and with or without SALT they easily could far outdistance us in the 1980s," Bush said in June 1979 before the World Affairs Council in Philadelphia. "Yet the United States continues to flounder."

● *Salt II.* Bush went on record opposing the second Strategic Arms Limitation Treaty (SALT II) in its originally negotiated form.

"The SALT treaty is seriously defective and should be corrected before it leaves Capitol Hill," Bush said in a speech at the National Press Club in Washington in early September 1979. Bush said he believed the treaty should be renegotiated and be made more verifiable.

● *Soviet troops in Cuba.* Bush criticized the Carter administration's handling of the revelation that Russian combat troops were located in Cuba, although he said he did not believe they were a threat to the United States.

● *Intelligence.* The former CIA director supported the strengthening of the American intelligence system, but with stringent protections for the rights of U.S. citizens. He criticized Carter for stopping in 1977 SR-71 flights over Cuba as a weakening of U.S. intelligence.

● *Middle East.* In a meeting Oct. 18, 1979, with the American Jewish Committee, Bush, who visited Egypt and Israel in July 1979, said one way "not to lower oil prices is to trade Israel's security for price cuts."

● *China.* The former envoy to Peking criticized the manner in which the Carter administration established diplomatic relations with the People's Republic of China. "For the first time in our history, a peacetime American government has renounced a treaty with an ally [Taiwan] without cause or benefit," Bush wrote in *The Washington Post* in late December 1978.

little known and from the East. In the runoff he beat — with 61.6 percent of the vote — the more widely known Jack Cox, who had come close to beating John B. Connally, then a Democrat, for governor in 1962.

Against Democratic incumbent Ralph Yarborough, Bush won a respectable 43.6 percent of the vote, but Lyndon B. Johnson swept the state in the presidential election and Bush lost by 330,000 votes. Bush then lowered his sights somewhat, and in 1966 won a newly created House seat in the Houston suburbs against a right-wing Democrat with 57.1 percent of the vote.

In his two-term House tenure, Bush voted a basically conservative line: His 7th District remains the most Republican congressional district in Texas.

During his four years in the House he generally scored high in the ratings of the conservative Americans for Constitutional Action and low in those of the liberal Americans for Democratic Action. On Congressional Quarterly's conservative coalition score, he earned a higher rating in general than the average Republican member of the House.

Nonetheless, Bush did support some civil rights legislation, most notably the Civil Rights Act of 1968 and the open housing requirements that it contained. But his backing of civil rights was not unqualified. In 1970 he told Congressional Quarterly that "no more major legislation is needed now."

In 1970 he voted for creation of the Environmental Protection Agency. The year before, he supported a proposed constitutional amendment, which passed the House, to abolish the Electoral College and provide for the direct election of the president.

Bush long advocated the disclosure of public officials' assets, liabilities and income, and in April 1979 he released a statement listing his net worth at $1.8 million. His income for 1979 was $109,543.

On fiscal policy questions Bush maintained a conservative voting record. He also was a friend of the oil industry. Although he had divested himself of his oil interests after

his election to the House in 1966, he favored retention of the oil depletion allowance.

In 1968 Bush was mentioned as a vice presidential possibility, but Richard M. Nixon bypassed the one-term representative, who that year won re-election to his congressional seat without opposition. In 1970 Bush tried again for the Senate. He had hoped to run against the liberal Yarborough, but the senator was defeated in the Democratic primary by the more conservative Lloyd Bentsen.

Bush received the help of Nixon and Vice President Spiro T. Agnew in the campaign against Bentsen. Bush also conducted a sophisticated television advertising effort and even got some help from liberal Democrats dissatisfied with Bentsen. Economist John Kenneth Galbraith and ex-Sen. Ernest Gruening (1959-69) of Alaska both wrote letters in Bush's behalf. Bush, however, lost by nearly 160,000 votes, receiving 46 percent of the vote.

Five years later, when Bush was nominated to head the CIA, an allegation surfaced that he had concealed a 1970 cash campaign contribution — one news account placed the amount at $55,000 — from an illegal Nixon White House slush fund. The charge, resurrected by the media in February 1980, was denied by Bush, who said he had reported all his donations.

Executive Career

Bush entered the second phase of his public career in December 1970, when Nixon appointed him ambassador to the United Nations. The appointment drew criticism because of Bush's lack of foreign policy experience. Nevertheless, the Senate confirmed him by voice vote in February 1971.

At the United Nations, Bush pushed unsuccessfully to keep Taiwan in the world body while seating the People's Republic of China. By advocating the two-China policy of the Nixon administration, he modified his 1964 campaign statement that the United States should leave the United Nations if mainland China were admitted.

Although Bush often touted his government background during the 1980 campaign, he actually spent very little time in any of the jobs he held.

This pattern emerged in December 1972 when Nixon moved him to the post of GOP national chairman. In that post, from which Sen. Robert Dole of Kansas had been ousted after losing the support of the Nixon White House, Bush had the unenviable task of chairing the Republican National Committee during Nixon's Watergate travail. He remained loyal to the embattled president, but in 1980 insisted that he had privately urged Nixon to resign, a statement that was greeted with skepticism in some quarters.

In August 1974, when Ford succeeded Nixon, Bush was mentioned as a possibility to fill the vacant vice presidential slot. Instead, Ford named Bush the U.S. envoy to Peking, an appointment that did not require Senate confirmation. Bush attracted little attention in his Peking job.

Slightly more than a year later, Ford fired William E. Colby as CIA director and named Bush to replace him. Democrat Frank Church of Idaho, chairman of the Senate Intelligence Committee, opposed the selection of Bush for the CIA post because of his past political roles, particularly as Republican National Committee chairman. Church also was concerned that it would be unseemly if Ford were subsequently to name Bush as his 1976 running mate.

Bush told the Senate Armed Services Committee in December 1975 that he would not refuse the vice presiden-

Bush takes oath as vice president.

tial nomination, but promised to discourage any campaign boosting him. Ford pledged that he would not ask Bush to run with him in 1976, and the Senate confirmed him, 63-27, on Jan. 27, 1976.

In early 1977, at the end of his stewardship of the agency, which was then under fire for domestic spying, assassination plots and other schemes, several Democratic senators who had voted against his confirmation praised his performance. During this period, Bush belonged briefly to the Trilateral Commission, an association of prominent figures from the United States, Europe and Japan concerned with international affairs. In the spring of 1980 Bush came under attack for this affiliation from conservatives, who viewed the group suspiciously, suspecting it of left-wing leanings.

Two-Year Presidential Quest

The independently wealthy Bush spent almost two years in his quest for the presidency. Following the script that won Carter the 1976 Democratic nomination, he assiduously worked states holding early primaries in hope of attracting attention by a good performance.

The plan worked well in the fall of 1979 when Bush won several non-binding straw votes at state and local party gatherings. The aim was to draw news media notice, and it worked.

At one well-publicized state convention in Maine, Nov. 3, 1979, he embarrassed a rival, Sen. Howard H. Baker Jr. of Tennessee. Baker had brought a planeload of reporters along to witness his expected victory, only to be narrowly upset by Bush.

The plan also worked well in the important Jan. 21 Iowa precinct caucuses, the first bona fide vote of the 1980 political season. When Bush bested the front-running Reagan, who did little campaigning in the state, he was catapulted to the top ranks of the GOP field.

In the polls, he found himself gaining on Reagan. Networks interviewed him and *Newsweek* magazine put him on its cover. Bush began extolling his "Big Mo," or momentum. The Iowa loss woke up Reagan, who had been avoiding the fray but now plunged into campaigning in New Hampshire.

Bush's performance in the Nashua debate was damaging and he spent the weekend before the primary resting at home in Houston, while Reagan busily worked the Granite State. The result was a better than 2-1 drubbing by Reagan, who moved firmly into the lead again.

From then on, Bush's campaign was erratic. Reagan would beat him in a string of primaries, Bush would resurface with a solitary victory, then his fortunes would submerge once again.

Bush's Background

Profession: Public official and former oil drilling company executive.
Born: June 12, 1924, Milton, Mass.
Home: Houston.
Religion: Episcopal.
Education: Yale University, B.A., 1948.
Offices: Member of U.S. House, 1967-71; ambassador to the United Nations, 1971-73; chairman of the Republican National Committee, 1973-74; head of the U.S. liaison office in Peking, 1974-75; director of the Central Intelligence Agency, 1976-77; vice president, 1981-___.
Military: U.S. Navy, 1942-45.
Family: Wife, Barbara; five children.

A big setback for Bush came in Illinois March 18, when he limped in with a poor third-place showing, partly due to Illinois Rep. John B. Anderson, who finished second.

Toward the end of the primary season, Bush got a break. Reagan, having spent too much money in the early months, neared the $14.7 million legal expenditure cap and had to cut back. Bush's success in the April 22 Pennsylvania primary and near victory in the May 3 Texas contest were largely the result of this financial advantage. He unveiled an effective paid television program called "Ask George Bush," in which the candidate fielded friendly questions from an audience of supporters. Nevertheless, Reagan had built up a formidable delegate lead.

Ironically, one of Bush's biggest nights proved to be his biggest letdown. Even though he beat Reagan May 20 in Michigan, some news media tallies projected that the Californian had enough delegates to win the nomination.

At this point, Bush's own finances started to dwindle. The large Reagan delegate margin had slowed Bush fund raising to a relative trickle.

Bush took the advice of a country and western song, "The Gambler" by Kenny Rogers, which was popular among his campaign entourage: "You gotta know when to hold 'em/know when to fold 'em." He withdrew from the race May 26.

Presidential Transition

Presidential transitions may represent "a triumph of hope over experience," in the words that Dr. Samuel Johnson, the 18th century British wit, once applied to second marriages.

Expectations run high during the transition from one administration to another, and criticism usually is muted while the president-elect and the federal government adjust to the prospect of living together.

The transition operation of President-elect Ronald Reagan appeared to do "a lot of things right," according to Stephen Hess, a presidential scholar at the Brookings Institution, the Washington, D.C., think tank. Hess said the Reagan team's effort to work simultaneously on "policy, process and personnel" was an admirable departure from the job scramble that had dominated past transitions.

There were some rough spots, of course. But whether these were just inevitable snags in a new and complex undertaking or deep, lasting flaws would not become apparent until the new administration began to take control of the government bureaucracy and tried to leave its imprint on foreign and domestic policies.

Nevertheless, previous transitions gave the nation an early glimpse of the presidential style of a new administration.

For example, President-elect Jimmy Carter's deep involvement in 1976 in his transition foreshadowed his insistence on mastering details of federal programs as president. He spent long days poring over briefing books and scouring the country by telephone for candidates for government posts. Reagan, by contrast, appeared remote from the operation that sprang up in Washington after his election, though top aides insisted he was in full charge of important decisions.

Transition Tasks

Reagan's first crucial task was to pick his Cabinet. With a few exceptions, his choices were noncontroversial, moderate Republicans drawn from the nation's business and professional communities. This was particularly true of the key economic posts that would have the greatest responsibility for implementing the president's campaign promises to reduce inflation and stabilize the economy.

In two instances — those of Alexander M. Haig Jr. for secretary of state and James G. Watt for secretary of the interior — Reagan decided to go ahead with the selections knowing that they were controversial and would be challenged in Congress. One other nomination was unintentionally controversial, that of Raymond R. Donovan, Reagan's candidate for secretary of labor. In this case, federal investigators looking into his fitness for the post uncovered allegations that a construction company he owned in New Jersey had been involved in criminal dealings.

The Reagan transition drew several other critical observations:

● The contrast between Reagan's objections to the massive cost of government and the fact that his transition was the largest and costliest ever.

● A proliferation of statements by Reagan advisers and groups on important foreign policy, economic and national security issues. The number of persons appearing to speak on behalf of the president-elect was far greater than in previous transitions, and their importance was unclear because transition officials such as press secretary James Brady sometimes disavowed their statements.

● A sprinkling of controversial transition appointments, such as the Cleveland Teamsters union official Jackie Presser, who was being sued by the Labor Department for alleged "imprudent use" of Teamster pension and welfare funds.

● Charges by Carter administration officials that some Reagan transition team staffers who were working in federal departments could have had conflicts of interest.

● Concern about how much control Reagan himself exercised over the process of staffing the administration and developing its policies.

Washington veterans warned against making too much of these shortcomings and criticisms. Attorney Clark M. Clifford, adviser to presidents since Harry S Truman, stated that "what people say" during the transition period would "be forgotten" after the new administration took over. Many political scientists maintain that it takes a year or more for a new administration to become fully in command of the executive branch.

Continuity and Responsiveness

Two tasks of any presidential transition are to assure continuity in the federal government while seeking to instill "responsiveness of the government to the new political leadership," according to Laurin L. Henry, author of a Brookings Institution study, *Presidential Transitions.*

A third function is the "care and feeding for the battle-scarred veterans of the campaign — a way of rewarding people," observed Harrison Wellford, who during Carter's term was the executive associate director for reorganization and management at the Office of Management and Budget.

Wellford, who served in the Carter transition operation in 1976 and stayed on temporarily to handle the "nuts-and-bolts" details of Reagan's, added that the process also "gives you a chance to try out a lot of people."

The latter two functions partially explained the startling growth of transitions in recent presidencies, in the view of Hess and others.

Sandwiches and the Cabinet

Formally organized and federally funded transitions are a recent phenomenon. In a much simpler era, President-elect Woodrow Wilson spent most of the months before Inauguration Day — which before 1937 did not take place until March in years following a presidential election — winding up his term as governor of New Jersey. Wilson picked potential Cabinet members while munching sandwiches with his close friend, Col. Edward M. House. (The 20th Amendment to the Constitution, ratified in 1933, moved Inauguration Day to Jan. 20.)

"Much to the disgust of the reporters who badgered him daily," wrote Henry in the Brookings study, Wilson refused to disclose his Cabinet until he introduced them at his swearing-in — a customary practice at that time.

Twenty years later, an attempt at improving the process failed. Outgoing President Herbert Hoover sought unsuccessfully to draw President-elect Franklin D. Roosevelt into joint action to stem the massive failures of the nation's banks during the four months between the November 1932 election and the March inauguration. Roosevelt's resistance had severely strained relations between the two men by the time they rode to the Capitol for FDR's swearing-in.

Truman, who had been thrust unprepared into the job by Roosevelt's death in April 1945, was more thoughtful to his successor, Dwight D. Eisenhower. Before leaving office, Truman turned over to him various budgetary and other information on government programs. But the first clearly organized transition was the changeover from Eisenhower to John F. Kennedy in 1960.

Kennedy Transition

In the summer of 1960, Kennedy asked Clark Clifford to prepare a general memorandum on "fundamentals," as Clifford remembers it. On the day after the election, Clifford sent off a 60- or 70-page guide, largely on governmental processes, to Kennedy and his "gang at Hyannisport." There also were a handful of "low-key, very small" groups preparing short issue reports after the election, and Clifford met daily with Eisenhower's White House chief of staff.

Cabinet announcements were handled with dispatch, Clifford said. The press was called to Kennedy's Georgetown house. Kennedy and the nominee would appear on the front step, and "the press would ask some questions. But it was kind of cold in December" so the queries didn't last long. Clifford recalled that the transition was "quite smooth" and "didn't cost anything" beyond donated time.

Cabinet nominees, once they were cleared by the FBI, were told by the Kennedy staff to immediately "get an office in their department and start meeting with people there," Clifford said.

Several years later, Congress decided that the process should be institutionalized, and the Presidential Transition Act of 1963 authorized $900,000 for expenses of incoming and outgoing administrations.

In 1964 Lyndon B. Johnson collected the first of such funds — some $72,000, according to a 1977 General Accounting Office (GAO) report. In 1968 Richard M. Nixon's transition spent $450,000 in federal funds and an additional $1 million from private sources. Congressional amendments passed in 1976 raised the ceiling to the existing level of $2 million for incoming administrations and $1 million for expenses of the presidential staff leaving office.

Carter Transition

The increase in funding authorized by Congress for the transition may have led to some of the problems President Carter encountered once he took office, according to Harvard Professor Richard E. Neustadt. Neustadt had written extensively on the presidency and had been an adviser to four presidents — Truman, Kennedy, Johnson and Carter.

In a 1980 update of his study *Presidential Power,* Neustadt wrote that the availability of generous transition funds ballooned the transition staff, setting the pattern for a larger White House than Carter had planned. Some 312 people were on the Carter transition payroll for varying periods, according to the 1977 GAO study. And the total cost of his transition was about $1.7 million of the $2 million provided by Congress.

In Neustadt's view, Carter underestimated how much the trend to a larger White House staff, begun in his transition, would undermine his plan for a decentralized "Cabinet government" where policy would be made largely in the departments.

The 1976 transition also was deeply troubled by an internal power struggle between Jack H. Watson, who had been overseeing planning and policy development for Carter for months before the election, and Carter campaign operatives led by Hamilton Jordan.

Precious time was lost to this jockeying for position, and "the inevitable triumph of the tried-and-true campaigners helped dilute the [Watson] planners' emphasis on governance," according to Neustadt. He concluded that "too many transitions like Carter's . . . might indeed make the presidency impossible."

Wellford conceded that the Carter transition was too large and that some of its work was not used. At the Department of Health, Education and Welfare, for example, Secretary Joseph A. Califano Jr. "just said 'thank you very much'" to the transition team and disregarded its recommendations, according to Wellford. But other transition recommendations, such as those on Civil Service and regulatory reform, became the core of major Carter administration legislative achievements, he said.

Reagan Transition

Reagan avoided some of these pitfalls, according to Hess. His campaign staff moved smoothly into transition positions.

Reagan Sworn In as Nation's 40th President

Ronald Reagan began his term as the nation's 40th president by renewing his campaign pledges to take swift action to deal with the economy — the issue that more than any other was identified with his drive for the White House. At the same time, he was blessed with an end to the nation's most excruciating foreign crisis.

As the new president delivered his inaugural address from the West Front of the Capitol, 52 Americans who had been held hostage for the last 444 days of the Carter administration were freed by their Iranian captors.

It was, the president declared, "a perfect day."

In his first official act Jan. 20, the new president made good on a campaign pledge by signing an executive order instituting a federal hiring freeze.

By week's end, 13 of his Cabinet-level nominees had been confirmed overwhelmingly by the Senate. But most sub-Cabinet-level positions, critical to the functioning of the government, still had to be filled.

Republican officials at the White House and State Department began their new jobs by poring over the details of the intricate agreement, worked out by the Carter staff, that provided for the return of frozen assets to Iran in exchange for the hostages' freedom. The president subsequently promised to honor the terms of the pact.

Assuming the Reins

Chief Justice Warren E. Burger administered the oath of office to Reagan at three minutes before noon. At 69, he was the oldest man to be sworn in as president of the United States. For Reagan it was the culmination of a 12-year effort to gain the presidency.

Breaking with custom, Reagan was inaugurated on the West Front of the Capitol overlooking the Mall and its monuments. Previously, inaugurations were held on the East Front, which looks out on the Supreme Court and the Library of Congress.

At the beginning of his inaugural address, Reagan praised the nation's history of "orderly transfer of authority" and thanked Carter for his "gracious cooperation" during the transition period. The 40th president repeated familiar economic and patriotic themes from his campaign speeches. He spoke in a warm and firm manner that seemed more suited to television audiences than to the crowd of 70,000 that had gathered to hear him. Rhetorical flourishes were limited.

Four years earlier, Carter had promised a "new beginning," too, but warned that "we can neither answer all questions nor solve all problems."

Reagan made the same "new beginning" pledge — it was the theme of his inaugural — but his speech seemed more reassuring than Carter's.

Transfer of Power

Government cannot solve the nation's problems, he said, because government "is the problem." But to his own question of whether answers could be found to those difficulties, Reagan answered: "an unequivocal and emphatic yes."

Addressing U.S. "friends and allies" abroad, Reagan promised to "match loyalty with loyalty." To "enemies of freedom," he vowed that to keep the peace "we will negotiate for it, sacrifice for it; we will not surrender for it — now or ever."

Return to Pomp

The pomp of Reagan's inauguration contrasted with Carter's efforts four years earlier to downplay ceremony. This time male members of Congress were asked to wear formal morning dress — gray jacket, pearl-gray vest and striped trousers.

After the ceremony, congressional leaders attended a traditional luncheon with the new president in the Capitol — where the president made the first official announcement of the release of the U.S. hostages. "Some 10 minutes ago," he told the legislators, "the planes bearing our prisoners left Iranian airspace, and they're now free of Iran."

After the luncheon, President and Mrs. Reagan rode in a limousine up Pennsylvania Avenue to a parade reviewing stand in front of the White House.

Later in the day, nine inaugural balls were held. They had been preceded by a lavish array of parties and concerts.

Inaugural planners thought the cost of official festivities would reach a record high — estimates ranged from $8 million to $11 million.

Another important difference was that Reagan's over-all governing philosophy was clearer than Carter's, which helped to reduce the internal power struggles. Carter picked strong-willed advocates from consumer, environmental and other public interest groups for many transition slots and permanent appointments in his administration. "These people each had very clear, competing agendas," while Carter was "ambiguous" on many policy questions; so "you had a lot of fighting for the heart and mind of the president," Hess observed.

Edwin Meese III, the Reagan transition director, who subsequently became White House counselor, repeatedly emphasized that loyalty to Reagan's philosophy was the first consideration in making appointments.

And the transition team created an elaborate structure for sifting through policy recommendations and putting them in some order before sending them on to Reagan. According to Hess, President-elect Reagan apparently saw his job as that of decision-maker rather than as manager of the federal government, "and frankly that's good," according to Hess.

Size and Organization

Officially, there were about 450 people working on the Reagan transition. But transition officials believed that perhaps an equal number were working informally on behalf of the president-elect in various advisory roles. About 10 percent of the 450 were salaried. The rest were volunteers or worked on a "dollar-a-year" basis.

The cost of Reagan's transition was estimated at between $2.3 million and $3 million by Verne Orr, deputy director for administration of the transition team. "The dollar just doesn't buy what it did four years ago," Orr lamented.

The process of surveying existing programs and policies, headed by the Reagan transition's deputy director, William E. Timmons, provided both data and a ready-made staff for incoming Cabinet members, John Nugent, Timmons' assistant, pointed out. Timmons was in charge of congressional liaison under Presidents Nixon and Ford. The transition program evaluation groups, or teams, provided "the nucleus of the staffs" for the new department heads, said Nugent.

Transition officials had made no commitments to move the various program teams onto department payrolls after Inauguration Day, but their expertise and loyalty to Reagan's viewpoints made them likely candidates for permanent appointments, Nugent said. While it worked this way in some departments, there were exceptions. Secretaries Haig and Weinberger, for example, dismissed the transition teams for their departments almost as soon as they were confirmed.

Another function of the program evaluation groups, of which there were 25 stationed in the 13 federal departments and various agencies throughout the executive branch, was to freeze implementation of programs that were not in accord with Reagan's priorities, according to transition official Darrell M. Trent.

Trent headed a 30-member Office of Policy Coordination that received issue papers from a second group of 48 transition task forces which began work in the summer of 1980. The group also received reports from about 20 congressional task forces and a substantial amount of unsolicited advice, including a 20-volume study of the federal government by the Heritage Foundation, a conservative, Washington-based research organization.

From these sources of information, Trent's group fashioned an "overall program" for the Reagan administration. The group's recommendations then were studied by five general "issue chiefs" and ultimately were given to senior policy advisers Martin C. Anderson, Caspar W. Weinberger and Richard V. Allen.

How the GOP platform fit into these deliberations was not altogether clear. Trent called the platform a statement of "general [Republican] goals and objectives" but not "specifically the document of the standard-bearer of the party."

During the transition period, Trent declined to speculate on how much of the policy apparatus ultimately would be incorporated in Reagan's White House staff. But the procedure initiated by the transition for processing information and setting priorities for the new president suggested that Reagan and his top advisers wanted sources independent of the permanent — and sometimes stubborn — federal bureaucracy.

Past presidents commonly complained of difficulties in instituting major new policies for the federal bureaucracy. Truman recalled thinking that Eisenhower would assume office and order officials to " 'Do this! Do that!' *And nothing will happen.* Poor Ike — it won't be a bit like the Army. He'll find it very frustrating," Truman wrote.

Staff

Carter relied largely on public interest groups and congressional staff members for his transition workers, many of whom were inexperienced in department management. Reagan workers within the departments generally were older and more knowledgeable.

Hess and Wellford indicated there was more focus on information gathering by the Reagan transition and less preoccupation with sparring for jobs. "For this group, there aren't that many great government jobs," because they had already seen the government from the inside and because their existing salaries in private industry or law practices probably were significantly higher, Hess added.

Because many of the Reagan transition staffers had worked either in or with the departments they were scrutinizing, the quality of the information they produced may have been more useful than that produced by the Carter transition staff, Hess speculated.

"The 'outs' have only been out for four years and now they're back in the departments, knowing how things work and where the bodies are buried," he said.

Conflict-of-Interest Charges

In the opinion of some Carter officials, however, the background of the Reaganites created potential conflicts of interest. The volunteers and dollar-a-year workers typically were on the payrolls of companies that may have had an interest in inside information on departmental contracts, regulations or lawsuits, they noted.

"We would never have sent defense contractors into the Department of Defense," remarked Wellford. By contrast, Ben Plymale, a Boeing Co. vice president on Reagan's defense transition team, was a leading proponent of an expensive modernization of the Boeing-made Minuteman intercontinental missile — a project for which the original manufacturer would be the likely contractor. Plymale, not surprisingly, was widely mentioned as a candidate for a top Pentagon post. But as of the end of February, Plymale had not been named to any such post.

The Reagan group was "very" sensitive to conflict-of-interest problems, according to Nugent. Transition counsel Peter McPherson and staff lawyers were ordered to inform each transition worker of potential conflicts and to avoid working on contracts or regulations where there were potential conflicts.

Within the departments, however, transition team leaders were given considerable latitude to bring in occasional consultants or "helpers from their law offices, Senate staffs, whatever," reported one staff member. These consultants did not necessarily go through the official screening by the transition counsel's office and thus may not have received the conflict-of-interest instructions.

Policy Pronouncements

When President-elect Roosevelt avoided Hoover's efforts to draw him into emergency action before his inauguration, he was acting in a well-established tradition. Wilson was conspicuously uninterested in a Mexican revolution that occurred after he was elected, even though rioting Mexicans sacked the U.S. Embassy and killed several Americans.

Half a century later, in 1968, President Nixon explicitly stated that Johnson administration officials should be viewed as spokesmen also for the incoming Republicans in the ongoing Paris negotiations over ending the Vietnam War.

Reagan, too, stressed the need for continuity, saying he would not comment on or interfere in policy matters until after he was inaugurated. But his reputation for delegating authority had heightened interest in the opinions of those advising him. His views on various issues pending in the lame-duck session of Congress that was held after the November election, such as the partial embargo on U.S. grain sales to the Soviet Union and the so-called Kemp-Roth income tax cut, were solicited and given. Within days of Reagan's election, reports began surfacing on recommendations of various Reagan advisory groups on economic, health, environment, defense spending and other issues.

And the State Department criticized in the waning weeks of the Carter administration the "unofficial statements and news leaks" from the Reagan transition team on foreign policy, particularly on Latin America. Patricia M. Derian, assistant secretary of state for human rights, suggested to the Associated Press that certain "imprudent statements" of some Reagan advisers had encouraged brutality and might have contributed to terrorist attacks on Americans in El Salvador, including the murder of four American women, three of them Roman Catholic nuns.

Different Work Habits

In 1976 Carter spent long hours during the transition reading detailed reports and huddling with his transition teams in Washington and Georgia. Wellford recalled that "when you realized that you had access to the president-elect and that he was intensely interested in what you did, you had less recourse to the newspaper."

Reagan appeared distant from his Washington transition operation after he was elected. For four days, Dec. 15-18, 1980, his California press schedule showed only that he would visit his barber, his tailor and a meat locker and that he would receive a Christmas tree.

But Meese had dismissed suggestions that Reagan was idle while staying in California or that he was uninterested in the details of the transition. And Trent said Reagan's involvement at a major briefing session with his economic advisers in mid-November was typical of his method of operation: "He went through the report line by line. He is always very interested in the details of specific proposals."

Cabinet: Mainstream Republican

In selecting his Cabinet secretaries, Ronald Reagan skimmed the top levels of the nation's law and business communities, particularly for key federal departments such as Defense and the Treasury.

In filling the positions dealing with the economy, for example, Reagan generally chose moderate, mainstream Republicans with years of management expertise.

These appointments were uniformly conservative, male and white. Several were drawn from Reagan's closest circle of confidants, and most attended Harvard or Yale.

Reagan also tried to assuage his Southern supporters by picking James B. Edwards, former governor of South Carolina, to be his Energy Department secretary. And he made a clear but controversial appeal to discontented land users in the West by designating as his secretary of the Interior Department a lawyer, James G. Watt, who had specialized in contesting the department's management of federal lands as well as the conservation efforts of environmental groups.

There were two other controversial choices besides Watt: for secretary of state: Alexander M. Haig Jr., whose reputation as a brilliant public servant was clouded by questions concerning his role in the Nixon White House on issues such as Vietnam and Watergate; and, for secretary of labor: Raymond J. Donovan, whose nomination was delayed by allegations that his New Jersey construction firm had made payoffs to union officials. (An FBI investigation failed to substantiate the charges, and Donovan was confirmed by the Senate.)

Reagan's choices generally brought praise from the business community and disappointed reactions from some liberal and consumer groups as well as from some of Reagan's far-right supporters.

Prime qualifications for being chosen were, above all, loyalty to Reagan's philosophy, and then "integrity," "competence," "toughness" and a "team-player" style of operation, according to transition chief Edwin Meese III.

"They share my philosophy and my belief in Cabinet government," Reagan said in announcing the first eight Cabinet nominees in December.

There was substantial government experience among them. Caspar W. Weinberger at the Pentagon had headed the Department of Health, Education and Welfare, the Federal Trade Commission and the Office of Management and Budget under Presidents Nixon and Ford.

Others, such as Reagan's attorney general, William French Smith, and Transportation Secretary Drew Lewis, were new to Washington and to the programs they would have to oversee.

Of the 13 Cabinet secretaries, only one, HUD Secretary Samuel R. Pierce Jr., was a black. None was a woman. However, Reagan's choice for U.N. ambassador — which had Cabinet-level rank — was Jeane J. Kirkpatrick, a woman and a Democrat.

Appointment Speed

Reagan waited longer than Jimmy Carter did in 1976 to announce his first Cabinet choices. Reagan announced his first eight choices on Dec. 11, 1980, but didn't complete the process until Jan. 7, 1981, when T. H. Bell was named to head the Department of Education.

Carter had made his first appointments on Dec. 3 and his last on Dec. 23. In 1968 Richard M. Nixon introduced his entire Cabinet on Dec. 11. John F. Kennedy announced his first selections on Dec. 1, 1960, and his last on Dec. 16. Dwight D. Eisenhower in 1952 made his first appointments on Nov. 20 and had completed the process by Dec. 5.

Reagan's Cabinet

Agriculture —John R. Block
Commerce — Malcolm Baldrige
Defense — Caspar W. Weinberger
Education — T. H. Bell
Energy — James B. Edwards
Health and Human Services —
    Richard S. Schweiker
Housing and Urban Development —
    Samuel R. Pierce Jr.
Interior — James G. Watt
Justice — William French Smith
Labor — Raymond J. Donovan
State — Alexander M. Haig Jr.
Transportation — Drew Lewis
Treasury — Donald T. Regan

Alexander M. Haig Jr.:
Secretary of State

By selecting Alexander M. Haig Jr. to be secretary of state, Reagan precipitated his first serious challenge from Senate Democrats, risking a political battle rather than giving in to Haig's critics.

Democratic leaders had promised even before Haig's nomination was formally announced Dec. 16, 1980, that they would use the retired Army general's Senate confirmation hearings to examine his role as a top aide to President Nixon during the Watergate period. Because of that association, Haig was considered probably the most controversial of Reagan's Cabinet nominations.

In the end, Haig won Senate confirmation handily by a vote of 93-6 on Jan. 21, but only after surviving five grueling days of hearings before the Senate Foreign Relations Committee and a Senate floor debate.

Sen. Lowell P. Weicker Jr., R-Conn., the lone Republican voting against Haig, provided the most vehement opposition, accusing the nominee of consistently choosing the "lowest road" in his conduct. "Gen. Haig has shown — shows — a contempt for both Congress and the individual rights and liberties of all Americans," Weicker said.

Sen. Barry Goldwater, R-Ariz., was just as vigorous in his support. "Those who want to associate Alexander Haig with Watergate are talking through a rather empty hat, and I might even go lower than that," Goldwater said.

Military, Government Record

Whatever the disagreements about his record, supporters as well as critics of the nomination agreed that Haig would be a driving force in the Reagan administration.

Born on Dec. 2, 1924, in Philadelphia, he attended the University of Notre Dame for one year, but then used an uncle's congressional connections to transfer to the U.S. Military Academy.

A 1947 West Point graduate — number 214 in a class of 310 — Haig served as an administrative assistant to Gen. Douglas MacArthur's deputy chief of staff in occupied Japan in 1949. In 1950 he married Patricia Fox, the daughter of his commanding officer. In 1951 Haig saw combat in several Korean War actions, including the Inchon landing.

Haig testifying at his confirmation hearings.

After various military assignments, he studied international relations at Georgetown University in Washington, D.C., earning an M.A. in 1961. He then worked in the Pentagon on European and Middle Eastern affairs and later became military assistant to Secretary of the Army Cyrus R. Vance.

When Vance was appointed deputy secretary of defense in 1964 he took Haig along. Then when Henry A. Kissinger was forming his National Security Council staff, just before the Nixon administration took office in January 1969, he was urged by the Army's general counsel, Joseph A. Califano Jr., to take Haig on.

As Kissinger's military adviser, Haig acted as liaison between the Pentagon and the State Department and screened all intelligence reports before they went to the president.

Haig's first brush with public controversy came on Sept. 7, 1972, when Nixon skipped more than 240 other top-ranking generals with more seniority and promoted Haig from a two-star major general to a four-star, full general. Nixon also appointed Haig as Army vice chief of staff.

When Nixon aides H. R. Haldeman and John D. Ehrlichman resigned from the White House April 30, 1973, Nixon selected Haig as his new chief of staff. Haig left his White House post in 1974 after Ford became president and appointed him commander of NATO. He retired from the Army on June 30, 1979. He spent six months testing his chances for the 1980 Republican presidential nomination but gave up, saying "it would not be constructive for me to seek political office in 1980."

On Dec. 27, 1979, he was named president and chief operating officer of United Technologies Corp., a multinational aircraft manufacturer that was the third largest U.S. defense contractor in fiscal 1979. Haig served less than a year in that job; he spent six weeks during the spring of 1980 recovering from heart surgery.

Senate Reaction

Haig reportedly had been Reagan's favorite for secretary of state ever since the November election. But *The Washington Post* Dec. 6 said "authoritative sources" had deemed the appointment in jeopardy because of Haig's activities in the Nixon White House, particularly his involvement in the Watergate scandal. Sen. Robert C. Byrd, D-W.Va., for example, said the questions about Haig's Watergate role were serious enough that "it is possible he would not be confirmed" by the Senate.

Other senators quickly joined the debate. Some said they were uncertain a military man should be made the nation's chief diplomat.

Alan Cranston, D-Calif., the new Senate minority whip and a member of the Foreign Relations Committee, said he was "disappointed" with Haig's 1979 Senate testimony against the SALT II arms treaty. "He seemed to me not to be very well prepared," Cranston said. "He hadn't studied the treaty with great care . . . and, while he came there as an expert witness, he was never willing to say what he found at fault with the treaty."

But Haig had strong support on the committee as well. The chairman of the committee, Sen. Charles H. Percy, R-Ill., said he did not want Haig's confirmation proceedings to be "a second Watergate hearing." Foreign Relations member and conservative leader Jesse Helms, R-N.C., also endorsed Haig.

After the nomination was announced, a reporter asked about the alleged "skeletons in his closet" from Watergate.

Haig responded: "Sometimes, I feel like it's Halloween, there are so many bones rattling around." Then he added, "I'm ready to set the record straight. I'm optimistic. Why shouldn't I be? I know what my record is."

Senate Hearings

The committee thoroughly probed the retired Army general's role as White House chief of staff during the later stages of the Watergate scandal. It also scrutinized Haig's foreign policy views, questioned his morality and judgments and tested the limits of his composure to a degree rare in Senate confirmation hearings.

Haig outlined and aggressively defended his world view — characterized by a hard line toward the Soviet Union and founded on the idea that "there are things worth fighting for. We must understand that. We must structure our policy under that credible and justified premise."

Consistent with this, Haig's testimony reflected a belief that, while international law provides standards by which policies were judged, in the final analysis it is the global balance of power that shapes events.

The hearings began Jan. 9 with panel members squabbling over how deeply to delve into Haig's involvement in Nixon administration scandals. Committee members argued over whether there should be a full-scale attempt to resurrect Watergate as a major issue in the confirmation process. Some Democrats had threatened to grill Haig on his roles in the Nixon administration's wiretapping of reporters and government officials and in the Watergate scandal. Haig himself moved to head off critics by offering to testify under oath and by agreeing to cooperate in the attempts to obtain evidence about his activities under Nixon.

Chairman Percy declared that past investigations of Haig had been "exhaustive." Percy said he had "no information which would justify an adverse conclusion or which suggests that this nomination should be delayed."

But Claiborne Pell, R.I., the senior Democrat on the committee, said Haig "carries with him — whether justified or not — political baggage, or scar tissue, if you will." As a result, Pell said: "I do not recall a nomination that has come to us that has caused the concern in the Senate that this one has."

Haig forcefully read a lengthy, carefully drafted opening statement in which he defended his conduct under Nixon, broadly stated his views of American foreign policy and offered subtle assurances to those who were apprehensive about a military man directing the nation's diplomacy.

Role in Watergate

At the insistence of its Democratic members, the committee Jan. 10 subpoenaed an index of tape recordings made in Nixon's office between May 4 and July 18, 1973, a crucial period during the Watergate affair. But the committee was sidetracked by Nixon, who asserted a legal right to deny release of the tapes.

Democrats wanted to subpoena the actual tapes, but Republicans — armed with a 9-8 committee majority in the 97th Congress — refused to go that far. They argued that it would be wrong, as Majority Leader Howard H. Baker Jr. of Tennessee put it, to indulge in "an orgy of Watergate." The rationale for the compromise was that, with the index, the committee could decide which tapes to subpoena.

Assisted by his attorney, former Health, Education and Welfare Secretary Joseph A. Califano Jr., Haig moved

to defuse the Watergate issue during the first day of his hearings. In an appendix to his opening statement he provided responses to a variety of specific charges.

Throughout the hearings, Haig, when asked about his conduct during the Nixon years, turned to that appendix — almost as if by reflex action — and answered by reading his original responses to the charges raised. As White House staff director in the Watergate era, Haig said, his goal was to protect Nixon "within the boundaries of the law and the advice of lawyers," and he viewed his "overriding duty as one to preserve [the presidency] in the national interest."

But such questions were infrequent, except in the fourth day of the hearings when Democrats Paul S. Sarbanes, Md., Paul E. Tsongas, Mass., and Joseph R. Biden Jr., Del., grilled Haig on the topic for 45 minutes. They repeatedly pressed the nominee to give them his "value judgment" on whether abuses during the Nixon era were morally right or wrong. As if struggling to restrain himself, Haig finally said there were "abuses on both sides" during Watergate. Then, raising his voice, he told Sarbanes: "Nobody has a monopoly on virtue — not even you, senator."

Tsongas told Haig the senators were searching for "reassurance" that he disapproved of abuses of power and illegal actions by White House officials during the Nixon administration. Haig responded that "the kind of *mea culpas* that I sense in your question you want, I just can't give, because I don't feel them."

However, after a break in the hearings Haig returned with a prepared statement in which he said, in part, that the Watergate break-in and cover-up were "improper, illegal and immoral. They were an affront to the fundamental values I cherish and we all share."

Despite the opposition of these Democrats, the committee overwhelmingly approved his nomination Jan. 15 by a 15-2 vote, leaving little doubt he would be confirmed. Sarbanes and Tsongas cast the two votes against Haig in committee. Cranston, who earlier had said "This is a nomination that should not have been made," ended up voting for Haig. "One by one," Cranston said, "most but not all" of his doubts about the nominee had been relieved.

Haig won his battle not on the strength of his rebuttal to questions about his ties to President Nixon, but by demonstrating a broad, studied grasp of dozens of foreign policy issues and, in many cases, by setting forth firm convictions on how to deal with them.

Foreign Policy Views

Haig outlined his general foreign policy views, but said it would be "premature here to set forth definitive policies or offer detailed programs." Haig — whose critics had questioned whether he possessed a global perspective — said the major dangers facing the United States ranged from the threat of Soviet military action in Eastern Europe to turmoil in Africa and Latin America. All foreign policy problems, he said, were "made more intractable" by massive increases in Soviet power over the last two decades.

The most "urgent task is to re-establish a foreign policy consensus" in the United States, he said. But beyond that, the conduct of American foreign policy must be characterized by "consistency, reliability, balance." Haig said he would set out to achieve those goals in three specific ways — each of which addressed criticisms that had been directed at the Carter administration:

● "The United States government must speak to other nations with a single voice." As secretary of state, Haig said he would be Reagan's chief foreign policy spokesman and the president's national security adviser would merely "fill a staff role for the president." Under President Carter, national security adviser Zbigniew Brzezinski had, according to foreign policy officials, repeatedly undercut Secretary of State Cyrus R. Vance.

● The executive branch must have an "effective partnership with Congress."

● There must be more reliance on career State Department officials "if the United States is to act reliably and consistently in the world arena."

Haig gave the following positions on specific issues:

Nuclear Balance

Haig repeatedly emphasized the need for a military buildup to counter Soviet arms gains in recent years and to enable the United States to succeed in the fundamental task of "the management of Soviet power."

However, despite a Republican Party platform call for "military superiority" over the Soviet Union, Haig declined to endorse superiority as a goal. In one exchange, he said "superiority" had become a "buzzword" that evoked "visceral reactions."

Arms Control

Haig consistently defended his belief that the Soviets would negotiate worthwhile arms control agreements only when persuaded that the United States had the strength to resist their "imperial foreign policy" even without them.

He also stressed his faith in "linkage" — the idea that arms control negotiations must be linked to general Soviet behavior and should be used as an inducement to them to conduct their foreign policy in ways acceptable to the United States. Arms control, he said, could not become "an end in itself."

More specifically, Haig said that despite the demise of the SALT II arms control treaty, preliminary talks with the Soviets about future negotiations might begin fairly early in the Reagan administration. However, he said: "I think there are matters to be settled between the Soviet Union and ourselves that, callous as it may sound, are more important" than arms talks. "I think there has to be some clearing of the air early on."

China-Taiwan

One delicate issue Haig consistently declined to discuss in detail was how to continue improving relations with the People's Republic of China without undermining Taiwan or antagonizing the Soviets. "We must not get into a triangle relationship that creates constant irritation to the detriment of East-West relations," Haig said. But, he added: "It is in our interest to continue the normalization process [with the PRC]."

Human Rights

Reflecting Reagan's announced intention to abandon the Carter administration's policy of holding U.S. allies accountable for their human rights records, Haig said:

"The assurance of basic human liberties will not be improved by replacing friendly governments which incompletely satisfy our standards of democracy with hostile ones which are even less benign." However, he said he saw no need to change provisions of the Foreign Assistance Act linking U.S. aid to recipient nations' human rights records. That law was "not overly restrictive," he said.

Intervention

Another event during the nominee's years as a Nixon aide that was repeatedly probed was Haig's role in White House decisions that led to U.S. covert operations in Chile in connection with the overthrow of Marxist leader Salvador Allende.

Asked whether there were circumstances under which he would support covert action to overthrow a constitutionally elected government, including a Marxist one, Haig said he would abide by an intelligence oversight law enacted in 1980. That measure relaxed a 1974 law requiring various House and Senate committees to be informed in advance of most covert intelligence operations. It did not broaden or curtail existing authority for U.S. agencies to conduct intelligence operations.

Persian Gulf

Haig identified the Persian Gulf as an area of vital U.S. interest, but declined to be specific about how the United States should attempt to assure the flow of oil out of the gulf.

He said that, in light of the revolution in Iran and other developments in the Middle East, the United States must show a "heightened interest," but added: "It is clear the United States does not have *carte blanche* to move into other nations [in the region] and establish bases."

Said Haig: "In general, I am comfortable with the current trend begun by the [Carter] administration to develop a rapid reaction force" to respond to a crisis in that area.

NATO

Haig defended the United States' NATO allies on the "burden-sharing" issue — a charge by some members of Congress that the European members of the alliance had failed to contribute enough to their own defense.

He said the way to get them to cooperate was not to complain. "I would much rather engage in . . . quiet, consultative discussion than . . . public bludgeoning about burden-sharing, which I have found counterproductive."

Other Issues

On other issues, Haig:

● Said he was "very suspicious of food embargoes" as a rule, but on the grain embargo against the Soviet Union, which Reagan promised to end during the presidential campaign, Haig said: "We're there now."

● Hinted he would support a resumption of military aid to El Salvador. (President Carter did so before leaving office.)

● Opposed the 1976 Clark amendment, named for its sponsor Sen. Dick Clark, D-Iowa (1973-79), which effectively prohibited U.S. intervention against the Marxist government of Angola. Haig said it was "a self-defeating and unnecessary restriction on the executive branch." He also said he would not support U.S. recognition of Angola as long as there were Cuban troops there.

● Said it would be "very, very difficult for me to move toward normalizing relations with Cuba as long as they are spawning, encouraging, manning and backing terrorist efforts in this hemisphere."

● Supported the multilateral development banks such as the World Bank. However, he agreed that the United States had to carefully consider, on an individual basis, how much to contribute to them.

• Called the Palestine Liberation Organization (PLO) a "terrorist" group. However, Haig said: "If you're talking about the PLO, you're talking about a broad range of [groups]. If you're talking about the Fatah wing of the PLO, then you're talking about a rather hard-core, tough bunch of terrorists."

• Supported foreign aid as "a very cheap investment in the interests we have."

David A. Stockman:
Office of Management and Budget

President Reagan's choice for director of the Office of Management and Budget (OMB) — David A. Stockman, a conservative, two-term Republican representative from Michigan — was given his long-sought chance to arrest the growth of the federal government's "social pork barrel."

To weed out and reform the myriad federal programs providing benefits for black lung victims, lunches for schoolchildren and aid for alcoholics or distressed cities had been a goal of the 34-year-old member of the House ever since he entered Congress in 1977.

Stockman resigned his seat on Jan. 27, the day he was confirmed by the Senate by a 93-0 vote.

"The vast increase in federal social welfare outlays ... has created in its wake a political maintenance system based in no small part on the cooptation and incorporation of Congress itself," Stockman wrote in a 1975 *Public Interest* article that became his trademark.

"As a consequence . . . , what may have been the bright promise of the Great Society has been transformed into a flabby hodgepodge, funded without policy consistency or rigor, that increasingly looks like a great social pork barrel."

This commitment to reduce the government's fiscal involvement in all walks of American life was expected to make Stockman one of the most activist OMB chiefs. And unlike his predecessors, he had a firsthand knowledge of Congress' spending habits and its six-year-old budget process.

In Congress Stockman worked steadfastly to oppose expensive new "entitlement programs" — those which by law must provide benefits for all who meet the eligibility requirements. He took over the reins of OMB armed with an inch-thick list of spending cuts he had prepared early in 1980 on the eve of a House debate on ways to balance the budget.

And with Rep. Jack F. Kemp, R-N.Y. — a key economic adviser to the new president — Stockman, the staunch defender of the free enterprise system, proposed that Reagan declare a "national economic emergency" immediately after taking office.

Stockman argued that declaring a state of economic emergency would calm the financial markets and give the administration time to design a recovery program, which, he said, should include major spending cuts, a 10 percent tax cut in fiscal 1981, relaxation of federal regulations and a tightening of monetary policy.

He and Kemp warned in a paper released late in 1980 that failure to adopt such a program could lead to an "economic Dunkirk" and disaster for the Republican Party.

'First-Class Mind'

The prospect of seeing a "supply side" economic thinker at OMB appeared to strike fear in the hearts of Capitol Hill liberals.

But many lawmakers, even some of those committed to programs established under the "Great Society," praised Stockman's nomination. They saw him as an intellectual who would apply his budget-cutting knife with an even hand: to the Defense Department as well as to domestic programs.

"He has a first-class mind," commented Rep. James R. Jones, D-Okla., who was elected chairman of the House Budget Committee for the 97th Congress. Another key member of the Budget panel, Leon E. Panetta, D-Calif., called the appointment an "excellent choice" because Stockman "knows the politics of what you can achieve" through budget-cutting efforts on Capitol Hill.

"He is very familiar with where the traps are," Panetta said, "and he is very willing to challenge these areas."

Other lawmakers cited Stockman for his "intellectual honesty" and pointed to his vote on the Chrysler loan guarantee bill as an example. Stockman, who opposed the bail-out on grounds that the free market should be allowed to work its will, was the only Michigan lawmaker to say "nay" to the Detroit-based auto manufacturer's plea for help.

One of Stockman's Republican colleagues, Rep. Barber B. Conable Jr., N.Y., ranking minority member of the Ways and Means panel, however, was worried that Stockman could be "inflexible" on issues. "He's one of the 'pragmatic populists' who sees the world in simpler terms than some of us who have been around Washington longer," Conable told a reporter.

Kemp, perhaps Stockman's closest friend on Capitol Hill and co-author of the proposed Kemp-Roth tax cut bill, had said of Stockman: "He operates from a constant model, the incentive-oriented school."

But it was this very model that could cause the former Harvard theology student his greatest headaches at the OMB. Reagan promised U.S. voters tax cuts, balanced budgets and higher military spending — promises many economists saw as an impossible dream.

Stockman and Kemp held that by permitting Americans to keep more of their earnings, they would be more productive. Thus, a tax cut would add, not subtract, revenues from federal coffers because it would stimulate the economy.

Many experts questioned this theory, however, and cautioned that providing tax cuts before inflation was brought under control would only put upward pressure on the cost of living. They urged that the budget be balanced before tax cuts were enacted.

Many budget observers also doubted that the budget could be cut as much as Reagan had promised: 2 percent to 3 percent in fiscal 1981, increasing to 7 percent by 1985. But Stockman had pledged when his nomination was announced that "The commitment has been made to cut, and there is no indication at this time that we would back off."

Nader's 'Mirror Image'

Born Nov. 10, 1946, in Camp Hood, Texas, Stockman grew up in St. Joseph, Mich., where his father ran a fruit farm. He graduated from Michigan State University with a degree in American history and then enrolled in Harvard University's divinity school.

It was there that he came to the attention of Rep. John B. Anderson, R-Ill. (1961-81), who brought him to Washington in 1970 as his special assistant and two years later named him director of the Republican Conference, the policy-making committee of all House Republicans. During his tenure under Anderson, he was known as a liberal party member.

In 1975 Stockman returned to Boston to study at Harvard's prestigious John F. Kennedy Institute of Politics. He left academia for the trenches of electoral politics in Michigan, winning election to the House in 1976 with 61 percent of the vote. He was re-elected in 1978.

Despite his short tenure in the House, Stockman played a major role in the development of several pieces of key legislation: hospital cost containment, child health care, synthetic fuels and the Energy Mobilization Board.

Stockman was known on Capitol Hill for working with almost single-minded dedication to achieve the goals he believed in — a characteristic that led *The Washington Post* to describe him as the "mirror image of Ralph Nader." That quality would come in handy for Stockman as OMB director, an often thankless post whose occupant on many occasions became a whipping boy for conflicting factions within the executive branch.

But the slightly built, prematurely gray young representative, who served as chairman of the Republican Economic Policy Task Force in the 96th Congress, was elated with his selection to OMB.

"I've been watching this process for 10 years, seeing the difficulty of injecting new ideas into the political structure," he told a reporter. "I've become convinced that OMB is absolutely the best forum possible to carry out that kind of agenda. Everything flows through there."

Confirmation Hearings

Only by cutting taxes could Congress hope to balance the budget, Stockman maintained at his confirmation hearings before the Senate Governmental Affairs Committee Jan. 8.

Stockman said a "debilitating" rise in taxes rather than congressional "spending sprees" had caused the huge federal deficits of recent years. "What has happened is that the economy has collapsed out from under the budget." But he said the effective date in 1981 for President Reagan's much-ballyhooed income tax cut (the Kemp-Roth bill) might have to be postponed from Jan. 1 to June 1. That would help to reduce the spiraling deficit for the fiscal year ending Sept. 30.

Stockman's support for the immediate enactment of Kemp-Roth, which called for a 30 percent cut in individual income tax rates over three years, put him at odds with many Republicans who felt the budget should be balanced before taxes were reduced. But it pleased the chairman of the committee that considered his nomination, William V. Roth Jr., R-Del., cosponsor of the legislation. Stockman also got a favorable reception from most other committee members, who praised him as "bright" and "talented."

Less happy with the prospect of Stockman as budget director was committee member John Glenn, D-Ohio, whose state was heavily dependent on government funds. Citing several articles Stockman had written about what he called the "social pork barrel," Glenn asked if he intended to do away with most welfare-type programs. "From your writings, I would guess you do," Glenn said.

Stockman replied that entitlement programs had to be "carefully" reviewed to determine whether they were meeting their original intent.

Malcolm Baldrige:
Secretary of Commerce

President Reagan's secretary of commerce, Malcolm Baldrige, was equally at home in a corporate suite or in the saddle. A successful businessman — the chairman of the board and chief executive officer of Scovill Inc. of Waterbury, Conn., and a board member of several other firms — Baldrige also was a member of the Professional Rodeo Cowboys Association and a prize-winning steer roper.

Baldrige said there was nothing unusual about being a corporate executive and having steer roping as a hobby. "I think it's strange [that] people play tennis and golf," he said.

Daniel P. Davison, a Scovill board member, noted that the rodeo circuit required "great accuracy and great experience." That background likely would prove useful as secretary of the Commerce Department, which administers such wide-ranging activities as the promotion of U.S. trade and the compilation of census data.

Although not well-known in Washington, Baldrige was widely respected in business circles and had strong Republican Party credentials. In 1980 he was chairman of the Bush for President Committee in Connecticut, one of the few states George Bush won over Ronald Reagan.

"I don't know him well," but "I think it's a very good appointment," commented Alexander B. Trowbridge, president of the National Association of Manufacturers (NAM) and commerce secretary for President Johnson.

Baldrige was credited with launching Scovill, formerly a brass manufacturing concern, on an ambitious program of product expansion and diversification that transformed it into "a mini-conglomerate" with sales of $941.6 million in 1979, according to Scovill board member Robert Kilpatrick. The manufacturing firm included well-known trade names such as Hamilton Beach appliances and Yale locks.

As an executive, Baldrige aimed at achieving results, Kilpatrick said. He was "very demanding" but "low-key" and "unflappable."

"He's the kind of guy people instinctively like," Davison said, but added that neither Congress nor other agency heads were likely to "push him around."

The Senate liked him, too, confirming the non-controversial nominee Jan. 22 by a 97-1 vote. William Proxmire, D-Wis., cast the only vote against him.

Decentralized Management

At the time of his selection, Baldrige said his management style was "very uncluttered and decentralized, with accountability as well as authority shared down to the lowest level."

Friends and associates said businessman Baldrige showed a willingness to make difficult decisions and a dogged determination to chip away at tough problems. They cited his ability to take a hard look at some of Scovill's less profitable ventures and to divest the company of them.

"He's steady rather than dramatic," commented John M. Henske, another Scovill board member.

Baldrige said his main aim at the Commerce Department would be to tackle tough economic problems. He said he intended to start "working on the problem of productivity, helping to increase our exports and trying to get rid of excessive government regulation." Baldrige declined to provide any details of his proposals.

He expressed optimism that he would become one of Reagan's key economic policy-makers — a role that traditionally had been denied to most commerce secretaries in the past.

Asked whether he thought he would be included in the proposed "super-Cabinet," Baldrige said: "I don't know about the 'super-Cabinet,' " but added, "I think I'll be part of the core economic team."

He said the "central theme of management of the administration is going to be a team effort to get the administration's policies through Congress so they can be effective. The president has told me he wants a strong Commerce Department. I'll do the best to give [him] one."

Baldrige expressed confidence that he would have a relatively free hand in filling sub-Cabinet posts. "I and other Cabinet officials have enough self-confidence so we're not going to worry about consultation" from White House officials, he said. "I have no fears I will have to take someone I don't want."

GOP, Midwestern Roots

Baldrige's roots in the Republican Party went back to his father, H. Malcolm Baldrige, who was a Republican House member from Nebraska in 1931-33.

Baldrige himself was very active in party politics. A delegate to the Republican National Convention in 1968, 1972 and 1976, Baldrige was Connecticut co-chairman of United Citizens for Nixon-Agnew. He also was a member of the National Republican Finance Committee.

Despite his Connecticut base, Baldrige had strong ties to the Midwest. Born in Omaha Oct. 4, 1922, Baldrige worked on a Nebraska ranch during the summers. He traveled East to attend the Hotchkiss School in Connecticut and Yale University, where he was graduated in 1944.

After serving in the Army in World War II, Baldrige joined Eastern Co. as a foundry foreman, rising to become president in 1960. He left Eastern to join Scovill as executive vice president in 1962, becoming president and chief executive officer in 1963 and chairman and chief executive officer in 1969.

Besides his direction of Scovill Inc., Baldrige was a director of AMF Inc., IBM Inc., Bendix Corp., Connecticut Mutual Life Insurance Co., Eastern Co. and Uniroyal Inc.

He also was a member of the Business Council, the Council on Foreign Relations, the International Chamber of Commerce and the Citizens Research Foundation.

Confirmation Hearings

At his confirmation hearings before the Senate Commerce Committee Jan. 6, Baldrige advocated opening trade talks with the Japanese to help solve the financial problems of the American auto industry. He said the main reason why the U.S. economy would be depressed in the first quarter of 1981 was because of the worsening financial condition of the domestic auto industry.

On other issues, Baldrige:

● Declined to comment on the potential status of the U.S. special trade representative in the new administration. (There had been speculation that the post might be downgraded from Cabinet rank, but William E. Brock III, who was offered the post by Reagan, had accepted it on the condition it would remain a Cabinet-level position. Brock was confirmed Jan. 21.) Baldrige said trade activities could be better coordinated within one department.

● Called for simplification of the foreign corrupt business practices act. Baldrige said its provisions had discouraged small- and medium-sized businesses from trading abroad.

● Said he supported attempts in the 96th Congress to allow manufacturers, distributors and other businesses to form self-insurance cooperatives to protect themselves against product liability damage suits.

Drew Lewis:
Secretary of Transportation

Reagan named Andrew Lindsay Lewis Jr., a Schwenksville, Pa., businessman and backstage politician, as transportation secretary despite Lewis' major role in denying Reagan the Republican presidential nomination in 1976.

Lewis, head of the Pennsylvania delegation at the 1976 GOP convention, supported Gerald R. Ford for president. Reagan needed the support of the major Eastern states, but

Lewis could not be swayed from his support for Ford, even by Sen. Richard S. Schweiker, R-Pa., a close friend of Lewis' and Reagan's running mate.

But Lewis was one of the first establishment Republican leaders to back Reagan for the 1980 battle, and he became a trusted aide. Lewis managed Reagan's primary campaign in Pennsylvania and succeeded in winning for him a majority of the delegates even though Reagan lost the popular vote.

Lewis, known as Drew, had been an influential member of the Reagan transition team. He was a member of the transition's executive advisory committee and the transportation task force. A successful businessman with a reputation for salvaging troubled firms, Lewis was the head of Lewis & Associates, a financial and management consulting firm in Plymouth Meeting, Pa., when Reagan picked him for transportation secretary.

Lewis met virtually no opposition in Congress, and the Senate confirmed him by a 98-0 vote on Jan. 22.

Railroad Experience

Lewis' only apparent link with transportation problems had been as a trustee for the previous 10 years of the bankrupt Reading Co., the holding company that used to operate the Reading Railroad. The company's railroad assets were folded into Conrail, the federally subsidized freight rail system, in the mid-1970s.

Business and political observers said Lewis would need his political and business skills perhaps even more than his railroad experience in handling the Transportation Department. Mass transit, railroad and highway interests were desperate for federal aid and little new money was expected to be available because of budget constraints. Also, political controversies in 1980 over auto safety and transportation deregulation were expected to carry over into the new Congress.

"He is ideally suited to the times," said a top aide to Pennsylvania Gov. Richard L. Thornburgh, a Republican for whom Lewis had raised funds.

"The secretary is going to have a massive job of organizing and managing the transportation infrastructure...; [Lewis] knows transportation and he knows business. Knowing business is even more important. He knows politics. He knows how to get things done," said John Snow, senior vice president of CSX Corp., the merged Chessie and Family Lines railroads. Snow was a member of Reagan's task force studying transportation issues during the transition.

Lewis' views on transportation needs were not known at the time of his selection. And the transition team's task force recommendations on transportation were not made public, although they reportedly called for 1) scaling back mass transit subsidies, 2) barring new Conrail subsidies and 3) increasing highway user taxes.

Lewis was thought to be an advocate of mass transit. But rather than push for new funds Lewis was expected to shift priorities from new highway construction to public transportation.

According to the *Philadelphia Inquirer*, Lewis once said he was "not an idea man, but I'm effective in evaluating other people's ideas." Lewis had a reputation for being a quick study. He absorbed information quickly and took decisive actions. Lewis was said to be particularly good at bringing opposing parties together to work out problems.

Reagan installed Lewis as deputy chairman of the Republican National Committee as a bridge between the Reagan diehards and the committee's chairman, Bill Brock. Before the convention, Reagan backers had agitated to remove Brock. Many Brock supporters feared Lewis would be a hatchet man, but they apparently were impressed by how he handled the assignment.

Career

Lewis, 49, received a masters degree from Harvard's Graduate School of Business Administration and did postgraduate work at Massachusetts Institute of Technology.

He went to work for a Philadelphia general contracting firm in 1955 and held various positions responsible for construction supervision, cost control and other matters. He ended up as a member of the board of directors in 1960.

Lewis was a corporate vice president and assistant to the chairman of the National Gypsum Co., aiding in corporate development and acquisitions. In 1969 he joined Simplex Wire and Cable Co. in Boston as president and chief executive officer, later assuming the chairmanship of the board. In that capacity he reorganized the company. In 1970 Lewis was brought in as president and chief executive officer of Snelling and Snelling, a personnel agency, to turn it around.

Lewis was chairman of Sen. Schweiker's successful House campaign in 1960 and chairman of his successful Senate campaign in 1968. He also was a local Republican leader as well as chairman of the state Republican Finance Committee from 1971 to 1973. He also had been a Republican national committeeman from Pennsylvania since 1976. An aide to Gov. Thornburgh described Lewis as one of two premiére fund raisers in the state.

Although Lewis was successful in working for the candidacies of others, he lost his only bid for public office in 1974 when he ran for governor.

Confirmation Hearings

Lewis assured the Senate Commerce Committee at his confirmation hearings Jan. 7 that support for deregulation of the transportation industries would continue under the Reagan administration.

"We don't plan to back off deregulation in any way," Lewis told the committee. He said, however, that one of his priorities would be to evaluate the impact of the rail, trucking and airline deregulation laws enacted in the previous Congresses, and to help those small communities that might have lost vital services as a result.

While emphasizing his and Reagan's preference for less government involvement in transportation, Lewis attemped to calm fears that the new administration would allow the Chrysler Corp. or the rest of the auto industry to collapse, the rails to shut down or mass transit systems to stop running.

The worsening condition of the auto industry was the nation's "single most important" transportation problem, and the new administration would have a policy for dealing with it at an early date, Lewis promised.

On mass transit, Lewis said he would like to reduce federal operating subsidies and focus attention on aid for new equipment. Operating subsidies — over which the government had no control — were "an unsound investment," he said, although he recognized the need for some additional aid to keep public transit systems in business. He declared that the new administration would not "take a walk from mass transit. I am supportive of mass transit."

As for Conrail and other financially troubled railroads, Lewis said he favored transferring economically viable lines to private industry and giving federal funds only to those problem lines that provided vital service. He pointed out that he had opposed creation of Conrail, but told the panel, "I realize Conrail had to continue to operate." Conrail was expected to run out of money in early 1981, and Lewis said he would prefer some short-term aid while the Reagan administration determined what to do with the rail line.

Lewis said he would recommend to Reagan that the federal government return to the states the decision on whether to maintain the 55-mile-an-hour speed limit. He said he personally supported the limit for Pennsylvania because it was safer in urban areas.

He also said he favored finishing the remaining links of the interstate highway system that were worthwhile and dropping those projects that were environmentally unsound or too costly.

Richard S. Schweiker:
Health and Human Services

Sen. Richard S. Schweiker, R-Pa., was in Ocean City, Md., that summer day in 1976 when he got the word that Ronald Reagan was calling. He returned the call from a pay phone on the boardwalk.

Reagan, making a last desperate effort to win the Republican nomination from incumbent President Gerald R. Ford, wanted Schweiker to be his running mate. He hoped the choice would swing enough of the 103 votes in the Pennsylvania delegation to him, and away from Ford, to give him the nomination.

The effort failed, but it touched off one of the most abrupt and thorough political conversions of modern times. Until then, Schweiker had been among the most liberal Republicans in the Senate — a favorite of labor, a maverick in his party. When he returned to the Senate after his 25 days as Reagan's No. 2 man, his voting record shifted dramatically.

His rating by the liberal Americans for Democratic Action dropped from 89 percent in 1975 to 15 percent in 1977. On labor-backed measures, he fell from 100 percent to 47 percent.

During the 94th Congress, he had supported the conservative coalition of Republicans and Southern Democrats only 16 percent of the time; in the 95th that figure jumped to 73 percent. One liberal group dubbed him the "disappointment of the year" in 1977.

In 1980 labor organizations, confused and angered by Schweiker's defection, launched an intense personal campaign against him after he introduced a bill to restrict the powers of the Occupational Safety and Health Administration (OSHA). They called for pickets at his home, and the Pennsylvania steelworkers scrapped plans to honor him at their annual dinner.

"Apparently his sights were on a more powerful office," Pennsylvania labor official Jim Moran said of Schweiker's transformation.

If so, that office came Dec. 11 when Reagan named Schweiker to head the massive Department of Health and Human Services (HHS). HHS administered more than $200 billion worth of health and welfare programs.

This time, only the most hard-boiled of conservatives were upset, and none in the Senate was upset enough to vote against him. The vote confirming Schweiker Jan. 21 was unanimous, 99-0. Schweiker had retired from the Senate only 18 days earlier, when the 96th Congress came to an end.

Shift on Health Issues

It was in the field of health policy primarily that Schweiker made his transformation to conservatism. Al-

though once a cosponsor with Sen. Edward M. Kennedy of a national health insurance bill, Schweiker had served as the perfect foil for the Massachusetts Democrat since 1976.

As the ranking Republican on the Labor and Human Resources Committee, its Health Subcommittee and the Appropriations Subcommittee on Labor, Health, Education and Welfare during the Carter administration, Schweiker had fought for less regulation and more private competition in the health care industry. Kennedy had consistently called for an expanded federal role.

Dividing Schweiker and Kennedy was chiefly a question of economics. Kennedy operated on the theory, which had largely prevailed in recent years, that the market for health services did not work like the market for manufactured goods or farm products. Consumers were unable to shop dispassionately or knowledgeably for the best buys in health care, and doctors could create demand for their services at almost any price. Government regulation, therefore, was necessary to hold down costs and ensure that care was available to all who needed it.

Schweiker, on the other hand, considered the market for health services similar to that for consumer goods and food. Competition could lower prices, and the market could assure proper distribution of doctors and hospitals, he maintained.

Sought Competitive Health Services

This theory was the underpinning for a bill (S 1590) introduced by Schweiker in 1979 that required large firms to offer employees a choice of health plans, some of which would have required workers to pay a hefty percentage of their own hospital costs. Employees would have received tax-free rebates if they chose this lower-cost, higher-risk option, and employers would have been required to provide health insurance for "catastrophic" medical costs (over 20 percent of the worker's annual income in a given year). The plan also would have offered tax incentives to firms that provided "preventive health benefits." The theory behind this and other competition-based health bills was that if people had to pay more of their own health care costs — instead of having them covered by insurance — they would be more likely to question the necessity, quantity and cost of medical services. And doctors, hospitals and health insurers, operating in a competitive market, would be forced to keep prices down and quality up.

The competition philosophy was reflected in Reagan's speeches and in reports on health given him by his transition team and by The Heritage Foundation, a conservative "think tank."

The Heritage Foundation study was directed by David Winston, Schweiker's health aide on the Labor and Human Resources Committee. Although Reagan had not endorsed it, its blueprint for a conservative Department of Health and Human Services was thought by many to be indicative of the direction in which the new administration would move.

The study called for scaling down government health planning efforts, encouraging competition among private insurers and, perhaps, eventually moving toward a voucher system of health care for the poor and aged, allowing them to shop among private providers for their federally financed care.

Schweiker himself said little in the weeks following his selection about his goals in his new post. "At this point I haven't formulated anything," he said Dec. 15, "and I shouldn't until I take office."

He did promise to cut the department's budget by decreasing fraud and abuse. "I think a lot of cuts can be made," he said, citing a 1978 inspector general's report that estimated $6 billion-$7 billion was lost each year to fraud and abuse. (The outgoing HHS secretary, Patricia Roberts Harris, called that a gross overestimate.)

Schweiker indicated he also planned to formulate a "preventive" health care agenda, which would include encouragement of exercise and good nutrition, but not promotion of clean air, clean water, automobile safety or a stronger OSHA. "Those are in somebody else's department," he said.

On the controversial issue of abortion, Schweiker while in the Senate had gone down the line with those opposing the use of federal funds to help pay for abortions for poor women. Anti-abortion groups had lobbied for his appointment as secretary of HHS.

Still Considered a Moderate

In spite of the shift in his voting record, Schweiker still was considered a moderate by many observers. Even liberals were not overly displeased by his appointment.

"I think on balance Schweiker will be very, very moderate, and perhaps helpful to us on some things," said United Auto Workers President Douglas A. Fraser, who chaired the Committee for National Health Insurance.

Jay Constantine, special health counsel to the Senate Finance Committee, called Schweiker a "second-look liberal," who had a deep commitment to providing people with appropriate health care but had come to question whether Great Society-type programs were the way to do it. If Schweiker recommended cutting HHS programs, Constantine predicted, it would be with "a scalpel rather than a saber."

Confirmation Hearings

Appearing before the Senate Finance Committee Jan. 6, Schweiker told his former colleagues his experience as a senator would strengthen his control over the department.

"I know where a lot of the bodies are buried. People are going to have trouble pulling the wool over my eyes," Schweiker said, referring to his past service as ranking Republican on the subcommittee on HHS appropriations.

Still, Schweiker admitted to some anxiety at taking over a department with a $222 billion budget, bigger than any government other than the United States or the Soviet Union. "It's an awe-inspiring managerial colossus," he said.

He said his first priority in his new job would be to protect the stability of the Social Security system, which was facing serious financial problems. But he conceded that efforts to improve the health of the system would involve painful choices — either reducing benefits or increasing payroll taxes.

Schweiker also promised quick action on welfare legislation. He indicated the Reagan administration's proposal would be similar to legislation introduced in past years by Sens. Robert Dole, R-Kan., and Russell B. Long, D-La., to convert the existing system of matching federal payments for state welfare costs into block grants.

Dole became the new chairman of the Finance Committee at the start of the 97th Congress, taking over from Long, who was now the ranking minority member.

As for national health insurance, Schweiker made it clear that the only proposal that might possibly be considered was one involving coverage of catastrophic illnesses, plus a program of "fill-in-the-gaps" insurance for people not currently covered. "Anything beyond that just wouldn't fit this administration's philosophy," he said.

Another area of possible health-related legislation, Schweiker said, involved changes in the "Delaney clause," which bans food additives that have been shown to cause cancer in humans or animals. "We really have to redefine the Delaney clause on some kind of risk-benefit ratio," Schweiker added.

Earlier Career

Schweiker, a descendant of early Pennsylvania settlers, was born June 1, 1926. After serving in the Navy and earning a degree from Penn State University, he went to work for the family business, American Olean Tile Co. He represented the 13th District of Pennsylvania in the House from 1961 to 1969. In 1968 he defeated incumbent Democrat Sen. Joseph S. Clark and moved over to the Senate. He was re-elected in 1974.

In December 1978 Schweiker announced plans to retire from the Senate at the end of the 96th Congress for personal reasons. Although some observers speculated that his alienation from organized labor had damaged him politically, others said his conservative shift would have helped rather than hurt him had he stood for re-election. "Our polls showed he would have been unbeatable if he had run," said an aide to Gov. Richard L. Thornburgh, R-Pa. If Schweiker had stayed in the Senate, he would have been in line to chair the Labor and Human Resources Committee.

William French Smith:
Attorney General

In selecting his close friend and personal lawyer, William French Smith, for the post of attorney general, President Reagan chose the prototypical corporate lawyer — well-educated, articulate, self-assured and, perhaps most important to Reagan, a political conservative.

The last time a president appointed an intimate adviser to head the Justice Department was 1968, when Richard M. Nixon selected campaign manager John N. Mitchell

for the post. That appointment turned sour. The image of the department under Mitchell suffered amid charges that the attorney general was misusing federal power at the behest of the president.

At a Dec. 11, 1980, news conference, Smith tried to cancel any thoughts that as a Reagan confidant he would abuse his office. He met head-on a question as to whether he could maintain an arm's length relationship with his friend in the White House.

"The question is the basic integrity of the persons involved," Smith told reporters. "You will not be disappointed."

Smith's colleagues in Los Angeles, where he had spent the previous 30 years practicing law, thought his self-confidence was well deserved.

"First, he's a good administrator. He also is very intelligent. He has a retentive, analytical mind," said Sharp Whitmore, a partner with Smith in the prestigious firm of Gibson, Dunn and Crutcher, one of California's biggest. "He really is conscientious and serious minded."

And from prominent California businessman Ed Carter, a moderate Republican whose company owned the Neiman-Marcus stores: "On balance, I think he'll be splendid. . . . He is essentially a conservative, but he approaches his conservative objectives slowly and constructively. He believes in evolution, not revolution."

The Senate appeared to be satisfied with Smith's record and his assurances that he would carry out his responsibilities with integrity. It confirmed the Californian Jan. 22 by a 96-1 vote. The lone vote against Smith was cast by William Proxmire, D-Wis.

Translating Philosophy to Practice

Just how Smith, 63, a Harvard law graduate, would translate his conservative philosophy into Justice Department policy was expected to take time to work out. Smith's professional record and personal life in California contained few clues about how he would handle the department.

Smith held one important public position in California. In 1968 Gov. Reagan appointed him to the Board of Regents of the University of California, a post he still held when Reagan chose him for attorney general.

Smith generally received good marks from fellow regents. John Henning, head of the California AFL-CIO and a former under secretary of labor in the Kennedy administration, called Smith "a very civilized person, a person of integrity. He does have a conservative direction, but I trust he will not be mean and harassing. I don't think he will loan himself to [those] who want to turn back the clock."

"It can't be argued that the president-elect put an incompetent in office for the sake of friendship," Henning added. "But a fair question is whether he is too conservative for this complex, pluralistic, open society we live in."

Smith worked primarily in labor law, frequently negotiating for management in labor disputes. But in recent years he also spent a good deal of time helping wealthy clients manage their finances. Reportedly, his advice helped make Reagan a millionaire.

As attorney general, Smith had to take charge of the nation's largest law firm, one responsible for a variety of legal matters much more diverse than his own private practice. The Justice Department's work included antitrust litigation, criminal prosecutions and the sensitive matter of civil rights enforcement.

He served on the board of a number of large companies, including Pacific Telephone & Telegraph Co., Crocker National Bank and Pacific Mutual Life Insurance Co. Pacific Telephone was a subsidiary of American Telephone & Telegraph Co. A Justice Department antitrust suit against AT&T was scheduled to go to court early in 1981.

In California Smith also headed the state's chamber of commerce at one time and was involved in philanthropic and civic work.

Sketchy Civil Rights Record

Unlike former Attorney General Griffin B. Bell, who had a long public career and a controversial civil rights

record as a federal judge, Smith's record on civil rights was sketchy. As a regent, he opposed efforts to require the university to dispose of its holdings in companies doing business in South Africa.

A spokesman for Smith said the attorney general believed that, as a regent, he had a duty to the endowment of the university to "maximize resources and income return" and that investment decisions "should not be based on political motives." Smith also helped lead efforts to fire black activist Angela Davis, an avowed communist, from the university faculty.

On the other hand, Smith supported the University of California's affirmative action plan that led to the controversial decision to reject medical school applicant Allan Bakke, a white, in favor of less qualified blacks. Smith also served on the board of the Legal Aid Foundation of Los Angeles, which provided legal services for the poor.

John H. F. Shattuck, head of the American Civil Liberties Union's Washington office, called Smith "a mystery man to us." And Verna Canfan of San Francisco, Western regional director for the NAACP, said civil rights groups in the West knew very little about Smith. "I am not aware that he has had a presence in the civil rights arena that would attract our immediate response," she said.

Confirmation Hearings

The only bone of contention at Smith's confirmation hearing Jan. 15, 1981, was his membership in two all-male clubs in California. But that did not deter the Senate Judiciary Committee from approving his nomination the following day by an 18-0 vote.

Despite a 10-minute lecture on the club issue from Sen. Joseph R. Biden Jr., D-Del., the committee's ranking minority member, and suggestions from two other senators that he resign from the clubs, Smith declared he had no intention of doing so. The nominee said he was "fully committed to vigorous enforcement of civil rights. . . . However, to me, belonging to a private all-male organization does not constitute a violation of that concept."

Shortly after Smith made that statement — which was in response to a question from Sen. Edward M. Kennedy, D-Mass., Biden gave Smith the lecture on the all-male clubs. He said he was trying to "sensitize" Smith to women's issues, suggesting Smith's views on the clubs "may be a reflection of a generational blind spot."

Smith responded that he really did not disagree with Biden, but added: "You would draw a line different from where I would draw the line."

Charles McC. Mathias Jr., Md., ranking GOP member of the Judiciary Committee, did not directly address the club issue, but told Smith his new office had a certain "vulnerability."

"What affects you also affects the president of the United States. Your own personal interests have to be subordinated," Mathias said.

In response to questions on a variety of subjects, Smith gave only general answers. He told the senators he was not sufficiently familiar with Justice Department operations to be specific. Smith made the following points:

• He generally favored extension of the 1965 Voting Rights Act, which was to come up for renewal in 1982, but said he expected debate on "the efficacy of some of its provisions." Judiciary Committee Chairman Strom Thurmond, R-S.C., for example, objected to the act's provisions that single out states in the South and West for Justice Department supervision.

• He believed "strongly" in the concept of fair housing, but declined to say how existing law should be changed to help reduce housing discrimination. The Senate killed a fair housing bill in 1980.

• His priorities would be working to curb violent crime, organized crime, drug trafficking and white-collar crime. This would be a departure from the Carter administration, which had made white-collar crime its top priority.

• He favored restoration of the death penalty for certain specified federal crimes.

Donald T. Regan:
Secretary of the Treasury

With the selection of Wall Street veteran Donald T. Regan as Treasury secretary, President Reagan pleased the nation's troubled financial markets but angered many of his most conservative backers. They feared the highly successful chairman of the giant investment firm of Merrill Lynch, Pierce, Fenner & Smith Inc. would abandon Reagan's election commitment to make sweeping changes in the country's tax structure.

Howard Phillips, director of the Conservative Caucus,

a private organization espousing conservative causes, went so far as to term Regan's appointment "a disgrace and insult to every person in America who worked for Gov. Reagan's election."

But the nomination of the brokerage executive pleased many traditional Republicans, who hoped it would help calm the inflation-buffeted financial markets. Business leaders such as George Ball, president of E. F. Hutton & Co., praised Regan as "probably one of the more erudite leaders when it comes to comprehension and imagination."

And *The Wall Street Journal* cheered Regan's selection as an "apt choice," citing the "daring and imagination" he had shown in directing his company and his familiarity with the credit markets.

Senators also expected him to bring new ideas to Washington for stabilizing the economy, voting to confirm him by a 98-0 vote Jan. 21.

Wall Street Career

The Harvard-educated Regan joined Merrill Lynch in 1946 and rose quickly in its ranks. In 1968 he was named president, and two years later he won the title of chairman.

As head of the investment firm, Regan became known as a maverick, developing Merrill Lynch into one of the largest and most innovative companies on Wall Street.

"He's not a traditionalist," New York Stock Exchange Chairman William M. Batten told a reporter. "He's intelligent, imaginative and aggressive and has been a leader in getting his firm into new areas and new ideas."

Although Regan was active in influential organizations such as the Business Roundtable, the Committee for Economic Development and the Council on Foreign Relations, he had not been active in politics.

He amassed a sizable fortune at Merrill Lynch: Records showed he owned more than 244,000 shares of stock in the investment firm, worth nearly $9 million.

Regan, who became 62 on Dec. 21, 1980, was born in Cambridge, Mass., and was graduated from Harvard University with a degree in English.

Conservative Objections

The brokerage chairman entered the running as Treasury chief after several other potential nominees were eliminated for personal reasons and because of possible conflicts of interest.

They included Citicorp Chairman Walter B. Wriston and former Treasury Secretary William E. Simon. Also mentioned as a possible nominee was Lewis Lehrman, Rite Aid Corp. chairman and a strong supporter of Reagan economic tenets such as across-the-board tax cuts and a return to the gold standard.

Conservative columnists Rowland Evans and Robert Novak charged that Regan's name was pushed on the president by William J. Casey, who was selected to head the Central Intelligence Agency (CIA). The attack was taken up on Capitol Hill by Sen. William L. Armstrong, R-Colo., and by Rep. Steven D. Symms, R-Idaho, who was elected to the Senate in the November 1980 election. Both lawmakers became members of the Senate Finance and Budget committees in the 97th Congress.

Some conservatives urged that Regan's nomination be blocked because his firm's political action committee (PAC) contributed to President Carter's re-election campaign and the campaigns of liberals such as Rep. Bob Eckhardt, D-Texas (1967-81), and Rep. Christopher J. Dodd, D-Conn., who was elected to the Senate in November.

But Merrill Lynch spokesman William Clark called Regan a "lifelong Republican" and said he was not responsible for decisions made by Merrill Lynch's political action group. He noted that the firm's PAC also had donated funds to Reagan's campaign and to Republican presidential hopefuls John B. Connally and George Bush.

Ironically, the Regan selection also came under fire from House liberals, who charged that Merrill Lynch had promoted tax-shelter schemes that were being investigated by the Internal Revenue Service. Democrats Charles A. Vanik, Ohio, William M. Brodhead, Mich., and Benjamin S. Rosenthal, N.Y., had urged the Senate Finance Committee to study the tax-avoidance plans at Regan's confirmation hearings.

Economic Policy

At a Dec. 11, 1980, news conference called to introduce Reagan's Cabinet choices, the Treasury secretary-designate said he believed inflation to be the No. 1 problem facing the nation. But he warned that "there is no easy solution to it; there's no magic wand. It took us 15 or more years to get to where we are. We're going to have to take a long time in getting out of it."

Regan acknowledged that the Federal Reserve Board had put such a squeeze on credit that interest rates jumped to record levels, threatening the economic recovery economists thought had begun in August.

He added, however, that the Fed's tight-credit policy was the policy of the day and promised that "when this administration takes over, we'll deal with inflation in several ways at once, rather than just one way."

The Wall Street executive also noted that tax cuts proposed by the administration would be offset by spending cuts — a policy that put him at odds with some backers of "supply side" economics. Though they also advocated cuts in government spending, supply side economists said tax reductions should be the Reagan administration's first priority. The cuts would generate so much economic activity that federal tax revenues would multiply rather than decrease, they maintained.

Regan also differed from supply side proponents on what kind of tax cuts would be best for the economy. They argued that individual income tax rates should be cut 10 percent across-the-board for three consecutive years, while Regan had told the House Ways and Means Committee in July it was more important to reduce business taxes.

"We must change from a bias toward consumption to a tax structure that generates jobs and promotes increased and more efficient production," he said.

Confirmation Hearings

Regan Jan. 6 dashed hopes for quick control of the federal budget, predicting that the Reagan administration probably would not be able to balance the budget until 1984. Appearing before the Senate Finance Committee at his confirmation hearing, Regan's short-run economic outlook was not very optimistic either.

The economic "recovery [from the 1980 recession] is aborting," he said, adding that the gross national product, adjusted for inflation, would decline in 1981 and that both high unemployment and high inflation would continue in the first half of 1981.

He told the committee that Reagan would propose budget cuts leading to a lessening of the deficit over the next two or three years. "If everything works well, and nothing else changes," he added, "we will see a balanced budget in the fourth year of the Reagan administration."

During the campaign Reagan had said he would balance the federal budget by fiscal 1983, and perhaps as early as 1982.

Despite the prospects for continuing federal deficits, Regan said it was his and Reagan's intention to carry out another campaign promise: full implementation of the Kemp-Roth income tax cut plus accelerated tax writeoffs for investments by businesses. The Kemp-Roth plan called for cuts in personal income tax rates of 10 percent annually for three years.

Regan opposed proposals suggested by Office of Management and Budget Director David A. Stockman that the administration declare an "economic emergency," but he promised quick action on the economy. The administration's economic package would be announced "within a few days or, at most, a few short weeks after taking office," he promised.

"It will be the highest priority of the Reagan administration to whip inflation somehow," he declared.

The only controversy during his testimony arose when Regan fended off a series of questions about his involvement with a tax-avoidance scheme called the "butterfly straddle," which Merrill Lynch recommended to some of its customers in the mid-1970s. Regan maintained that he had never personally used the straddle or suggested its use to any customer.

Caspar W. Weinberger:
Secretary of Defense

To run the government's largest bureaucracy, President Reagan chose a close adviser with diversified experience in high-level government administration. Two of the most prominent qualities of Defense Secretary Caspar W. Weinberger's previous government experience were his reputed managerial prowess in a variety of roles and his loyalty to Reagan.

The overwhelming 97-2 vote for him in the Senate — despite his lack of experience on defense issues — reflected senators' confidence in this record. The only votes against Weinberger, who on Jan. 20 became the first Cabinet nominee confirmed, came from North Carolina's two Republicans, Jesse Helms and John East, both from the party's right wing.

Helms told the Senate before the vote that Weinberger did not have the necessary resolve or vision for the job. And he criticized Pentagon appointees, particularly Weinberger's choice of Frank Carlucci as his deputy, for not having credentials that were sufficiently conservative.

On the other hand, Armed Services Committee Chairman John Tower, R-Texas, praised Weinberger's government experience, calling the Californian "highly qualified because he has the right instincts."

Defense Spending Issue

In his years with the federal government, Weinberger had dealt with defense policy only in the context of budget management. He was not among the Republican defense specialists battling for control of Reagan's defense policy. So his nomination sent no clear signal as to Reagan's positions on specific defense policies or the development of new weapons.

Longtime GOP defense spokesmen, including Tower and former Defense Secretary Melvin R. Laird, had argued for annual increases of $25 billion-$30 billion in the Carter administration's projected defense budgets, with a heavy emphasis on increasing the combat-readiness of conventional war forces. Increases higher than this, Laird argued, would jeopardize domestic support for a defense buildup.

But congressional and academic defense experts prominent in the Reagan administration's transition lobbied for a much more expensive buildup, with a heavy emphasis on rapidly increasing the number of U.S. nuclear weapons.

Moreover, Weinberger reportedly was one of many in the Reagan inner circle backing the formation of a "super-Cabinet" — a small group of generalists who would advise Reagan on all types of policy questions. Such a system might provide close scrutiny of alternative defense policies.

On the other hand, Weinberger's earlier career provided no basis for assuming that he would oppose a substantial increase in defense spending. During his tenure as the Nixon administration's highest-ranking budget official, Weinberger insisted repeatedly that the country could not prudently reduce its military posture. This was a period in which Congress was being pressured to cut Pentagon spending because of the increasingly unpopular war in Vietnam.

Earlier Career in Government

Born in San Francisco in 1917, Weinberger received his undergraduate and legal education at Harvard, served in the Army during World War II and began practicing law in San Francisco after the war.

He was a Republican member of the California Legislature from 1952 to 1958, then vice chairman and chairman of the Republican state central committee from 1960 to 1964.

After Ronald Reagan's election as governor in 1966, Weinberger served as chairman of a state commission on governmental organization and economics (1967-68) and state finance director (1968-69). It was in this period that he acquired the nickname "Cap the Knife," a reference to his flair for budget-cutting.

In January 1970 Weinberger became chairman of the Federal Trade Commission (FTC), then in turmoil from the just-ended chairmanship of Paul Rand Dixon. In his brief tenure there, Weinberger won general acclaim for bringing harmony to the commission. And he became a favorite of liberals for staking out a more aggressively pro-consumer position than had been taken in the first year of the Nixon administration.

One Weinberger proposal was to give the FTC a wider range of enforcement tools to increase the deterrent value of threatened commission action.

Service in Nixon Administration

After less than six months at the FTC, Weinberger was tapped by Nixon as the deputy director of the newly created Office of Management and Budget (OMB). Under OMB Director George Shultz, Weinberger directed the administration's budget process. One aspect of the new arrangement was that Shultz and Weinberger fielded all appeals by Cabinet officers of proposed reductions in their budget requests.

Weinberger became OMB director in 1972 when Shultz became secretary of the Treasury. During his OMB years, Weinberger was a point man in Nixon's battle to establish the president's power to impound congressionally appropriated funds. The fight began in early 1971 when Democrats in Congress charged that the administration was refusing to spend some $8 billion in appropriated funds, much of it for highway construction and water pollution control projects. Weinberger and other administration spokesmen called the move an anti-inflation tactic, citing rising costs in the construction industry. Critics demanded that the funds be spent to stimulate the lagging economy.

Over several months, Weinberger was a frequent witness on Capitol Hill, defending the administration position. The administration was withholding a smaller percentage of appropriated funds than Presidents Kennedy and Johnson routinely had done, he maintained. And most of the money was not being spent, he said, because of technical problems having to do with the schedule on which contracts routinely were let.

But although he insisted that Nixon never would use his claimed authority to thwart Congress, Weinberger conceded that policy judgments had entered into the selection of some of the funds proposed for impoundment.

Role of Congress Criticized

In a March 1973 newspaper column, written just after he left OMB to become secretary of health, education and welfare (HEW), Weinberger attacked the congressional position with a vengeance.

He dismissed as a "media-made 'crisis'" talk of a clash over basic constitutional issues. What was really at stake, he maintained, was whether federal taxes should be raised to pay for the programs funded by a profligate Congress. He criticized Congress for lacking any institutional focal point at which spending ceilings could be set and monitored to assure "fiscal sanity."

"Until Congress gets its budget-making house in order," Weinberger declared, "strong presidential leadership is the only weapon the people have to prevent higher taxes and ruinous inflation."

Just over a year later, Congress took up Weinberger's gauntlet, passing the Budget and Impoundment Control Act of 1974, which established a process for setting congressional spending ceilings and imposing strict limitations on presidential impoundment powers.

Support for Defense Spending

Weinberger's OMB tenure coincided with the peak of the domestic turmoil over the Vietnam War. In 1970 Weinberger became a frequent spokesman for the administration's effort to reverse moves in Congress to cut defense spending. He pointed out that Nixon's fiscal 1971 defense budget of $71.8 billion was $6 billion less than the previous year's budget, largely because of the continuing withdrawal of U.S. forces from Vietnam.

But Weinberger argued that such cuts could not be continued: Pay and prices would continue to rise, thus boosting the cost of keeping the forces combat-ready, even if they remained at the current size. Newer weapons were more complex and thus more expensive. The increased unit-cost could not be completely offset by reducing the number of weapons put into the field, he said.

Super-Cabinet Role

When Weinberger moved to HEW in January 1973, he was one of three Cabinet officials simultaneously named White House counselors. In this capacity the three counselors divided among themselves responsibility for oversight over all domestic policy. Other domestic Cabinet secretaries reported to the president through these super-secretaries.

Nixon had proposed such a consolidation of the government's senior ranks by legislation in 1971, but Congress ignored it. The 1973 streamlining implemented as much of the proposal as possible by executive order. But as the Watergate scandal eroded Nixon's authority, the much-touted reorganization faded from sight.

Despite a flurry of rumors that he would be dumped, Weinberger remained at HEW after Gerald Ford replaced Nixon in August 1974.

But in 1975 he followed his old boss, George Shultz, to the Bechtel Corp., a San Francisco-based engineering and construction firm. Shultz had left Treasury for the firm in 1974, and in 1975 he became president of Bechtel. Weinberger joined the firm as general counsel.

Confirmation Hearings

After battling for two years to extract from President Carter a pledge to increase defense spending at a set annual rate (after allowing for inflation), the Senate Armed Services Committee Jan. 6 accepted without demur Weinberger's refusal to make a similar commitment.

At his confirmation hearings, the longtime budget manager expressed a definite skepticism of arbitrary percentages as a budgeting tool. But he dismissed as unfounded speculation that his Pentagon tenure would reflect the tightfistedness that had won him his budget-cutting nickname.

U.S. defenses needed a substantial boost, Weinberger said, to increase the combat-readiness of forces already in the field. Those forces were suffering from insufficient manpower and inadequate training, due in part to shortages of fuel, ammunition and spare parts.

Increased military pay and benefits also had to have a high priority, Weinberger said, to give the all-volunteer force a better chance to succeed. He confirmed that a new GI Bill giving educational benefits to armed forces personnel was under consideration.

Although noting that President-elect Reagan wanted to avoid resumption of peacetime conscription if possible, Weinberger said he would recommend resumption of the draft if it were needed. He hedged Reagan's campaign attacks against the draft registration program resumed by Carter in 1980. Interrupting the registration once it had begun would pose a "severe administrative problem," he said.

Jeane J. Kirkpatrick:
United Nations Ambassador

Jeane J. Kirkpatrick, the disaffected Democrat President Reagan chose to lead the U.S. delegation at the United Nations, neatly fit the intellectual mold of a previous U.N. ambassador, Daniel Patrick Moynihan.

Moynihan unabashedly defended the United States and lambasted its critics when he served at the United Nations in the mid-1970s. His defense of the United States contrasted sharply with the attitudes of other prominent Democrats in those years, and it helped the New Yorker win election to the U.S. Senate in 1976.

Whether Kirkpatrick, 54, possessed the fire or desire to follow in Moynihan's footsteps at the United Nations was yet to be seen. But the views of Prof. Kirpatrick of Georgetown University in Washington, D.C., contrasted sharply from those of President Carter's U.N. ambassadors, Andrew Young and Donald McHenry, who took a generally soft and quiet line toward Third World anti-Americanism.

Like Moynihan, Kirkpatrick came from a school of thought known as "neoconservative" — a group of intellectuals, mostly Democrats, whom she regarded as the "traditional liberals" and who rejected the "counterculture liberalism" of the Democratic Party in the 1970s.

In a 1979 article in the Republican journal *Commonsense*, Kirkpatrick explained her differences with the dominant forces in her party during the 1970s:

" 'We' affirmed the validity of the American dream and the morality of the American society. 'They' adopted the characterizations of intellectuals . . . who described the United States as a sick society drunk on technology and materialism. 'We' rejected the effort to revise American history, making it a dismal tale of dead Indians and double-dealing white settlers, imperialism and war. 'They' rejected facts and truths we hold dear."

There was no opposition to her nomination in the Senate, which confirmed her Jan. 29, 1981, by a vote of 81-0.

Earlier Career

Kirkpatrick was born Nov. 19, 1926, in Duncan, Okla. She received undergraduate degrees from Stephens College in 1946 and Barnard College in 1948, then earned a master's degree in political science at Columbia University in 1950. She worked briefly as a research analyst at the State Department in the early 1950s and was a French government fellow at the Institut de Science Politique in Paris.

In 1955 she married Evron Kirkpatrick, the executive director of the American Political Science Association, and interrupted her career to raise three sons.

She resumed her career in 1962, teaching part-time at Trinity College in Washington, D.C. She eventually completed her doctorate at Columbia in 1968, writing her dissertation on the Peronist movement in Argentina. With her knowledge of French and Spanish she was selected by the U.S. International Communication Agency to give speeches overseas.

Kirkpatrick joined the Georgetown faculty in 1967 and became a resident scholar at the Washington-based American Enterprise Institute for Public Policy Research in 1977.

Meanwhile, she was highly active in the Democratic Party, serving on various national party commissions. But her disillusionment with "McGovernism" in the 1970s led her to help found the Coalition for a Democratic Majority — a coalition of organized labor and "traditional liberals" such as Sen. Henry M. Jackson, D-Wash., who stressed American strength in foreign and defense policy as well as social welfare programs.

Reagan Adviser

In choosing Kirkpatrick for the U.N. post, Reagan delivered on campaign promises to try to put at least one woman and one Democrat in his Cabinet. More significantly, the appointment reflected Reagan's vow to abandon Carter's policy of judging authoritarian allies of the United States on their human rights records rather than on their anti-communism.

Kirkpatrick came to Reagan's attention because of her views on that subject, which she outlined in a 1979 article in *Commentary* magazine called "Dictatorships and Double Standards."

"The failure of the Carter administration's foreign policy is now clear to everyone except its architects," Kirkpatrick wrote, arguing that right-wing authoritarian regimes were more susceptible to democratization than left-wing totalitarian governments. "Although there is no instance of a revolutionary 'socialist' or Communist society being democratized, right-wing autocracies do sometimes evolve into democracies," Kirkpatrick wrote.

Reagan's top foreign policy adviser, Richard V. Allen, sent Reagan a copy of Kirkpatrick's article, and Reagan requested a meeting with her. Soon after their meeting, Kirkpatrick became a member of Reagan's foreign policy task force for the 1980 election campaign.

James G. Watt:
Secretary of the Interior

Reagan's selection of James G. Watt as secretary of the interior stirred up a controversy that nearly equaled in magnitude that of Alexander Haig's for secretary of state. Even before Reagan formally announced Watt's appointment Dec. 22, 1980, environmentalists mobilized to oppose him on the strength of rumors that the 42-year-old president of a conservative law foundation in Colorado was the likely choice to head the department.

As in the Haig nomination, though, the Senate finally backed the controversial nomination, and Watt was confirmed without difficulty Jan. 22, 1981, by a 83-12 vote. All 12 votes against him were cast by Democrats.

During the three years preceding his nomination, Watt headed the Mountain States Legal Organization. It had spent much of its time challenging the Interior Department's methods of administering the 519 million acres of publicly owned land. The foundation had fought attempts by the Bureau of Land Management to limit access to public land by a number of industries. The organization was funded partly by oil, gas, timber and mining companies.

It challenged the government's authority to limit livestock feeding on over-grazed land, to review national forest lands for wilderness potential and to prohibit motorized rafts on the Colorado River in the Grand Canyon. It also had fought extension of the deadline for approving the Equal Rights Amendment; the granting of rate reductions for the handicapped, the poor and the elderly by a Colorado utility; and the use of tax money to help high school dropouts.

According to its literature, the Denver-based organization was a non-profit, tax-exempt organization dedicated to helping combat "excessive bureaucratic regulation and the stifling economic effects resulting from the actions of extreme environmentalist groups and no-growth advocates."

Soon after the nomination, Rep. John F. Seiberling, D-Ohio, chairman of the Interior Subcommittee on Public Lands, said one of the most "disquieting" aspects of Watt's appointment was the list of financial supporters of the foundation:

"These are people whose primary interest in the public lands is to exploit them for their own profit. Their idea of multiple land-use is to have everything with any conceivable value to be developed, even if its primary value is wilderness."

Brock Evans, executive director for the Sierra Club, said a list of those who contributed $500 or more to the foundation "sounds like a 'Who's Who' of exploitation industries in the West." Among the major supporters were Chevron U.S.A., Amax Inc., Boise Cascade, Gulf Resources and Chemical Corp., Husky Oil, Exxon, Day Mines Inc. and the Kemmerer Coal Co.

Watt wrote in the organization's 1978-79 annual report that it was committed to fighting "those bureaucrats and no-growth advocates who create a challenge to individual liberty and economic freedoms as expressed through the private enterprise system."

In a May 18, 1979, *Wall Street Journal* story, Watt explained his primary thesis that environmentalists were "the greatest threat to the ecology of the West." By preventing the orderly development of Western energy resources now, he said, environmentalists would cause those resources to be developed later in a crisis atmosphere, resulting in the "ravaging of our land and the destruction of our natural environment."

Supporters of Watt pooh-poohed the alarmist reaction. Sen. Alan K. Simpson, R-Wyo., a friend of Watt's, called environmentalists' concern "hysterical hoopla. I have never seen a cloven foot on him or a horn growing out of his head. I assume he is not the personification of evil."

Earlier Career

Despite the controversy over Watt's ideology, no one disputed his record as an experienced administrator of programs and problems likely to come before the Interior Department. Born in Lusk, Wyo., Watt had a lifelong involvement in controversial Western issues of land and water rights.

After he graduated from law school at the University of Wyoming in 1962, Watt became legislative assistant and counsel to Sen. Milward L. Simpson, R-Wyo. (1962-67), father of Sen. Alan Simpson.

In 1966 Watt joined the U.S. Chamber of Commerce, where he directed the natural resources section. From 1969 until 1972 he served in the Interior Department as deputy assistant secretary for water and power resources. He then served for three years as director of the Bureau of Outdoor Recreation, whose name later was changed to the Heritage Conservation and Recreation Service, where he administered the Land and Water Conservation Fund.

While at the bureau, Watt advocated tripling the fund, a popular program for buying parks and wilderness lands. As director, Watt was a "strong delegator" and "one of the most effective managers we've ever had," said a department official who asked not to be named.

"He was a pretty good politician. He knew which way the political winds were blowing," said Daniel Beard, who had Watt's old job as deputy assistant secretary for water and power and worked under him at the Bureau of Outdoor Recreation. "He was fair and open."

Watt served as vice chairman of the Federal Power Commission (FPC) from 1975 until 1977, when he resigned to join the legal foundation.

The only controversy involving his activities in Washington centered on his work at the FPC. In March 1977 the Oversight and Investigations Subcommittee of the House Commerce Committee held hearings on whether two FPC employees had been demoted because they had "blown the whistle" to the panel in 1976 about alleged unauthorized diversion of natural gas from federal fields by private companies. Watt was questioned about allegations that shortly after he joined the commission he tried to get an FPC attorney demoted because he had testified at the 1976 hearing. Watt said the attorney, who had been on the staff for 11 years, was transferred not because he had testified but because his work was unacceptable.

The subcommittee found no violations by Watt of a federal law prohibiting harassment of congressional witnesses, but it said the employees' testimony had "contributed significantly" to their transfers or demotions. It also said the "unjustified transfer" of several of the FPC's most experienced natural gas attorneys had hindered the regulation of natural gas during a period of severe natural gas shortage.

In his testimony, Watt said he was not afraid to make waves, even as a new member of the commission. He said he was "appalled" at what he considered the lack of accountability of the general counsel's staff and simply tried to make the office accountable. "I like to think I left tracks at the commission," he said. "I try to have an impact."

Confirmation Hearings

Watt faced critical questioning by the Senate Energy and Natural Resources Committee before he received the panel's endorsement Jan. 14 by a vote of 16-0, with three Democrats abstaining. Sen. Wendell H. Ford, D-Ky., said he was voting for Watt with "grave reservations," because he was not satisfied with many of Watt's answers to committee questions. He said he felt Watt represented a 180-degree shift in philosophy from Carter administration Secretary Cecil D. Andrus. "I hope Mr. Watt comes to realize that his jurisdiction extends east of the Mississippi River."

During the hearings, Watt pledged not to try to change federal environmental and land-use laws, but to improve their implementation to allow the orderly development of coal, oil, gas and minerals on federal lands.

"I don't see a need for massive overhaul of existing laws. I see a need for massive attention toward good management of those laws," he told the committee's members.

Watt said he would implement a "good neighbor policy," in which the Interior Department would cooperate more with landowners and local governments affected by its actions. Only by doing so would he be able to defuse the anger and frustration that had prompted the so-called "sagebrush rebellion" among Westerners, he said. Watt, who previously had embraced the controversial sagebrush movement to transfer millions of acres of federally owned land to Western states, said he would not push for legislation mandating the transfer.

"It would be premature and a divisive force in the Congress, and there's not much chance of it passing," he said. But he warned that the movement had developed because of "inept, arrogant management" by the Interior Department, and if that did not change Congress would be under intense pressure to pass such legislation later.

Watt sought to convince senators that the environmentalists were unduly concerned and that he would take positions more moderate than the foundation's. "My loyalties are totally shifted because of my commitment to Reagan," he replied when senators pointed out that the foundation had taken positions contrary to Reagan's.

In an effort to deflect conflict-of-interest charges, Watt agreed not to participate in current or future suits brought by the foundation involving department policies. Watt said he had met for 15 to 20 minutes with Reagan to discuss his mission at the department and that Reagan outlined four goals he wanted him to pursue: 1) to make public lands available for more uses, such as oil exploration and coal mining, not just wilderness or recreation; 2) to develop a policy for producing strategic minerals; 3) to upgrade the national parks and increase public access to them; and 4) to improve management of the department's programs.

While groups representing timber, ranching, farming and energy interests backed Watt, the environmentalists were not assuaged. "What I am hearing is more and more exploitation of what natural lands are left," Sierra Club spokesman Brock Evans said of Watt's testimony. And former Sen. Gaylord Nelson, D-Wis. (1963-81), representing the Wilderness Society, was not convinced Watt would have a "balanced" approach to managing federal lands. Watt "brings to his office what we believe to be a strong anti-environmental bias," said Nelson.

Called Tough Administrator

Supporters described Watt as a tough administrator who demands accountability.

"He is very reasonable, articulate, extremely bright, and — almost to a fault — thorough. He doesn't make mistakes because of lack of information," said David C. Russell, a Senate Energy Committee staffer and a member of Reagan's Interior Department transition team.

An Interior Department official who worked with Watt, but asked not to be identified, said environmentalists need not be alarmed at Watt's appointment. "I don't think he would have a knee-jerk reaction to anything," the official said. "He always wanted to examine all the alternatives."

Joseph Coors, president of the Adolph Coors Co. and a founder of Watt's legal foundation, said environmentalists should not be upset, because Watt is "an environmentalist . . . who believes in properly controlled growth."

Former Sen. Clifford P. Hansen, R-Wyo. (1967-79), said Watt understood the energy potential of the West and would proceed with development "in an orderly, but timely, fashion."

Simpson agreed with Reagan, who said Dec. 17 that the environmentalists who were upset about Watt's appointment were the "environmental extremists."

"They're the 100 percent environmentalists," said Simpson. "You're either with them 100 percent of the time or they'll cut your bicycle tire." He said the real reason the environmentalists didn't like Watt was that he learned to beat them at their own game. "They're after him because he took them on their own turf. [He's] learned how to use the judicial system to get results. They've gotten a little petulent and pouty about all that."

Simpson said Watt was chosen because of his affinity toward the laws of the Western states, particularly regarding water, and that Watt believed strongly in the multiple use of public lands. That concept called for making the land available for timbering, farming, oil and gas development, and mining, as well as recreation.

Watt's nomination did not mean a return to the "pre-World War I attitude of ripping up the public domain," Simpson said. He predicted that the Bureau of Land Management would be made "more responsive to the public" under Watt.

Environmental Values Questioned

Environmentalists were particularly upset that Reagan broke a recent Washington tradition of seeking their backing for the interior secretary. "For 10 years we've been saying the secretary of interior is the No. 1 environmental position in the country because of all the parks and trusts he is in charge of," said the Sierra Club's Evans. "We would hope that the secretary would at least have environmental values. Watt appears to have no environmental values whatsoever."

Reagan's selection of Watt was "rather an astounding choice from our perspective," said Liz Kaplan, assistant legislative director for the Friends of the Earth. "As far as we can tell, he has spent the last few years ardently representing the anti-environmental point of view."

Elvis Stahr, senior counselor for the National Audubon Society, said: "I am apprehensive, but I am willing to reserve judgment. From what I have read, he apparently does not take the balanced approach that we believe in between environmental protection and a sound economy, but tips the balance in favor of short-term economic considerations."

John R. Block:
Secretary of Agriculture

The Illinois farmer and state official chosen by President Reagan to be secretary of agriculture was headed for a quick baptism by the 97th Congress with some of the nation's most difficult farm issues.

The first legislative order of business to face John R. Block, 45, who was the director of the Illinois Department of Agriculture when Reagan picked him, was the 1981 farm bill extending nearly $22 billion worth of agriculture pro-

grams. The complex legislation required early decisions by the department on price supports, conservation, research and the food stamp program.

Block, who was new to Washington, quickly had to grapple with the need to balance the perennial demands of farmers for higher price supports against pressures from budget-conscious Reagan economic advisers to cut farm credit and other federal subsidy programs.

Debate on the bill was certain to play against a backdrop of soaring food prices and consumer discontent. And anticipated food price increases in 1981 of up to 15 percent were expected to hasten the date on which the food stamp program would exceed the $9.7 billion spending ceiling set by Congress and thus run out of money.

Block also faced early decisions on the partial embargo on sales of U.S. grain to the Soviet Union imposed by the Carter administration and on renewal of an agreement that had guaranteed the Soviets a minimum purchase of American grain — even during the embargo.

There were strong pressures within the Reagan administration to use American farm commodities more explicitly as a tool of foreign policy than in the past. That trend would make many farmers and officials in the food industry uneasy because it implied government intervention in the market.

Many farm experts predicted that projected worldwide grain shortages would make allocation of scarce food resources another important and explosive issue in 1981. That would be a sharp departure from U.S. farm policy, which for decades had sought to compensate farmers for low prices caused by surpluses. And creating a method for allocating short supplies was expected to be difficult given Reagan's "free market" philosophy.

Major farm groups and the National Governors' Association said Block had been unusually able and aggressive in the Illinois state government post. The governors' group and Sen. Robert Dole, R-Kan., strongly backed Block's nomination.

"He's a fast learner, he surrounded himself with good people [in state government], and he's not afraid of hard work or new ideas," said Len Gardner, executive director of governmental affairs at the Illinois Farm Bureau.

Joseph A. Kinney, staff director of the committee on agriculture at the National Governors' Association, praised Block as an effective manager with experience in international trade and a good record on conservation and farm programs. Block served on the agriculture committee and on the association's agricultural export task force.

Block was well received by the Senate Agriculture Committee, which considered his nomination, and he was unanimously confirmed by the Senate Jan. 22, 1981, by a 98-0 vote.

Opposition From Nutrition Groups

Food and nutrition groups such as the Community Nutrition Institute (CNI) objected to the choice of Block, however. Ellen Haas, director of CNI's consumer division, said Block had identified himself with "a very narrow promotion of agriculture interests." For example, in testimony before Congress Block had strongly criticized Agriculture Department moves against the meat preservative sodium nitrite, which had been linked to cancer in rats. He also objected to controversial USDA dietary guidelines. These positions were very "disappointing" to consumer groups, Haas said.

On food stamps and other federal food programs, Block was an "unknown quantity, but we're worried," she said. The Agriculture Department's stress on consumer issues under the Carter administration had been a sore point with many farmers. Hog producers, for instance, protested that the department's warnings against the nitrites used to preserve bacon, sausage and other processed meats caused them to lose money.

During the campaign, Reagan objected to "unfounded attacks on nutritious, farm-produced foods unleashed by . . . activists" in the Carter administration. He had promised to restore the department to "farmers and those who understand farming." The choice of Block appeared to fulfill that promise.

A Working Farmer

Block, a 1957 graduate of the U.S. Military Academy at West Point, left the Army in 1960 to take over his family's farm near Galesburg, Ill. He expanded it to 3,000 acres, from 300. He raised hogs and soybeans and was a former board member of the Illinois Farm Bureau.

When Block was appointed state agriculture director in 1977 he was a strong advocate of revisions in Illinois' conservation law. The program he drew up was voluntary and relied on financial incentives to reward farmers for protecting land from erosion. It had less "teeth" than environmental groups would have liked, but Illinois Farm Bureau director Gardner praised it as a good start on a serious problem.

Gardner also said Block played a major role in setting up a 1980 state conference on the problem of conversion of prime farm land to non-farm uses such as shopping centers or industrial development. After the conference, Illinois Gov. James R. Thompson issued an executive order requiring state agencies to evaluate the impact of their actions on farm land use.

Block also pushed for development of state trade promotion offices abroad to act as "middlemen" for sales of Illinois farm products and the production of gasohol. A physical fitness buff, Block had competed in a number of races, including the Boston Marathon.

Confirmation Hearings

Block described himself as a "free-market man" who believed high prices for farm goods — not price supports — were the best guarantee of high farm income. He promised the Agriculture Committee at his Jan. 6 confirmation hearing that he would "aggressively" promote sales of American farm goods abroad. Strong export markets would boost farmers' earnings and strengthen the whole economy, while fostering more "efficient" farming, Block said.

Block felt U.S.-produced food was a "valuable tool" to "promote greater stability in the world and . . . peace." But he said he would be "very reluctant" to impose any embargo because, in "turning the faucet on and off, we will fail in our effort to create better relations with other countries."

He told the panel embargoes "generally [were] not effective," should be used only "as a last resort," and, if used, should apply to all American products, not just food.

Responding to a question by Sen. Walter "Dee" Huddleston, D-Ky., Block said he saw no contradiction between his disapproval of embargoes and his strong belief in using U.S. food as a diplomatic tool. As his precedessors also had pledged, Block promised to be a "strong voice for agriculture" in the Reagan administration. His stress on "agriculture production" was "not to the neglect of consumers," he assured committee members, because "they would be best served" by a healthy and efficient farm industry.

In response to committee questioning, Block gave his position on the following government programs:

● The food stamp program should be "carefully scrutinized" and made "more efficient" to ensure benefits for the "truly needy."

● Programs to protect farm land from erosion and conversion to non-farm uses were best carried out at the "local level" with the federal government providing "leadership and some money for the states."

● Federal restrictions on the amount of acreage that farmers planted — such as the Carter administration's "normal crop acreage" regulations — generally were undesirable.

● The federal government should "stay out" of publishing nutrition advice — such as the Carter administration had done — because the information was "not conclusive" and because "people are pretty good at figuring out what to eat" on their own.

Block's answers clearly pleased committee members, including Chairman Jesse Helms, R-N.C. The committee later voted without opposition to recommend that the Senate approve Block's nomination.

Raymond J. Donovan:
Secretary of Labor

President Reagan's controversial labor secretary, Raymond J. Donovan, a New Jersey construction contractor, had few ties to the nation's business and labor leaders. The 50-year-old business executive, who was chairman of the Reagan-Bush campaign in New Jersey, was credited with rounding up blue-collar support that helped ensure Reagan's election victory in the state.

In confirming him Feb. 3, 1981, the Senate rejected  allegations that Donovan was linked to labor racketeers and organized crime. The vote for Donovan was 80-17 — the largest number of votes against any of President Reagan's Cabinet nominees. Only Democrats voted against Donovan.

Approval of the nomination completed the confirmation process for heads of Cabinet departments.

Senate action on Donovan had been delayed for nearly two weeks while the FBI and the Senate Labor and Human Resources Committee, which considered the nomination, investigated Donovan and his firm, the Schiavone Construction Co.

The investigations looked into charges, made by FBI informer Ralph Picardo, that Donovan and Schiavone had provided illegal payoffs to corrupt union officials to maintain "labor peace." Other informants said the company had close ties with organized crime. But an intensive FBI investigation did not uncover any evidence to substantiate the various charges. On the other hand, the FBI said it could not disprove some of the allegations.

Donovan was the executive vice president of the construction firm, located in Secaucus, N.J. He was responsible for negotiating contracts with the firm's unionized construction workers. The firm, one of the nation's largest construction concerns, primarily built tunnels and bridges.

Link With Labor

Donovan had a reputation for being a hard-nosed, but fair, negotiator. "I'm told he's tough as hell on those [union] contracts," said Victor Kamber, former head of the AFL-CIO building and construction trades department.

"His ability as a negotiator is fantastic," commented John J. Messinger, business manager and financial secretary to the New York City-based Local 14 of the International Union of Operating Engineers, who had sat across the bargaining table from Donovan for years. "He gets a lot done without a lot of noise. He's very quiet and very sure of every step he's ever made," Messinger added.

Donovan's experience as a unionized laborer and brewery worker during summers off from college helped him in his efforts to forge ties to workers, according to friends and associates. "He can talk their language," commented Roger

Bodman, an aide to Rep. Jim Courter, R-N.J., who represented Donovan's congressional district.

But most business and labor leaders in Washington had little information about him. "I never heard of Mr. Donovan before I read about him" in press reports, said Arnold Mayer, vice president for government relations of the 1.3-million-member United Food and Commercial Workers International Union.

Donovan was born on Aug. 31, 1930, in Bayonne, an industrial town in the northeast region of New Jersey. One of 12 children, Donovan attended St. Andrew's parochial school and graduated in 1952 with a bachelor's degree from Notre Dame Seminary in New Orleans. From 1953 to 1958 he worked for the American Insurance Co. in New Jersey, leaving to join Schiavone as a shareholder and vice president. He became executive vice president in 1971.

Few Positions on Issues

"It's unclear to anybody where he stands" on important labor issues, said former AFL-CIO official Kamber. Charles T. Carroll Jr., associate director of legislation for the Associated General Contractors of America, of which Donovan was a member, said: "We are as in the dark on his background as anyone."

And Frank E. Fitzsimmons, president of the 1.9 million-member Teamsters union, said the group would "look forward to working" with the New Jersey businessman. The Teamsters, who supported Reagan for president, had backed Betty Southard Murphy for labor secretary. Murphy, former chairman of the National Labor Relations Board (NLRB), also was backed by the U.S. Chamber of Commerce and Sen. Orrin G. Hatch, R-Utah, chairman of the Labor and Human Resources Committee.

Donovan's positions and future policy directions were largely unknown. But Donovan was expected to closely reflect Reagan's views on labor, according to Raymond Bateman, for whom Donovan worked when Bateman was the Republican candidate for governor of New Jersey in 1977. Bateman pointed out that Donovan had personal ties to the Reagans.

Business groups hoped Donovan would support their efforts to reduce workplace health and safety regulations imposed by the Labor Department's Occupational Safety and Health Administration (OSHA). But union leaders who knew him said Donovan was not likely to try to dismantle OSHA.

He may "do a little snipping, pruning and trimming, but always with an attitude of trying to improve [OSHA] rather than destroying" it, according to Messinger of the Operating Engineers.

Donovan's record of good relations with New Jersey union members seemed to point to a receptive attitude toward some of labor's concerns. But union leaders said his strong backing from the National Right to Work Committee cast some doubt on his labor sympathies. That group supported Section 14(b) of the Taft-Hartley Act permitting states to pass "right-to-work" laws forbidding union shop contracts, making the group anathema to labor unions.

Carter Clews, a spokesman for the National Right to Work Committee, said the group submitted a list of questions to Donovan about his views on key labor issues. Donovan "was very strong in his support for right-to-work issues," Clews said. Clews said the group mailed 100,000 cards and letters to the Reagan transition office outlining its opposition to various candidates for labor secretary. The group mounted a lobbying campaign against Murphy.

Confirmation Hearings

At his confirmation hearings before the Labor and Human Resources Committee, Donovan was questioned in detail about previous criminal investigations into links between the Schiavone Construction Co. and political corruption and labor racketeering.

But while Donovan's defense of his business record left doubts in the minds of some committee Democrats, it appeared to satisfy most Republicans enough to remove any serious obstacle to his confirmation.

Charges of Criminal Activity

On the isssue of criminal activity by his construction firm, Donovan was asked specifically about two incidents: a 1967 payment by the Schiavone Co. to a dummy company that allegedly served as a conduit for illegal payoffs to politicians, and a 1977 investigation into alleged extortion of the Schiavone Co. by a New York City Teamsters union official.

Donovan explained that the 1967 payment, for $13,000, had been made by Schiavone for the right to dump highway excavations on property supposedly owned by the dummy company, although it was later discovered that the land was owned by the city of Newark. As for the 1977 incident, which involved Schiavone's hiring of a Teamster "ghost employee," Donovan said the company had been forced to employ the man because of a provision in its contract with the union.

Labor Issues

In testimony Jan. 12, Donovan conceded he was not familiar with a variety of Labor Department programs. But he expressed a definite opinion about the general trend of policies at the department, which he said involved too much confrontation and "adversarial attitudes" toward business.

"You need the stick, but you need the carrot, too," he said of departmental regulations imposed on businesses. One way to change that attitude was to shift to "result-oriented" regulations, rewarding businesses with good performance in areas such as occupational safety and health.

Turning to specific programs, Donovan backed administrative changes in, but not repeal of, the Davis-Bacon Act, which set wages for workers on federal construction projects. He said he supported Section 14(b) of the Taft-Hartley Act, but did not favor such a law at the national level.

Donovan called for major changes, however, in federal employment and training programs. He said that public service employment had not been successful and that the federal effort should concentrate more on encouraging private sector job training. But Donovan shied away from direct support of proposals to establish a subminimum wage for young workers. He said he would support a youth differential if it did not harm older workers.

Committee Report

After questioning FBI agents and Donovan again on Jan. 27, the Labor Committee Jan. 29 approved the nomination by an 11-0 vote. Five committee Democrats voted "present."

The committee Jan. 30 issued a written report (Exec Rept 97-3) on the nomination — a step seldom taken on a Cabinet-level presidential nomination. The report included the additional views of committee Democrats, who argued that the nomination was "almost unique in the history of presidential nominations to the Cabinet because of the number and gravity of the allegations against Mr. Donovan."

Senate Debate

During the Senate debate on the nomination Feb. 3, Donovan supporters stressed that he was entitled to a presumption of innocence if a detailed investigation could not produce any hard evidence of wrongdoing.

"We do not feel that unsupported, hearsay, conclusionary allegations made by a convicted murderer or unnamed source should overcome all the other evidence that the committee had to consider," said committee Chairman Hatch. (Picardo had been convicted of murder in 1975, but the conviction later was reversed.)

Ranking committee Democrat Edward M. Kennedy, Mass., backed away from Picardo's allegations as a reason for opposing the nomination. Instead, he pointed to two charges — involving alleged payoffs to corrupt political and union officials — that had been raised at the Jan. 12 committee hearing. Donovan's actions in the two cases aired at that hearing "indicate a flawed sensitivity to the dangers of the criminal activity," Kennedy argued.

James B. Edwards:
Secretary of Energy

In choosing former South Carolina Gov. James B. Edwards to be his energy secretary, Reagan found someone who shared his basic philosophy on energy development: Get government out of the way so private industry could produce more.

But other than being a fervent supporter of nuclear power, Edwards had not been involved in or taken public positions on most energy issues.

Edwards assumed control over a three-year-old, $10-billion-a-year agency that often had been criticized by Republicans and Democrats alike for bureaucratic ineptness. Edwards said he was not an energy expert but rather a "problem solver."

Edwards, an oral surgeon who also was considered by Reagan's transition team to head the Department of Health and Human Services, said that as governor he had been heavily involved in energy. He chaired an energy subcommittee of the National Governors' Association in 1978.

Environmental groups opposed his confirmation because of his unwavering pro-nuclear position.

Edwards was selected after Southern senators, led by Strom Thurmond, R-S.C., complained that the South had been ignored in Reagan's initial Cabinet selections.

Shortly before he was named, Edwards said: "I'd like to go to Washington and close the Energy Department down and work myself out of a job." Abolishing the department was an early Reagan campaign pledge, but at a press conference Dec. 22, 1980, Edwards ducked the question, saying he needed direction from Reagan before making any decision on dismantling the department. Edwards had said that "the less the federal government has to do with problems, the better I like it."

Sen. J. Bennett Johnston, D-La., a senior member of the Senate Energy Committee, which considered Edwards' nomination, criticized the choice, saying it was unfortunate since Edwards had little background in the field.

Despite his lack of energy experience, the Senate Jan. 22 overwhelmingly approved his nomination, 93-3.

Career in Government

Edwards was born June 24, 1927, in Hawthorne, Fla. He received a B.S. degree from the College of Charleston in 1950 and a D.M.D. from the University of Louisville School of Dentistry in 1955. He went to sea with the U.S. merchant marine during World War II and served as a Navy dentist from 1955 to 1957, remaining in the Naval Reserve until 1967.

Party colleagues credited Edwards with building up the local Republican organization. He was chairman of the Charleston County Republican Party from 1964 to 1969 and was the 1970 Republican chairman for the state's 1st Congressional District.

In 1971 Edwards ran for Congress and lost. In 1972 he was elected to the state Senate, and in 1974 he won the governorship. In 1978, prohibited by law from seeking a second term, he returned to his dental practice in Charleston. The day after being named to Reagan's Cabinet, he performed a full day of surgery.

Edwards did not escape controversy as governor. In 1977, on returning from a trip to South Africa that was paid for by the South African government, he said: "The black influence in American politics prevented the white South African government from getting its fair share of sympathy and understanding." The remarks drew fire from South Carolina blacks, but Edwards refused to apologize, saying he had been misunderstood.

Edwards' 1974 election as South Carolina's first Republican governor since Reconstruction was regarded as something of a fluke. He defeated retired Army Gen. William C. Westmoreland in the primary, but was expected to lose the general election to Democrat Charles "Pug" Ravenel. However, state courts ruled Ravenel off the ballot because he did not meet the state's residency requirements, and Edwards faced a weaker opponent, former Rep. William Jennings Bryan Dorn, in the general election. Dorn failed to unite his party, and Edwards won with 50.9 percent of the vote.

As governor, Edwards strongly supported Reagan's 1976 bid for the Republican presidential nomination against President Gerald R. Ford. But in 1980 he, like Thurmond, backed John B. Connally. When Connally quit the race after losing the South Carolina primary, Edwards helped Reagan carry the state in November.

William Brantley Harvey Jr., lieutenant governor under Edwards, and a Democrat, described him as a "committed conservative" and "completely honest and fair." State GOP Chairman George Graham called him "a great one-on-one politician," good at "disarming his enemies."

Lamar Priester, state energy director under Edwards, said Edwards was often frustrated by the long time it took the Energy Department to get things done. He said Edwards considered energy the "basic thread of this country's economic base" and believed improved energy production was necessary to provide jobs for young Americans.

Nuclear Cheerleader

Edwards, an unabashed supporter of nuclear energy, as governor set up a state Energy Research Institute to study ways to expand nuclear power. It recommended building a 12-reactor nuclear power park in the state to supply electricity for the region, but the controversial project was not built.

Edwards' strong backing for renewed commercial reprocessing of nuclear fuel was the position that most dismayed environmental groups. Presidents Ford and Carter banned reprocessing, which involves turning burned nuclear reactor fuel into fresh fuel, plutonium and highly radioactive liquid waste. The ban was based on the fear that the plutonium could be used to produce nuclear weapons.

Edwards said in 1977 that "this idea that a high school kid can go into the kitchen and manufacture a plutonium bomb is hogwash." He promoted a reprocessing facility, which was built in South Carolina, but it never was put into operation because of the ban. Testifying before a Senate subcommittee in 1978, he said reprocessing would reduce U.S. dependence on foreign oil.

At a hearing in 1978, he said that "the only answer we have [to the U.S. energy shortage] is nuclear energy," which he described as safer than oil, coal or natural gas. He also urged that something be done about radioactive waste: "Everyone has wanted to put it off, and we are getting constipated with nuclear waste and have no real way to dispose of it [and thus allow us to] move ahead [with nuclear power]. Let us do something, even if it isn't the ideal situation in years to come. We can move back and correct it as technological advances are made."

Edwards said he was happy to have the problem of disposing of millions of gallons of highly radioactive waste from making nuclear weapons because, without it, "we would probably all be slaves working in the Siberian salt mines today."

Confirmation Hearings

The energy industry should be deregulated, and the marketplace should determine oil and gas prices, Edwards told the Senate Energy Committee, chaired by James A. McClure, R-Idaho, at his confirmation hearing Jan. 12.

Edwards said he would urge Reagan to immediately end crude oil price controls. Echoing Reagan's campaign speeches, Edwards told the panel the federal government should "unshackle" the "sleeping giant" of American private industry to "produce, produce and produce" more energy. Free market economics — not the federal government —should control energy production, he said.

With dozens of industry lobbyists jamming the huge Senate Caucus Room, Edwards had a relatively easy time with most of the questioning. Only two members, Dale Bumpers, D-Ark., and Howard M. Metzenbaum, D-Ohio, pursued tough lines of questioning about the nominee's attitudes toward consumers and the environment.

Edwards acknowledged that the incoming administration was "rethinking" Reagan's campaign pledge to abolish the Energy Department. Edwards said he could not promise to reduce the department's budget, only to restrain its growth. Saying he needed to give the issues more study,

Edwards ducked questions on whether to repeal the multi-billion-dollar windfall profits tax on oil companies or continue massive subsidies to private firms seeking to produce synthetic fuels. Both programs were enacted by the 96th Congress in 1980.

He did say, however, that "I've always stood for less taxes" and that government should subsidize only research on synthetic fuels, not their commercialization.

As governor of South Carolina, Edwards strongly supported nuclear energy. He was just as vigorous at his confirmation hearing, advocating reprocessing of burned reactor fuel, construction of breeder reactors and storage of nuclear waste in monitored vaults near the earth's surface. Environmental groups opposed all of these steps.

Edwards also rejected the idea, backed by environmentalists, of giving states veto power over the location of nuclear waste dumps. Edwards said the 1979 accident at the Three Mile Island nuclear plant in Pennsylvania showed that "the system worked, and no one was harmed or killed."

The committee Jan. 14 by voice vote without dissent recommended his confirmation.

Terrel H. Bell:
Secretary of Education

For his secretary of education, President Reagan selected an experienced administrator with longstanding ties to the education community.

Terrel H. Bell, the 59-year-old Utah commissioner of higher education, was named Jan. 7 to become the second head of the department, which was established in 1980.

Unlike the first education secretary, former California Judge Shirley M. Hufstedler, who had virtually no experience in education, Bell had spent his entire career in that field, from high school athletic coach to U.S. commissioner of education.

His selection was greeted enthusiastically by most education groups. Some lobbyists saw it as an indication Reagan might have had second thoughts about his campaign promise to abolish the department.

Bell supported the establishment of the Department of Education, which was carved out of the old Department of Health, Education and Welfare. Educators familiar with his record said he was not the type of person who would have taken the job just to oversee its dissolution. Reagan advisers reportedly were considering retaining the agency's separate status, but demoting it from Cabinet rank.

The delay in naming Bell (the other Cabinet members had been announced in December) was ironic because Bell was the first choice suggested by Reagan's transition team after the November election. In an attempt to add more balance to the Cabinet, however, Reagan advisers apparently searched for a month for a woman or minority representative to take the post.

Several potential candidates contacted by Reagan officials declined to accept the position. After that the final decision came down to a choice between Bell and former Rep. Marvin L. Esch, R-Mich. (1967-77), both white males.

No opposition was expressed to Bell during his confirmation hearings, and he was overwhelmingly confirmed by the Senate Jan. 22 by a 90-2 vote.

Support From Education Groups

Education groups were pleased at the selection of a fellow educator with long experience, detailed knowledge of education programs and a reputation as a competent administrator. While generally supportive of Hufstedler, the education community never really took her to heart as one of its own. J. W. Peltason, president of the American Council on Education, said she was "a lay person who was a quick learner. But Bell is the finest representation of another kind — the experienced professional."

Bell was well known in Washington and familiar with federal education programs through his service as U.S. education commissioner from 1974 to 1976. In that job Bell oversaw some controversial decisions, especially the 1975 "Lau remedies" that required school districts to provide bilingual instruction to children from non-English-speaking families. The new administration was expected to block similar bilingual regulations.

But Bell's personal concerns as commissioner generally were directed toward goals more compatible with the Reagan administration's perspective, particularly his mandates to reduce paperwork and strengthen the parental role in education. "He was the first one to say there was far too much red tape in education. That was one of his pet peeves back then," noted August Steinhilber of the National School Boards Association.

Bell's support for a strong parental role got him into trouble with education groups in 1974 during a violent protest by West Virginia parents against textbooks used in the state's schools. In a speech to textbook publishers, Bell said they should "chart a middle course" between academic freedom and "the legitimate expectation of parents that schools will respect their moral and ethical values."

"He suggested they tone down the textbooks. We objected to that because it was an inappropriate role for the commissioner of education to take," said Paul Salmon of the American Association of School Administrators.

Bell spent the early part of his career in public school systems in Idaho and Utah, first as a teacher, later as a school superintendent. From 1963 to 1970 he was Utah's superintendent of public instruction. After a short term as deputy commissioner in the U.S. Office of Education and three years as head of a school system near Salt Lake City, he was named commissioner of education.

His reason for leaving that job reflected the relatively low status of the office at that time. With three sons in college, Bell said he could not afford the job's $37,800 salary. So he returned to Utah to run the state's higher education system, at $48,600 annually.

Confirmation Hearing

Bell told the Senate Labor and Human Resources Committee at his confirmation hearing Jan. 15 that the Reagan administration was committed to the abolition of the Department of Education. But Bell made it clear to committee members that he did not want to see a return to the days when education was a low-status part of the massive Department of Health, Education and Welfare.

"My support of the separate Department of Education grew out of the frustration I had as education commissioner in the huge structure of HEW. There were times when I felt I was the lowest form of life," he said. Bell was head of the old Office of Education from 1974 to 1976. "I'm open to other organizational structures," Bell added. "We've got to look at the alternatives."

After the confirmation hearing, the committee unanimously approved Bell's nomination, 16-0.

In addition to supporting changes in the department's status, Bell called for reductions in its size and complexity. "I'm fully committed to reducing the structure. We have a large number of assistant secretaries — we can streamline that considerably," he promised.

As an example of excessive federal regulation, Bell cited the Education of All Handicapped Children Act. "The bill specifies a bit too much. It gets into instructional methodology to an extent that exceeds good federal policy," he said, raising the possibility of new legislation to ease the act's requirements.

Acknowledging the heavy budget pressures there would be on the department, Bell singled out the rapidly growing program of federally guaranteed loans for college students as a prime target for spending cuts. "Maybe we don't need interest subsidies for the wealthy. We've got to make sure that aid for college goes only to the needy," he said.

Samuel Riley Pierce Jr.:
Secretary of Housing,
Urban Development

Samuel R. Pierce Jr., President Reagan's choice for secretary of housing and urban development (HUD), had made a lifelong habit of being "the first."

Before he became Reagan's first and only black Cabinet appointee, Pierce broke barriers to become the first black named to a sub-Cabinet-level position in the Treasury Department, the first black to become a partner in a major New York law firm and the first black named to the

boards of directors of two major U.S. corporations.

Pierce, a native New Yorker and lifelong Republican, had never had any direct involvement in housing issues. But supporters said his academic background, government experience and administrative abilities would serve him well in his management of one of the largest federal agencies.

Pierce was not opposed by anyone on the Senate Banking Committee, which considered his nomination, or in the full Senate, which confirmed Pierce by a unanimous 98-0 vote on Jan. 22, 1981.

Industry in Bad Shape

Pierce took over the sprawling department at a time when the housing industry was in the worst shape it had been in for many years.

Sales of private homes had dropped 40 percent during much of 1980, compared with the previous year, and were expected to drop even further in the early months of 1981, according to Jack Carlson, executive vice president and chief economist of the National Association of Realtors. Carlson added that he expected the budget and economic policies being discussed by incoming Reagan administration officials to hurt the industry even further.

"From what we can tell, Pierce has been an outstanding attorney and judge," Carlson said, but added that he was "disappointed that he [Pierce] does not have firsthand familiarity with housing and urban development." Not to have someone familiar with housing issues heading HUD was "clearly a handicap," he said.

Members of the National Housing Conference board of directors who knew of Pierce's background spoke "very highly of his administrative abilities and dedication to the types of programs controlled by HUD," according to Gene Schaefer, executive vice president of the group. The conference was an umbrella organization of businesses and groups involved in housing issues, ranging from savings and loan institutions to tenants' rights organizations.

But Schaefer warned that it would be difficult for any incoming HUD secretary to protect many of the existing housing programs with "the constraints of a very, very strict Office of Management and Budget."

Schaefer predicted a "serious curtailment of HUD programs," given the strong inclination of OMB Director David A. Stockman to slash funds in the housing and urban aid area. In the OMB director's "Stockman Manifesto," outlining an economic blueprint for Reagan's first 100 days in office, Stockman singled out for cutbacks the UDAG program (Urban Development Action Grants), the community development program and the Economic Development Administration.

Simon Obi Anekwe, who as political editor of the *Amsterdam News* had watched Pierce operate as an attorney and on the board of the New York chapter of the National Association for the Advancement of Colored People (NAACP), said he thought Pierce's background made him better prepared than most recent HUD secretaries to handle the job.

Anekwe stressed Pierce's academic background, his financial experience in the Treasury Department and as a corporate director, and the fact that Pierce lived in New York "where all the housing problems are concentrated." He also cited Pierce's work with the NAACP in which he dealt "with the suffering of the people HUD serves."

Earlier Career

Pierce was born in Glen Cove, Long Island, Sept. 8, 1922. His father was in the dry cleaning and real estate businesses. According to Anekwe, Pierce grew up in what was not "just an ordinary black family."

During his undergraduate days at Cornell University, Pierce was a star halfback on the football team and was elected to Phi Beta Kappa in his junior year. After time out for service in the Army during World War II he received his A.B. degree from Cornell in 1947 and his J.D. from Cornell's law school in 1949. In 1952 he received a master's degree in tax law from New York University School of Law.

He also did postgraduate study as a Ford Foundation Fellow at Yale Law School.

After finishing his education, Pierce served as an assistant district attorney for New York County and later as assistant U.S. attorney for the Southern District of New York. In 1955 he was named assistant under secretary of labor in the Eisenhower administration. He later became associate counsel and then counsel of the House Judiciary Antitrust Subcommittee.

Pierce returned to New York in 1957. Gov. Nelson A. Rockefeller, R, named him to the Court of General Sessions, which later became part of the New York Supreme Court. When the post became elective, Pierce ran for election but was defeated by a Democrat.

In 1961 Pierce joined the prestigious New York City labor law firm of Battle, Fowler, Stokes and Kheel, primarily as a labor mediator. He did another stint in Washington from 1970 to 1973, serving as general counsel of the Treasury Department in the Nixon administration.

Pierce served on the boards of directors of six major corporations — Prudential Insurance Company, General Electric Co., International Paper Co., U.S. Industries, First National Boston Corp. and the First National Bank of Boston. He was a trustee of the Rand Corp. and a governor of the American Stock Exchange.

Confirmation Hearings

Pierce sailed through his Jan. 13 Senate confirmation hearings without being buffeted by a single tough question. Even the usually persistent Sen. William Proxmire, D-Wis., did not grill Pierce on Reagan administration plans for the nation's housing and community development programs.

As an indication of the Banking Committee's confidence in Pierce, only three committee members stayed throughout the hearing to ask him questions. A handful of other senators came in long enough to congratulate Pierce and wish him good luck. Then they departed for hearings on more controversial nominees.

During questioning by committee Chairman Jake Garn, R-Utah, ranking minority member Harrison A. Williams Jr., D-N.J., and Proxmire, Pierce said he thought the paramount issue in improving the supply of housing was improvement in the performance of the nation's economy. Pierce pledged to cut the HUD budget, but said that did not mean that "I intend for HUD to turn its back on the poor."

He said he would like to reduce the number of regulations that applied to housing programs and the amount of control HUD exercised over local governments.

Pierce added that he did not think the federal government should prohibit local governments from enacting rent control ordinances. "HUD may find it can't economically go into an area if rents are set too low," he said. But he stopped short of saying HUD should not invest in communities with rent control policies, a proposal that had been considered in the 96th Congress.

In response to a question from Garn, Pierce said he favored tightening the eligibility requirements for federally subsidized rental housing. Pierce also said he favored revising existing law to give the federal government more power to crack down on housing discrimination, but he did not offer a specific proposal. An effort to enact a fair housing bill in 1980 fell short in the closing days of the 96th Congress.

William J. Casey:
Central Intelligence Director

President Reagan got off on the right foot with the American intelligence community by naming a 67-year-old lawyer and self-made millionaire, William J. Casey, as director of central intelligence.

Indeed, many prominent former intelligence officials were elated by the choice of Casey. They said they hoped he would be just the right tonic to fortify the anemic morale at the Central Intelligence Agency and in the U.S. intelligence community at large.

The non-controversial nomination was approved by the Senate Jan. 27 by a 95-0 vote.

William E. Colby, a former CIA director who was practicing law in Washington, said Reagan's choice was "a very good one" because Casey "has a unique background and one very appropriate for the job."

That background included:

• World War II service in the Office of Strategic Services (OSS), the CIA's wartime predecessor, working to infiltrate U.S. agents into occupied Europe.

• Successful careers as a tax lawyer, teacher, writer and businessman that had earned him a fortune.

• Long and close associations with establishment Republicans that led to his appointment to various posts in the Nixon administration in the early 1970s: chairman of the Securities and Exchange Commission, under secretary of state for economic affairs and president of the Export-Import Bank.

• A continuing, and highly visible, interest in intelligence matters, as demonstrated by his participation in groups such as the Veterans of the OSS and the Association of Former Intelligence Officers, plus service on President Ford's Foreign Intelligence Advisory Board in the mid-1970s.

• A brief but successful stint as Reagan's presidential campaign manager that earned him Reagan's respect and his ear, and got Casey the job he had coveted for years.

Such experience, concluded John Bross, a former OSS and CIA officer who knew him, made Casey an "ideal choice for this job."

Mixed Reception

Although he was generally admired among his intelligence community contemporaries, one active CIA officer said Casey was a stranger to younger intelligence personnel.

"I can tell you honestly, the reception's going to be mixed [at the CIA]," this officer said. "Nobody knows anything about him. It's really a 'wait and see' attitude."

And Casey also had his doubters, including some who wondered whether a man who had done no intelligence work since World War II could run a modern spy agency.

Another question was whether Casey, whose rumpled, relaxed manner and wispy white hair made him look every bit his 67 years, had the energy to oversee the CIA and some 10 other intelligence community components.

Lawrence Houston, an OSS veteran and former CIA general counsel, was one skeptic. "People that worked with him seemed to think pretty highly of him," Houston said. "I've always frankly been a little puzzled by Bill. He knows all the right names to call. I've never been particularly impressed by him otherwise."

According to author Joseph Persico, Casey's appearance always was deceiving. In *Piercing the Reich*, a book about the OSS operation Casey worked in, Persico wrote:

"In Casey, the OSS had a man with an analytical mind, tenacious will and a capacity to generate high morale among his staff. He delegated authority easily to trusted subordinates and set a simple standard — results. He had no patience with the well-born effete who had flocked to the OSS, people he dubbed the 'white-shoe boys.'"

The criticism that Casey might be "out of touch" with modern intelligence operations was similar to the doubts that were expressed when he became Reagan's campaign manager in February 1980. Campaign insiders said Casey did not understand modern media campaigns, the heart of modern political contests.

Casey responded at the time: "I'm not supposed to know everything. I'm bringing into the campaign guys who have been there before, who know all these mysterious things I'm not supposed to know."

A lack of recent intelligence agency experience could prove a political virtue. Casey was not tainted by the CIA abuses of the 1960s — such as spying on Americans and attempting to overthrow or assassinate foreign leaders — that smudged the agency's image when they were exposed in the 1970s.

OSS Service

Born on March 13, 1913, and raised in New York City, Casey earned a B.A. degree from Fordham University in 1934 and a law degree from St. John's University Law School in 1937. He began practicing law the following year when he was admitted to the New York State Bar.

He was commissioned a lieutenant in the Navy when the war began in 1941, but poor eyesight confined him to a desk job in Washington. Through friends in legal circles, Casey came to the attention of Maj. Gen. William J. "Wild Bill" Donovan, the Wall Street lawyer President Franklin D. Roosevelt tapped to form and run the OSS. This led Casey into the OSS. Casey left the OSS with a reputation as a forceful manager who could make tough decisions with speed and see that they were carried out.

Casey was in and out of government after his war service. In 1947-48 he was special counsel to the Senate Small Business Committee. Then he was appointed associate general counsel for the Marshall Plan.

He taught tax law at New York University between 1948 and 1962. In this period he wrote and published some 30 manuals for lawyers and executives, including: *Tax Planning on Excess Profits* and *Tax Sheltered Investments*. Later, he also wrote *How to Raise Money to Make Money* and *How Federal Tax Angles Multiply Real Estate Profits*.

Casey practiced law throughout his career, but also was active in GOP politics. He worked in Thomas E. Dewey's 1940 and 1948 presidential campaigns, and he ran a foreign policy group during Vice President Richard M. Nixon's 1960 presidential campaign.

In 1966 Casey ran unsuccessfully for the House of Representatives. He worked again in 1968 for Nixon, who put him on the Advisory Committee on Arms Control and Disarmament in 1969.

President Nixon named Casey to the Securities and Exchange Commission (SEC) on Feb. 2, 1971. After a sometimes stormy tenure as SEC chairman, Casey was named under secretary of state for economic affairs in 1973. However, when Henry A. Kissinger became secretary of state, Casey was named to head the Export-Import Bank.

Controversies During Nixon Years

Casey's publishing ventures led to one dispute that caused him difficulty when he had been nominated by Nixon to the SEC. One suit involved a plagiarism charge against one of Casey's publishing ventures. Another charged that a firm in which Casey was a director and principal stockholder had sold unregistered stock, a violation of securities laws.

The suits were settled out of court, and Casey contended before the Senate Banking Committee in 1971, during his confirmation hearings for the SEC post, that he was unaware of the actions of his subordinates. The committee ultimately confirmed Casey to the SEC.

While Casey was at the SEC, some congressional Democrats charged that he had attempted to conceal information about the relationship of the Nixon administration to the International Telephone and Telegraph Corp. (ITT).

A special House subcommittee was investigating reports that ITT had offered to trade a $400,000 campaign contribution to Nixon for settlement of an antitrust suit, and Casey shipped 34 cartons of SEC documents to the Justice Department before the panel could subpoena them. Justice said it would refuse to turn over the documents because they were being used in a criminal investigation.

It was later disclosed that some of the documents contained information about conversations between ITT officials and Attorney General John N. Mitchell, Secretary of the Treasury John B. Connally, Vice President Spiro T. Agnew and White House domestic adviser John D. Ehrlichman.

In another case, Casey met in 1972 with a lawyer for Robert L. Vesco about a pending SEC investigation of the financier. The meeting was on the day Vesco secretly gave $200,000 to the Nixon re-election campaign, but Casey maintained he learned of the donation only later from news accounts. There was conflicting testimony in each case, and Casey never was charged or penalized.

Confirmation Hearings

Casey won a warm welcome at his confirmation hearings Jan. 13 from the Senate Intelligence Committee. Pledging to revive morale at the CIA, Casey said he would work to "minimize" restrictions placed on the CIA by Congress in the 1970s. However, he pledged "care and diligence in protecting the legal rights of American citizens."

Apparently satisfied with its background investigation of Casey, the committee paid scant attention to questions raised in the press about Casey's handling of the documents that had been sought by the House committee in 1971 and about his meeting with an aide to Vesco.

Casey expressed little interest in proposals to split the CIA into separate agencies for analysis and for covert operations. "This is not the time for another bureaucratic shakeup of the CIA," he said. He promised instead that intelligence community analyses would be presented to the president and the National Security Council "without subjective bias and in a manner which reflects strongly held differences within the intelligence community."

William E. Brock III:
U.S. Trade Representative

Former Republican National Committee Chairman William E. Brock III was picked by President Reagan to be U.S. trade representative. The post had been given Cabinet rank by President Carter, and Reagan, despite some opposition within his administration, assured Brock the office would continue to have Cabinet status. The Senate routinely confirmed him Jan. 21 by a vote of 99-0.

Brock was elected GOP national chairman in January 1977 and was praised for a very ambitious and successful effort to rebuild the party following the Republicans' election debacle in 1976. The grass-roots rebuilding effort was coordinated with the National Republican Congressional Committee. Brock also won high marks as the architect of the November 1980 Republican sweep at the polls.

Despite this success as national committee chairman, Brock continued to be anathema to many conservatives in the party because he had refused to use his position as national chairman to oppose ratification of the Panama Canal treaties in 1978 or to take positions on other issues of importance to them.

Earlier Career

Born in Chattanooga, Tenn., Nov. 23, 1930, Brock graduated from Washington and Lee University in Lexington, Va., in 1953 and then spent three years in the Navy. He launched his political career in 1962, winning the Tennessee 3rd District House seat by barely 2,000 votes. He was the first Republican elected from that district in 42 years. After four terms in the House, Brock ran for the Senate in 1970 and won, beating Sen. Albert Gore, D (1953-71).

In the Senate, Brock compiled a conservative voting record, although he was not a strict partisan. He lost the seat to James R. Sasser, D, in 1976.

The broad brush of Watergate touched him in 1975 when questions emerged about a report that he had received an illegal contribution from the Gulf Oil Co. in his 1970 Senate campaign. He returned to Gulf a cash donation of $3,000 that had been paid to a campaign aide and an additional $2,000 that he claimed was a legal contribution.

After losing his re-election bid, Brock ran for the Republican National Committee chairmanship. He won as the compromise candidate over Richard Richards, who was to succeed him in the post in 1981, and James A. Baker III, who was the choice of President Ford.

White House Staff

For his top White House aides, President Reagan picked two lawyers known as low-key, effective managers, and he decided to vest broad powers in them. They headed a staff of several hundred persons appointed to support the president's foreign and domestic policies, control the federal bureaucracy, lobby for his programs in Congress, conduct his relations with the media, brief him on sensitive foreign intelligence operations, provide him with expert advice on the laws of the land and settle political problems within his administration and with his Republican constituents.

Reagan designated Edwin Meese III, his closest aide when he was governor of California and in his presidential campaign, as counselor to the president. Meese, a member of both the Cabinet and the National Security Council, was expected to oversee the Cabinet, the council and the Domestic Policy Staff. The San Diego criminal lawyer and law professor, who turned 49 in December 1980, directed Reagan's transition operation.

Reagan chose as White House chief of staff Texas lawyer James A. Baker III, who was the campaign chairman for Reagan's chief opponent, George Bush, before Bush dropped out of the presidential primary race. Baker, 50, was given responsibility for congressional and press relations, administration and the White House personnel office.

Pragmatic Managers

As part of the coterie of close advisers to Reagan, both Meese and Baker were expected to "participate as a principal in all policy group meetings," according to the Nov. 14, 1980, announcement of the appointments.

The Meese and Baker appointments prompted the prediction of a smoothly run, relatively invisible White House management. Both men shared Reagan's conservative political philosophy, associates said, but they also were viewed as highly pragmatic individuals who put management ahead of ideology. Both were said to be very pleasant to work with.

"Meese and Baker are professional alter egos," said one transition official, "and they're very good at it."

President Carter had no chief of staff for the first two and a half years of his presidency, although Hamilton Jordan, as assistant to the president, in fact headed the White House staff and held a relationship to the president similar to that of Meese. In mid-1979, Carter broadened Jordan's powers and made him chief of staff, thus giving him the responsibilities held under Reagan by Baker as well as those held by Meese.

Other Key Appointments

To fill other top White House posts Reagan turned to longtime aides, officials of past Republican administrations and scholars known for their conservative positions on domestic and international issues.

Richard V. Allen was named assistant to the president for national security affairs, the post held by Zbigniew K. Brzezinski in the Carter administration, and Martin C. Anderson as chief assistant to the president for policy development, Reagan's chief adviser for domestic affairs. This position had been held by Stuart E. Eizenstat under Carter.

Both Allen and Anderson had similar positions during Reagan's election campaign, although Allen resigned temporarily a week before the election after allegations were made in the *The Wall Street Journal* that he had used his previous White House connections for private gain.

Other top White House aides included James S. Brady, assistant to the president and press secretary, the post held by Jody Powell in the Carter administration; Michael K. Deaver, deputy chief of staff; Elizabeth Hanford Dole, assistant for public liaison; Fred F. Fielding, counsel to the president; Max L. Friedersdorf, assistant to the president for legislative affairs; David R. Gergen, assistant to the president and staff director of the White House; Edwin L. Harper, assistant to the president and deputy director of the Office of Management and Budget; E. Pendleton James, assistant to the president for personnel; Franklyn C. "Lyn" Nofziger, assistant to the president for political affairs; and Murray L. Weidenbaum, chairman of the Council of Economic Advisers. *(Biographies: Allen, p. 66, Anderson, p. 68; Baker, p. 68; Meese, p. 67; Brady, p. 70; Friedersdorf, p. 70; Weidenbaum, p. 69; others, p. 70)*

Administration spokesmen indicated that the overall size of the White House staff would be kept smaller than it was under Carter, in keeping with Reagan's goal of smaller government.

But a month after the inauguration it was not clear that this objective would be achieved. The staffing of the White House had not been completed and a comparison was not possible.

Richard V. Allen:
National Security Adviser

For his national security adviser, Reagan chose Richard V. Allen, a hard-line conservative with a flair for publicizing his views on world affairs. But Allen, unlike his predecessors, Henry A. Kissinger and Zbigniew K. Brzezinski, vowed to stay out of the limelight.

Along with two of Reagan's other top foreign policy appointees — Secretary of State Alexander M. Haig Jr. and CIA Director William J. Casey — Allen had been subjected to questions about his activities during the Nixon years. *(Haig, Casey profiles, pp. 40, 63)*

Allen served the Nixon White House in several

capacities between 1969 and 1972, and *The Wall Street Journal* charged in 1980 that he had "used his White House connections" to profit his lucrative international consultant business. The Journal questioned the propriety of Allen's actions, which Allen defended as perfectly legal and ethical.

The newspaper published its allegations about Allen shortly before the election, on Oct. 28, while he was serving as a Reagan campaign adviser on defense issues. The questions raised by the Journal resulted in Allen's temporary resignation from the campaign. He rejoined the Reagan team two days after the election, when Reagan aides said their own investigation had cleared him.

Allen faced no further formal investigation because his post did not require Senate confirmation.

Role Redefined

The job of assistant to the president for national security affairs was created to administer the National Security Council, a Cabinet-level executive committee established in 1947 to coordinate foreign policy. But despite the job description, Kissinger and Brzezinski elevated the post to the policy-making level; they rivaled and often dominated the secretaries of state with whom they served.

These public conflicts provoked enough criticism and debate to enable Sen. Edward Zorinsky, D-Neb., to get legislation through the Senate in 1977 to require Senate confirmation for the position. Zorinsky said there were "two secretaries of state," and that the Senate should have a hand in approving both of them. The proposal died in a House-Senate conference committee.

Nevertheless, Allen promised to deflate the high profile of the national security adviser, acting more as a "liaison" between the State and Defense departments than as a policy-maker competing with them. In fact, he told reporters when his appointment was announced: "You're seeing a disappearing act right now."

Despite such disclaimers, many observers expected the ambitious Allen to remain an important influence on Rea-

gan's national security policies. While both Haig and Defense Secretary Caspar W. Weinberger possessed strong personalities, Allen knew Reagan better than Haig did before his appointment. Allen also was a defense expert whose mastery of military issues contrasted with Weinberger's inexperience in that area. *(Weinberger profile, p. 51)*

Early Career

Allen is a tall, silvery-haired father of seven who was born on Jan. 1, 1936, in Collingswood, N.J. He attended preparatory school in Pennsylvania and spent his early adulthood in academia. He earned a B.A. degree in 1957 and an M.A. in 1958 at Notre Dame University, then worked for a doctorate at the universities of Freiberg and Munich in Germany. His dissertation was rejected for what he has said were "political" reasons having to do with his anti-communism.

In 1961-62 Allen was an assistant professor of international studies at the Georgia Institute of Technology. He then moved to Washington as a senior staff member of Georgetown University's Center for Strategic and International Studies, a conservative think tank. He left Georgetown in 1966 for the Hoover Institution on War, Revolution and Peace at Stanford University in California, another conservative think tank.

In 1968 Allen worked for Nixon's presidential campaign as a senior foreign policy adviser, a position similar to his post in Reagan's campaign. Washington political lore holds that Allen had his sights on the national security adviser's job in 1969 but was squeezed out by Kissinger, who impressed Nixon more and was pressed on Nixon by Nelson A. Rockefeller. Allen became Kissinger's deputy, a relationship that ended when Allen resigned after only 10 months in the job.

Various explanations have been offered for Allen's resignation. Allen told *The Washington Star* in 1980 that when he left Kissinger's staff, "partly it was that the immediate environment of the NSC [National Security Council] people was politically hostile."

Allen worked in 1970-71 for International Resources Ltd., a Denver firm owned by John King, a major Nixon campaign contributor. At the same time, Allen was an unpaid member of the President's Commission on International Trade and Investment Policy.

Allen returned to the White House full time on July 15, 1971, as deputy assistant to Nixon for international economic affairs, but left that position on July 31, 1972, to found his own consulting firm, Potomac International Corp. His consulting work kept him occupied until 1980.

Foreign Policy Views

As Reagan's top foreign policy spokesman during the transition, Allen often was circumspect in answering specific questions about world affairs. For example, on ABC-TV's *Issues and Answers* Dec. 7 he was asked whether Reagan might follow through with his campaign suggestion of blockading Cuba in retaliation for the Soviet Union's invasion of Afghanistan.

"I wouldn't care to speculate now in these troubled times about the measures he might take," Allen said.

Allen's political career left little doubt that, like Reagan, he counted himself a "realist" who viewed U.S.-Soviet relations as the central problem facing America. Allen has said the United States must embark on a substantial military buildup to counter the Soviet gains in military might in the 1960s and 1970s.

He has advocated scrapping the SALT II treaty and demanding new arms control talks with the Soviets. He told ABC he was "quite optimistic" that the Soviets will accept Reagan's offer "to sit down for as long as it may take to negotiate balanced, verifiable, equitable arms control agreements."

Washington Post columnist Stephen S. Rosenfeld wrote in April that he had known Allen for years as "an instinctive right-winger." Rosenfeld said Allen had "borne the label of cold warrior easily."

Allen was among the Reagan aides who said the new administration would be more lenient than was Carter toward pro-U.S. dictatorships, especially in Latin America. Carter's pressure on those regimes to improve their human rights records only weakened them and encouraged revolutionaries backed by Cuba and the Soviet Union, Allen has said.

The Allegations

The portion of Allen's career that *The Wall Street Journal* questioned began when Allen quit the Nixon White House and went into private work, serving at the same time on Nixon's international trade commission. The Journal said that Allen, in letters written during 1970, leaked secrets from commission proceedings on U.S. export-import policy to an influential Japanese business associate with close ties to the prime minister of Japan.

In his letters to Professor Tamotsu Takase, the Journal said, Allen urged Japan to establish an American-run lobby to counter protectionist sentiment in the United States. He urged that an American friend, David Fleming, be hired to head it. Allen later said there was nothing secret in the letters, and that he was free to engage in private business.

The lobbying firm was not established, but Fleming later got a $120,000 consultantship from Nissan Motor Co. Ltd., the maker of Datsun automobiles. In 1973, when Allen was a private consultant, the Journal said, he wrote a letter demanding that Fleming give him half the fees from Datsun "inasmuch as your introductions to Japan were arranged by me."

The newspaper said Fleming refused to pay when his lawyer advised him that such a payment "could be considered a violation of the the law" because of Allen's former government service. Allen dropped his claim, but Fleming "subsequently lost the Datsun account, and Datsun's American subsidiary hired Mr. Allen," the Journal said.

The Washington Post quoted Allen as saying his claim to half of Fleming's fee "was based on a trip the two men made to Japan in March or April 1971, when Allen was privately employed and was not on the government payroll." The Post said Fleming agreed.

The Journal also revived a charge raised against Allen in a 1976 Senate hearing. Thomas B. Cheatham, a former Grumman International Corp. executive, accused Allen of having sought a $1 million contribution for Nixon's 1972 campaign from Grumman, a major defense contractor, in return for White House pressure on Japan to buy a Grumman airplane. Allen denied the accusation.

Vesco Connection

Building on charges raised by *Mother Jones*, a muckraking magazine, the Journal also reviewed Allen's connections with Robert L. Vesco, the financier indicted for bilking millions of dollars from the Geneva-based mutual fund, Investors Overseas Services (IOS) Ltd.

When Allen went to work in 1969 for International Resources Ltd., John King, the head of the firm, was struggling against Vesco in an attempt to take over IOS Ltd. — a struggle Vesco won.

Allen's work for King did not involve the IOS campaign, which landed King in prison for securities violations. However, Allen told the Journal that he did go to Geneva to watch the "fascinating" negotiations.

In 1972-73, according to the Journal, among the clients of Allen's consulting firm was Vesco's lawyer, Howard Cerny. Cerny paid Allen $60,000 in 1972 for what Allen told the Journal was an assignment to explore the establishment of an "offshore," unregulated financial center on one of the Azores' islands.

Allen also acknowledged to the Journal that, in 1972, he introduced Cerny to William Casey, then chairman of the Securities and Exchange Commission. By all accounts, Cerny began discussing the SEC's investigation of Vesco. The meeting took place on the same day that Vesco secretly gave the Nixon re-election campaign $200,000.

Allen told the Journal: "Cerny said he wanted a meeting with Bill Casey, and Bill Casey was a friend of mine. I had no idea what the purpose of the meeting would be." When Cerny brought up Vesco, Allen said, he "literally walked out of the meeting" and later apologized to Casey for having set it up.

The Journal also said Allen remained on the government's payroll as a special *per diem* consultant while he was working for Cerny. Allen denied that charge, and *The Washington Post* said its own check of civil service records substantiated his denial.

Edwin Meese III:

Counselor to the President

To one historian of the presidency, Edwin Meese's projected role would appear to be that of "minister without portfolio" — "the fellow who walks around thinking, and who always knows what the president wants on any issue." When Reagan was once asked who he would turn to first on any problem, he promptly named Meese.

The position of counselor to the president was created  by President Nixon but Carter did not use this slot, relying for advice on his chief of staff, Hamilton Jordan, and Zbigniew K. Brzezinski and Stuart E. Eizenstat, chiefs of national security and domestic affairs, respectively.

Like Baker, Meese had gained the reputation of an unflappable but determined administrator. He was largely responsible for the ouster from the Reagan campaign of John P. Sears, whom he replaced. In the campaign Meese served as chief of staff and also directed policy development and research.

As Sears described Meese's method of operation, it was not to "propose a lot of things himself. He's there to digest information and sum it all up."

Meese graduated from Yale in 1953 with a degree in public administration and from the University of California Law School at Berkeley in 1958. He was a deputy district attorney in Alameda County, Calif., before becoming Reagan's legal affairs secretary in 1967, and later chief of staff.

When he left state government in 1975 Meese became vice president of a California aerospace and transportation company, Rohr Industries Inc., before returning to law practice. He also has taught law at the University of San Diego and was on leave as director of the university's Center for Criminal Justice Policy and Management.

James A. Baker III:
White House Chief of Staff

Baker's responsibilities as chief of staff placed him in the position of earlier presidential aides who became very powerful "gatekeepers," deciding which issues and which individuals were brought to the president's attention.

In recent history the most influential gatekeeper was Eisenhower aide Sherman Adams, whose control over the presidential agenda was legendary until he was driven from the White House by a scandal.

Baker's personality and past service in government suggested that he would likely be more a facilitator than a controller. "Impeccable," "unruffled" and "decent" were adjectives typically used by observers of Baker's performance as an under secretary of commerce under President Ford, as Ford's campaign chief in 1976, Bush's campaign director in 1980 and then as a late addition to Reagan's campaign.

Frank Hodsoll, a transition official who was Baker's top aide at Commerce, attributed to his former boss an exceptional "sense of people, a sense of making everybody feel they play a role." Baker's talents were for touching "appropriate bases, designing appropriate actions, and following up" to make sure those actions are carried out, Hodsoll said. Baker reportedly disliked confrontations, but was also quite persistent in pursuing his goals.

Baker's appointment was widely seen as an effort by Reagan to broaden his inner circle, as well as a recognition of Baker's organizational and political talents.

Baker, a native Texan born April 28, 1930, came relatively late to the political expertise for which he was to become so highly respected. After graduating from Princeton in 1952, Baker served two years in the Marine Corps and then received a law degree with honors from the University of Texas Law School in 1957. He practiced with the Houston firm of Andrews, Kurth, Campbell & Jones until his 1975 appointment to serve under Rogers C. B. Morton,

secretary of commerce. Shortly after Baker went with Morton to the Ford presidential campaign in 1976, he became its national chairman.

In 1978 Baker launched an unsuccessful bid to become the Republican nominee for attorney general of Texas, and from 1979 until May 1980 he directed Bush's presidential campaign. In the Reagan campaign he served as a general troubleshooter and handled negotiations for the Carter-Reagan television debate.

Martin C. Anderson:
Chief Domestic Adviser

For those conservatives whose chief goal was to curb the role as well as the size of government in American society, Ronald Reagan's choice of political intimate Martin Carl Anderson as chief domestic policy adviser was good news.

Judging by his writings and policy pronouncements, Anderson could be classified as a libertarian. He viewed government as having a role in people's lives only when

they themselves or the private sector are unable to provide essential services. He had advocated this philosophy throughout his career, and was certain to continue to do so as the president's assistant in charge of supervising federal programs in areas such as health, education and welfare.

The power of the domestic policy adviser has shifted in intensity from president to president. Anderson's duties and responsibilities in that position had not been laid out precisely when Reagan took office: whether to be a conduit for the ideas of others, or the chief of the administration's domestic policy.

Anderson, 44 at the time of his appointment, was considered the "house intellectual" and "quiz kid" during the early years of the Nixon administration. Known as a conservative scholar, he has written frequently and persuasively on why there should be less government involvement in social welfare programs.

His 1978 book *Welfare: The Political Economy of Welfare Reform in the United States* was used by Russell B. Long, D-La., then chairman of the Senate Finance Committee, to convince the panel to drop President Carter's welfare reform proposal that featured a federally set minumum benefit, which some said was the equivalent of a modified guaranteed annual income.

Anderson initially caught Richard M. Nixon's eye with his book *The Federal Bulldozer — A Critical Analysis of Urban Renewal, 1949-1962*, which was developed from his doctoral thesis in industrial management at the Massachusetts Institute of Technology (MIT).

Anderson, who also wrote *Conscription: A Select and Annotated Bibliography*, is credited with selling Nixon on the idea of an all-volunteer army and maintaining Reagan's opposition to reinstituting the draft, despite pressure from some of his supporters on the pro-military right.

Welfare Theories

Although Anderson has written on a variety of subjects, welfare is his area of expertise. His welfare book made the case against this social program, but not in the classic conservative manner of attacking the cost to the working man. Instead, Anderson contended that it is the welfare recipients who suffer from the program because it works against their attempts to earn their own living and make their way in the world.

In the same book, Anderson states: "With scarcely anyone noticing it, the poor people in this country have been deeply entangled in a welfare system that is rapidly strangling any incentive they may have had to help themselves and their families by working to increase their incomes."

Anderson also argued that the "number of people remaining in poverty is very small, and it grows smaller every day." Only a very small percentage of the needy go without any aid, according to Anderson, and they are people whose pride doesn't allow them to ask for help and those who are unfairly denied benefits.

Anderson insists the biggest problem with welfare is finding the means for recipients to earn their own way. One of his solutions is to require beneficiaries, who are able, to work so "only those who truly cannot help themselves receive aid." While Reagan was governor of California, an experiment to put this philosophy into practice never got off the ground.

Also, Anderson suggests that welfare be turned over to the states and that charities assume a larger role in caring for the poor.

Edward T. Weaver, executive director of the American Public Welfare Association, which represents federal, state and local public welfare agencies in Washington, said Anderson's written position that the "War on Poverty" has been won raises more questions than answers.

"In the context of welfare," Weaver said, "I have questions about where he takes this position into the real world when there are millions of Americans on the welfare rolls."

Asked what he saw as the future for welfare programs under the Reagan administration and Anderson's influence, Weaver said: "It seems to me in most of these initiatives the bottom line will be where it puts the federal government in five years in terms of financial viability."

Weaver said he assumed that Reagan's changes in the welfare program would likely be directed at reducing the federal budget.

Background

Born Aug. 5, 1936, in Lowell, Mass., Anderson has traditional Eastern establishment credentials. He was a Phi Beta Kappa and was graduated summa cum laude from Dartmouth College in 1957. He then went on to earn master's degrees from Dartmouth in 1958 in engineering and business administration.

After a stint in the Army, Anderson in 1961 became a research fellow at the Joint Center for Urban Studies of MIT and Harvard. In 1962 he was awarded a Ph.D. in industrial management by MIT, and then taught finance at Columbia University until 1968.

Anderson joined Nixon's 1968 campaign as director of research and after the election worked at the White House,

first as a deputy to Arthur Burns, who was a counselor to the president. When Burns left to chair the Federal Reserve Board, Anderson became a White House special consultant for systems analysis.

In 1971 he left the White House to join the Hoover Institution on War, Revolution and Peace at Stanford University and in 1976 was tapped to be Reagan's issues adviser. In 1980, on leave as a senior fellow of the Hoover Institution, he filled the same role for the Reagan campaign and often was found at the candidate's side briefing him on issues.

Anderson's wife, the former Annelise Graebner, worked in the Reagan transition personnel office.

Murray L. Weidenbaum:
Economic Advisers Chairman

Selected to serve as chief economic adviser to the president and the Cabinet in the Reagan administration was a leading critic of government regulation, Murray L. Weidenbaum.

Weidenbaum, 53, director of Washington University's Center for the Study of American Business in St. Louis, was assistant Treasury secretary for economic policy under President Nixon.

In that post, he became the first official to publicly recommend adoption of wage-price controls and was the

administration's chief advocate for the general revenue sharing program.

As chairman of the regulatory task force during the transition, Weidenbaum urged Reagan to declare a one-year moratorium on new regulations and pressed him to issue an executive order requiring agencies to weigh the costs and benefits of major regulations before issuing them.

Weidenbaum supported the Kemp-Roth tax cut plan, which he saw as the "centerpiece of the administration package."

In a 1978 speech to the American Retail Federation, however, Weidenbaum questioned whether an across-the-board tax cut would spur enough economic activity to increase tax revenues, as some supply side economists claimed. The main benefit of such a reduction, he said, would be its impact on limiting the flow of tax dollars and forcing Congress to cut spending.

Born in the Bronx, N.Y., Feb. 10, 1927, Weidenbaum was graduated in 1948 from City College of New York. He received a master's degree from Columbia University in 1949 and a Ph.D. from Princeton University in 1958. After working as an economist for the Bureau of the Budget, the Boeing Co. and Stanford Research Institute, he joined the faculty of Washington University in 1964. He was chairman of the economics department until he went to the Treasury Department in 1969, returning in 1971 to the university, where he founded the center for business study. As an adjunct scholar of the American Enterprise Institute for Public Policy Research, he wrote frequently on regulation for AEI's *Regulation* magazine, as well as for other publications. He was also a member of *Time* magazine's board of economists and *Challenge* magazine's board of editors.

James S. Brady:
Press Secretary

President Reagan chose as White House press secretary James Scott Brady, a veteran Republican relations specialist who had been Reagan's press spokesman in Washington during the transition.

In announcing the appointment Jan. 6, Reagan said Brady would have full access to the Oval Office. Brady told reporters he would not lie to them, but that he also might not always respond to questions to which he knew the answers.

Brady, 40 at the time of his appointment, was known to Washington reporters as "Diamond Jim," the wry and able former aide to Sen. William V. Roth Jr., R-Del., who salted his boss's press releases with one-line jokes.

Besides working for Roth, Brady had substantial experience in other Washington jobs. From 1973 to 1981 he had served variously as a communications consultant to the House; special assistant to the secretary of housing and urban development; top aide to James T. Lynn, former director of the Office of Management and Budget; and assistant to former Defense Secretary Donald Rumsfeld.

From the Pentagon, he moved to a post as Roth's executive assistant, leaving in 1979 to serve as press secretary for presidential candidate John B. Connally. In the 1980 election campaign Brady was director of public affairs.

Brady was graduated in 1962 from the University of Illinois (Champaign-Urbana) where he majored in communications and political science. He attended the university's law school and did graduate work in public administration at Southern Illinois University, where he served on the faculty in 1964-65.

His other experience included stints on the staff of Sen. Everett M. Dirksen, R-Ill. (House 1933-49; Senate 1951-1969), in 1961-62; as assistant national sales manager of Lear-Seigler in 1965-66; as legislative and public affairs director for the Illinois State Medical Society in 1966-68; as manager of Whitaker and Baxter's Chicago office in 1968-69; and as executive vice president of James and Thomas advertising and public relations firm in 1969-73.

Named as deputy press secretary was Karna Small, a broadcast journalist who recently had been working for the U.S. Chamber of Commerce.

Max L. Friedersdorf:
Chief White House Lobbyist

To help sell his programs to Congress, President Reagan brought Max L. Friedersdorf back to the White House in a capacity similar to one he filled during the Nixon and Ford administrations.

As assistant to the president for legislative affairs, Friedersdorf was taking up where he left off in 1977 after serving since 1971 in the congressional liaison office for the two previous Republican presidents. At the time of his new appointment Friedersdorf was chairman of the Federal Election Commission (FEC), to which he was named by President Carter on March 1, 1979.

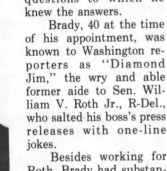

A native of Indiana, Friedersdorf began his career as a newspaperman in that state. After nine years as a reporter, first in Indianapolis and then in Louisville and Chicago, he became administrative assistant in 1961 to Rep. Richard L. Roudebush, R-Ind. (1961-71). He was appointed associate director for congressional relations of the Office of Economic Opportunity in 1970 and joined the Nixon White House congressional liaison staff in 1971. He became deputy head of the office in May 1973 and, after Ford replaced Nixon, was placed in charge of it at the beginning of 1975.

After Ford lost the 1976 election, Friedersdorf became staff director for the U.S. Senate Republican Policy Committee, a post he held until being appointed to the FEC.

Friedersdorf received degrees from Franklin College in Indiana and American University in Washington, D.C. He also attended Butler University in Indianapolis and New Mexico Western University in Silver City.

Other Top Aides

President Reagan completed the selection of his top White House staff Jan. 29, 1981. Besides Meese, Baker, Anderson, Brady and Friedersdorf, others sworn in as presidential assistants included:

Michael K. Deaver

As deputy chief of the White House staff and assistant to the president, Deaver was expected to have easy access to the Oval Office. His close association with the president dated to Reagan's first term as California governor when, in 1967, Deaver joined the administration to assist the Cabinet secretary. Later that year he became assistant to the governor and director of administration. He served in that capacity until the end of Reagan's second term. During the 1976 and 1980 presidential campaigns, Deaver was Reagan's chief of staff. He also acted as deputy director of the 1980 campaign, taking a leave of absence from his job as

Senior White House staff members brief President Reagan prior to first Cabinet meeting held Jan. 21, 1981. From left are: Edwin Meese III, Michael K. Deaver, Richard V. Allen, James S. Brady, James A. Baker III.

president of Deaver and Hannaford Inc., a Los Angeles-based public relations firm. Deaver received a degree in political science in 1960 from San Jose State University.

Elizabeth Hanford Dole

Reagan named Dole as his assistant for public liaison, a job that traditionally centers on women's and minority issues. Dole, a former Federal Trade Commissioner, is married to Sen. Robert Dole, R-Kan. She was national voter chairman in the Reagan campaign and served as transition director of human services. A Phi Beta Kappa graduate of Duke University, Dole received a master's degree as well as a law degree from Harvard University.

Fred F. Fielding

White House counsel Fielding was deputy to John W. Dean III from 1970 to 1974 when Dean held the counsel's post. As a member of the Reagan transition staff, Fielding served as counsel on conflict-of-interest matters and headed the transition team for the office of government ethics. Prior to his work in the Nixon administration, Fielding practiced law with the firm of Morgan, Lewis and Bockius, where he became a partner after leaving the White House. He received an undergraduate degree from Gettysburg College in 1961 and was graduated from the University of Virginia School of Law in 1964.

David R. Gergen

Gergen was appointed assistant to the president and staff director of the White House, reporting to the president through chief of staff James A. Baker III. His responsibilities included helping to coordinate activities of the staff and assisting in the development of policy.

Before going to the White House Gergen was a resident fellow of the American Enterprise Institute for Public Policy Research and managing editor of its *Public Opinion* magazine. He held positions on the Ford and Nixon staffs, and worked during 1975 at the Treasury Department under Secretary William E. Simon. A native of North Carolina, Gergen was graduated from Yale University with an A.B. in 1963 and obtained a law degree from Harvard University in 1967.

Edwin L. Harper

Reagan gave Harper the dual titles of deputy director of the Office of Management and Budget and assistant to the president. This action was intended to provide a strong connection between the White House policy development activities and the operations of the Office of Management and Budget. During Reagan's 1980 campaign, Harper served as a member of the spending control task force; during the transition, he was a member of the economic policy coordinating committee and served as deputy director of the policy coordination staff. In the Nixon administration, Harper was assistant director of the White House Domestic Council.

Harper was graduated from Principia College in 1963 and received his Ph.D. from the University of Virginia in 1968. He has taught at Rutgers University and was a fellow of the American Society for Public Administration.

E. Pendleton James

As assistant to the president for presidential personnel, James was continuing his transition team duties. He also had similar responsibilities under President Nixon when he was a deputy special assistant. Prior to his appointment to the Reagan White House staff, James ran his own executive search firm headquartered in Los Angeles. He was graduated from the University of the Pacific in 1954 and did graduate work at the University of California, Berkeley, and at the University of Santa Clara.

Franklyn C. "Lyn" Nofziger

The former press secretary to Gov. Reagan, Nofziger was named assistant to the president for political affairs. He was to provide general political counsel, with special responsibility for coordination and liaison with the Republican National Committee, the Senate and House GOP campaign committees and other organizations. A longtime Reagan loyalist, Nofziger worked in every Reagan campaign.

Nofziger first came to Washington in 1958 as correspondent for the conservative Copley newspaper chain, then worked for Nixon as a campaign operative and White House congressional liaison aide. When Reagan lost the GOP primary in 1976, Nofziger ran the political action committee, Citizens for the Republic, which kept the Reagan machine running. Nofziger served in the Army in World War II and graduated from San Jose State College with a B.A. degree in journalism in 1950.

Reagan and the Courts

The day after Mississippi federal Judge J. P. Coleman announced he was stepping down from his seat on the U.S. 5th Circuit Court of Appeals, a Republican state judge from Mississippi called his Republican senator, Thad Cochran, to say he was available for Coleman's job.

His call helped to illustrate the changed political scene in Washington caused by the election of Ronald Reagan to the presidency: For the first time in years, Republicans, rather than Democrats, had the opportunity to be appointed to the federal bench in substantial numbers.

The judge's call to Cochran demonstrated as well the role of senators in the judicial selection process. With a member of their own party in the White House, Senate Republicans gained the responsibility both for recommending potential judicial nominees to the president and for fulfilling their constitutional role in confirming the president's choices.

Despite the chance to reward a friend or political ally with a lifetime job, many senators have bemoaned this congressional task. The late Sen. Patrick McCarren, D-Nev. (1933-54), for example, once said of judicial appointments, "It's the lousiest duty in the world because what you end up with is 100 enemies and one ingrate."

Troublesome as nominations may be, they have assumed greater political significance since conservative groups started attacking federal judges for intruding too much into Americans' lives.

In addition, the makeup of the federal bench has become an issue in presidential politics. During the 1976 race, President Gerald R. Ford and candidate Jimmy Carter each pledged to reduce the politics involved in picking judges and to appoint more women and minorities to the bench.

After he was elected president, Carter tried to make good on his promises, creating panels to select judges on the basis of merit and appointing more women and minorities than any previous president. *(Box, p. 76)*

Republican Philosophy

During the 1980 presidential race, Republicans seized on the judiciary issue. The factor crucial to the GOP was not a potential judge's ethnic characteristics, but his legal philosophy. The Republican Party platform adopted by a Reagan-dominated convention took aim at two issues, judicial activism and abortion.

It called for appointing judges who believed in "the decentralization of the federal government and efforts to return decision-making power to state and local elected officials."

In addition, the platform pledged Republicans would "work for the appointment of judges at all levels of the judiciary who respect the traditional family values and the sanctity of innocent human life."

Despite the platform language, Reagan said during the campaign that he would not use any single issue, such as abortion, as a threshold test for judicial nominees. "The whole philosophical viewpoint of the individual would be considered," he said in pledging to appoint a woman to "one of the first Supreme Court vacancies."

Politicians, academics and lawyers familiar with Reagan's judicial appointments as governor of California agreed that Reagan likely would appoint judges who mirrored his conservative political philosophy.

In judicial terms, this suggested Reagan would seek judges who were reluctant to order judicial solutions — such as drawing school attendance lines — for social problems and who would try to avoid throwing out criminal convictions on technical procedural grounds.

Compared with Carter, "no doubt there will be a tremendous difference in the attitudes and viewpoints of judges [Reagan] puts on the bench," said Washington civil rights lawyer Ann Macrory, a member of the Judicial Selection Project. The selection project was an ad hoc organization of public interest groups formed to monitor Carter's judicial selections.

Macrory said she expected to see new judges who showed "conservatism on fiscal matters, a different kind of view of state *vs.* federal power, a different concept of judicial restraint."

Guessing Game

As Reagan was preparing to fill the existing 43 federal bench vacancies, major questions about his judicial selection process remained unanswered. Attorney General William French Smith and presidential counselor Edwin Meese III served as key judicial advisers to Reagan when he was governor, and both declined to discuss the issue.

An administration source said top officials had not yet had time to decide just how Reagan would handle the judiciary. "I can tell you they haven't done a thing," the source said.

Larry C. Berkson, director of educational programs for the Chicago-based American Judicature Society, a legal research organization, called the issue of Reagan's judicial appointments "sort of a wait-and-see game."

"Unlike Carter, Reagan did not make a bold statement, a bold commitment. This gives Reagan a considerable amount of leeway," he said.

Another important element in the judicial appointment process is the Senate Judiciary Committee, which came under the chairmanship of Strom Thurmond, R-S.C., with the GOP takeover of the Senate. The committee investigates each nomination and votes on whether it should be reported to the floor. About one month after the inauguration, one of Thurmond's aides said Republicans still were developing the questionnaire for judgeship candidates. The aide said that in contrast to the questionnaire developed by former Judiciary Chairman Edward M. Kennedy, D-Mass., Republicans would not concentrate on nominees' "demonstrated commitment to equal justice," or their membership in clubs that may have discriminatory policies.

"We're not too interested in social clubs," the aide said.

Although Attorney General Smith declined to discuss specifically how the Reagan administration planned to handle judicial nominations, he said at his Senate confirmation hearing the president probably would use a system similar to one used when he was governor of California.

"The only instruction we received from the governor at that time, and I am sure the only instruction we will receive at this time, is to find the most able and qualified people we can find to fill those positions," Smith told senators.

California Model

In California, the governor appoints state judges. And Reagan, as governor, generally used two methods for selecting jurists, according to Paul Haerle, a San Francisco lawyer who handled Reagan's appointments during his first two years as governor.

To fill trial court vacancies, Reagan set up judicial selection advisory boards in the counties where the vacancies occurred. The boards were made up of the chief judge of the area, a local lawyer recommended by the local bar association and two or three non-lawyers appointed by the governor's office. For seats on the intermediate appeals court and the California Supreme Court, Reagan did not use screening panels, Haerle said, but appointed persons with previous judicial experience.

Through an informal arrangement, now required by law, the State Bar of California reviewed each nominee to determine if the candidate was qualified. Finally, all candidates had to be approved by a three-member panel of state officials.

"The governor never appointed anyone the state bar found not qualified," said Mary Wailes, secretary of the bar.

Reagan did have one controversial appointment, however — William P. Clark, a close associate the governor put on the California Supreme Court. Clark never graduated from college or law school and became a practicing attorney by passing the state bar exam. The three-member panel voted 2-1 to confirm Clark, with the sitting chief justice, Donald Wright, another Reagan appointee, voting against

the nomination. As president, Reagan nominated Clark to be deputy secretary of state, and although questions were raised about his competence and qualifications, Clark was confirmed by the Senate Feb. 24 by a 70-24 vote. At his nomination hearings, Clark had been unable to answer many of the questions senators asked him about world affairs.

One Washington lawyer who practiced in California when Reagan was governor characterized Reagan's state performance as "a pretty good job. He listened to a fairly broad spectrum of advice. . . . He appointed reasonably good people."

Another lawyer, one who was still practicing in California, agreed that Reagan appointed qualified people. But John Cleary of San Diego, a public defender and board member of the National Legal Aid and Defender Association, added this observation: "Those who went on the bench were those who earned their spurs in the courtroom and bar associations. The euphemism was 'the best and the brightest,' but only as the senior members of the bar defined that."

It remained unclear how Reagan's California plan would translate to the federal judiciary, in large part because presidents must take into account the senatorial prerogative to "advise and consent," as outlined in the Constitution.

Merit Panels

Some senators apparently planned to continue the practice of setting up merit panels to recommend candidates, whether or not Reagan suggested continuance of the practice urged by Carter. For example, shortly after the November election, Sen. Richard G. Lugar, a Republican from Indiana, set up a merit selection panel with freshman Republican Sen. Dan Quayle, also from the Hoosier state, and had sent Reagan, by mid-February, three names recommended by the panel for a vacant judgeship.

Sen. S. I. "Sam" Hayakawa, R-Calif., said he, too, intended to use advisory panels to help him fill judicial vacancies. In rather strong language, Hayakawa said he expected to use criteria different from that of his Democratic colleague, Alan Cranston, in selecting nominees.

"I want jurists who are learned, experienced, wise and disinterested, a lot of objectivity as well as learning. Therefore, I will not use the criteria so often used by Sen. Cranston. He picked people because they were black, Asian or Hispanic," Hayakawa asserted. "That's no reason at all. If they are outstandingly learned, intelligent and impartial I don't care what color they are, whether they are men or women."

A Justice Department official close to Attorney General Smith said no decision had been made after Reagan's first month on whether Reagan would issue an executive order on a merit selection process.

Lobbying for Judicial Posts

Interest groups representing women and minorities expressed disappointment at Reagan's selection of so many white men to fill top government jobs. Spokesmen said they intended to watch Reagan closely in an effort to maintain the ground gained during the Carter years. They agreed in interviews that their task would be difficult, but all expressed optimism that Reagan would not return the federal bench to "white-male-only" status.

Supreme Court Speculation

As president of the United States, Ronald Reagan likely will have an unusual opportunity to shape the Supreme Court of the 1980s.

Simple facts of age and health seem to indicate that the early 1980s will be a period of change on the court. Over its history, the court has had at least one new member every two and one-half years; it has been almost twice that long since John Paul Stevens succeeded William O. Douglas.

Seventy is the average age at which death or terminal illness has removed members from the court in this century. Five of the current members of the court are several years beyond that milestone. Of these, four have suffered periods of poor health in recent terms.

On Inauguration Day, 1981, William J. Brennan Jr., the court's most senior service justice, was 74. Chief Justice Warren E. Burger and Justice Lewis F. Powell Jr. were 73. Justices Thurgood Marshall and Harry A. Blackmun both were 72.

These statistics suggest that Ronald Reagan conceivably could select several and perhaps even a majority of the members of the nation's highest court.

How is Reagan expected to use this opportunity to mold the direction of the Supreme Court in the 1980s, and possibly beyond?

Many presidents have selected Supreme Court justices in an effort to mirror their own outlooks. Reagan probably would not be an exception.

But one striking fact of Supreme Court history is that presidents rarely have been successful in stamping their own philosophy on a court.

Reagan is expected to pick judicial conservatives. The 1980 Republican platform pledged to work for the appointment of judges "at all levels of the judiciary who respect traditional family values and the sanctity of human life." Such coded language suggested a clear preference for the appointment of judges who support the "pro-life," anti-abortion movement.

Some have suggested that Reagan would pick conservatives who might undo some of the court's controversial "liberal" or "progressive" decisions. In recent years, the court has been closely divided on a broad range of issues, handing down many decisions by 5-4 margins. In view of this, a single Supreme Court appointment could be quite significant.

Pehaps the best way of predicting the judicial selections Reagan might make is to look at the appointments made by him as governor of California, where he named three justices of the state Supreme Court, widely considered one of the nation's most progressive.

When Reagan had the opportunity to name a new chief justice for the state Supreme Court, he chose a sitting state judge, Donald Wright. He was a man of top academic and legal credentials, substantial judicial experience, and fine reputation. Wright had a moderate-to-conservative voting record as a state judge. But Wright, unanimously praised by those who observed his tenure closely, turned out to be Reagan's Earl Warren. He surprised Reagan with his moderate-to-liberal votes, just as Warren had surprised Dwight D. Eisenhower two decades earlier.

Court watchers point out that the Wright experience is likely to make Reagan particularly careful to scrutinize the views of any person he was considering for the U.S. Supreme Court.

Reagan's second choice for the state Supreme Court could hardly have been more different from Wright. Never having graduated from law school, William P. Clark became an attorney by passing the state bar exam. He served on Reagan's staff during his first term as governor until he was promoted to a seat in the state court system where he stayed for several years. After considerable controversy focusing on his lack of qualifications for the post, Clark was finally confirmed. Clark, whose conservative views were well known to Reagan, pulled no judicial surprises. Clark was nominated by President Reagan to the post of deputy secretary of state and confirmed by the Senate.

Reagan's third choice, Frank Richardson, had fine credentials — academic and legal. He had served in various state judicial posts, and a close observer of Richardson's career commented that it is very hard not to respect or admire him, whatever one thinks of "his quite conservative views."

"We're not going to automatically assume that the new administration is going to be anti-black, anti-minority," said Althea T. L. Simmons, director of the NAACP's Washington office. "We are going to press our issues and use the resources of our 1,800 branches."

Susan Ness, who was head of a judicial appointments project for the National Women's Political Caucus, said her organization and other women's groups were settling in for a long four years. "I think we're going to have to work much harder [to get women on the bench]. It's not going to come as a natural course," Ness said. Echoing the views of others, Ness added, "I don't think ultimately we're going to find the same genuine commitment that President Carter had." Macrory, the Washington lawyer, urged liberal interest groups to be practical in pushing for judicial appointments, given the Republican takeover of the Senate and White House. "In order for us to have a dialogue [with the administration], it is important for people to consider supporting moderate Republicans," she said. "We're going to have to shift ourselves more to the middle."

Carter Court Revamping: Tough Act to Follow

Aided by a legislative plum that created 152 new federal judgeships, President Carter dramatically changed the face of the federal judiciary during his administration. He appointed more women, more blacks and more Hispanics to the federal bench than any other president.

Justice Department figures show that Carter made and the Senate confirmed 56 appointments to the U.S. courts of appeals and 206 to the U.S. district courts — a total of 262.

Of Carter's 56 appeals court appointees, 11 were women, nine were blacks and two were Hispanics. One of the nine blacks was a woman. Of the 206 district court appointees, 29 were women, 29 were blacks and 14 were Hispanics. Six of the 29 blacks were women, and one of the Hispanic appointees was a woman.

For all his judicial selections, though, Carter was denied the chance to alter the nation's highest court. Because he was not re-elected, he became the first president to serve a full term who did not appoint anyone to the Supreme Court.

Antonia Hernandez, director of the Washington office of the Mexican American Legal Defense and Education Fund, expressed the belief that practical politics would be a help to prospective Hispanic judges. Noting that Hispanics voted in large numbers for Reagan, she asserted, "I think the Reagan administration is going to have to be responsive to the Hispanic Republican electorate. And so, my feeling is you cannot very easily sweep [those voters] under the carpet. It is in the interest of the Republican Party to begin to see the Hispanic community as a viable political force."

The traditionally liberal interest groups expected competition on the lobbying front from conservative groups such as the American Family Institute and the Moral Majority.

The American Family Institute is a private research organization whose president, Carl A. Anderson, is a legislative assistant to conservative Republican Sen. Jesse Helms of North Carolina. The Moral Majority is a conservative, Lynchburg, Va., organization headed by evangelical minister the Rev. Jerry Falwell.

In a statement Dec. 2, 1980, announcing formation of a judicial screening advisory panel, the American Family Institute said efforts to get a new breed of federal judge "could open a new era in American jurisprudence."

"Surely the survival of the American family is sufficiently important that its interests should be safeguarded in the nominating process, especially in light of the growing tendency of federal courts to disregard the traditional rights and immunities of the family and to negate parental authority," the statement said.

The conservative groups likely will have important allies in the Senate such as Republicans Orrin G. Hatch, Utah, and Paul Laxalt, Nev., both members of the Judiciary Committee. In the 96th Congress (1979-81), the senators prepared a questionnaire that asked prospective judges about their views on "judicial activism" and their experience, if any, with public interest legal work.

In an article published in the conservative monthly *American Spectator*, Hatch said he was concerned about a judiciary that was departing from traditional American values. "As an American who believes strongly in the constitutional principles of checks and balances, federalism, and the separation of powers," Hatch wrote, "I am concerned by the school of jurisprudence now taking deep root in our judiciary that does not, to my mind, respect these principles."

Judiciary Committee

Hatch and Laxalt were only two of the 18 members of the Judiciary Committee, but along with Chairman Thurmond they were likely to exert considerable influence in handling judicial nominations. Few details had emerged about how the committee would operate during the Reagan administration. Unlike Kennedy, who held hearings on judicial selection, Thurmond had not scheduled any sessions on the subject by mid-February 1981.

During an informal committee meeting Jan. 29, Thurmond suggested that he would follow Kennedy's lead in abandoning a practice that allowed senators quietly to kill a judicial nomination. Under the old "blue slip" system, employed by former Chairman James O. Eastland, D-Miss. (1941; 1943-79), a senator could kill a nomination by refusing to return a blue slip to the Judiciary Committee with the nominee's name on it.

Kennedy, whose policy never was tested, said that if a blue slip were not returned, the committee would decide how to handle the nomination.

In brief remarks Jan. 29, Thurmond said that if a senator failed to return a blue slip "within a reasonable time, then I would not necessarily consider that fact a bar to the nomination, but it would be a significant factor which should be considered and taken into account prior to any hearing on the nomination."

Thurmond added that if a senator did not voice a specific objection to a judge and simply did not return a blue slip, "we assume, as Sen. Kennedy did, there is no objection."

Democratic members of the committee, led by Joseph R. Biden Jr., Del., early in the 97th Congress did little in a collective sense to gear up for handling nominations. One minority staffer said Democratic aides were working with Thurmond's staff to make sure Democrats would have sufficient access to FBI reports on nominees and enough time to examine nominees' backgrounds. Democrats, though, were prepared for more questioning by Republicans on nominees' views about the federal judiciary's role.

Reagan's Election Victory

Ronald Reagan was elected the nation's 40th president Nov. 4, 1980, in a stunning victory, the proportions of which looked improbable even a day before the election.

The incumbent President Carter was overwhelmed in every section of the country. Public opinion surveys noted a trend to Reagan in the final week of the campaign, but virtually all had said the election was too close to call. This made it all the more surprising when the voters gave Reagan an absolute majority of the popular vote.

By carrying 44 states, Reagan's advantage in the Electoral College was even more pronounced. He won 489 electoral votes to just 49 for Carter, who carried only six states and the District of Columbia. *(Map, p. 87)*

Independent candidate John B. Anderson did not win any states. But with 6.6 percent of the vote, he exceeded the 5 percent threshold needed to qualify for post-election public financing.

Falling well below the threshold were the other third-party candidates. Libertarian Ed Clark drew 921,188 votes (1.1 percent) in official results published in January 1981. Trailing him were Citizens Party entry Barry Commoner with 234,279 votes (0.3 percent) and Right to Life candidate Ellen McCormack with only 32,327 votes (0.04 percent).

Carter campaign leaders had feared that Anderson would draw the support of enough liberal Democrats to deny the president re-election. But even if Carter had won every vote that went to Anderson, Reagan still would have carried a majority of states and received more than 300 electoral votes. Only 270 were needed for victory.

Magnitude of Carter Defeat

In rejecting Carter, voters for the second consecutive election turned their backs on an embattled incumbent president to elect a challenger promising a fresh approach to government and a dynamic new brand of leadership.

But unlike the close contest in 1976 in which Carter narrowly defeated President Ford, the results in 1980 were emphatic. Since the Civil War, only two presidents — William Howard Taft in 1912 and Herbert Hoover in 1932 — had been denied re-election by popular vote margins larger than Carter's.

Taft was crippled by the Republican Party split that produced the Bull Moose candidacy of Theodore Roosevelt. Taft finished third in the 1912 election, 19 percentage points behind Democratic winner Woodrow Wilson. Hoover unsuccessfully sought a second term in the midst of the Depression and was beaten by Democrat Franklin D. Roosevelt by 18 percentage points. Still, Hoover won more electoral votes (59) than Carter.

Carter was the first Democratic incumbent president denied re-election since 1888, when Grover Cleveland was beaten by Republican Benjamin Harrison even though Cleveland ran ahead in the popular vote.

Carter's defeat underscored the Democrats' difficulty in winning presidential elections. Since the end of World War II, the Republicans had won five elections to the Democrats' four. But only twice — in 1964 and 1976 — had the Democratic candidate drawn a clear majority of the popular vote.

The Presidential Primaries

Before he could capture the presidency he had sought for so long, Reagan first had to win the nomination of his party. This he accomplished with a campaign that, after some initial stumbling, systematically removed the competition and left Reagan the only serious contender at the GOP national convention.

From the day President Gerald R. Ford was defeated by Jimmy Carter in 1976 until Reagan formally kicked off his campaign on Nov. 13, 1979, the Californian had carefully cultivated an image as the presumed GOP front-runner for 1980. Aware of the fate of previous early leaders, such as Democrat Sen. Edmund S. Muskie in 1972 and Republican Gov. George Romney in 1968, Reagan's campaign team tried to steer a cautious course.

From 1977 until late 1979 Reagan taped radio editorials and wrote a newspaper column that earned him more than $100,000 a year. He gave dozens of speeches around the country, charging an average of $5,000 apiece. And he set up a political action committee, Citizens for the Republic, that contributed $615,385 to federal, state and local Republican candidates during the 1978 elections.

Reagan's contributions far exceeded efforts by other GOP presidential hopefuls who established similar committees. Reagan's group gave to 234 House candidates, 25

Senate contenders, 19 gubernatorial hopefuls and another 122 candidates for other offices ranging from lieutenant governor to county clerk.

Reagan gave only to Republicans. In many cases, the recipient had little or no chance of winning. Sometimes the money went to incumbents who faced little opposition. Reagan's interest in these races established valuable political IOUs that he was able to cash in once his presidential campaign got under way.

From the beginning it was clear Reagan's 1980 presidential effort would be more broadly based than either of his two previous tries for the White House.

When campaign chairman Paul Laxalt, a conservative Republican senator from Nevada, announced the formation of an "exploratory campaign committee" in February 1979, he distributed a 23-page list of those who backed Reagan. It included many officials of the Ford administration as well as 28 senators and representatives. When the former California governor began his campaign in 1976, Laxalt had been the only member of either legislative chamber willing to publicly lend his name to Reagan's effort.

The Sears Strategy

Even after his nationally televised declaration of candidacy, Reagan kept a low profile. This was part of the strategy designed by John Sears, who had directed Reagan's nearly successful campaign against Ford. Since the 1976 defeat, Sears had maneuvered himself into a position of almost unquestioned authority in the Reagan camp by firing several longtime Reagan advisers.

It was generally agreed by Sears and others that, because he was the front-runner, the nomination was "Reagan's to lose." To avoid that, Sears maintained that candidate Reagan needed to remain above the fray and avoid taking a hard-line conservative tack, which had long been his political trademark. And he needed to avoid the blunders that had embarrassed him during the early stages of the 1976 campaign.

The Reagans signal victory on election night.

The best way to meet these dual objectives, Sears thought, was to keep Reagan off the campaign trail as much as possible, particularly while the other GOP candidates were scrambling to become known.

But Reagan's absence from the political hustings became a major issue, particularly at a Jan. 5, 1980, GOP candidates' debate in Des Moines. Coming just 16 days before Iowa's precinct caucuses, which kicked off the national delegate hunt, the debate produced no clear winner. But Reagan, by his absence, universally was declared the loser.

Sears had underestimated both the harm caused by Reagan's seemingly imperious attitude and the amount of media attention focused on the Iowa caucuses.

So when former U.S. Rep. George Bush topped Reagan in the Iowa straw vote, 33,530 to 31,348, the headline writers took the front-runner's crown from Reagan and presented it to Bush.

The next month was one of re-evaluation and upheaval in the Reagan camp. And many political observers later expressed the view that it was the changes Reagan made in his campaign in February that enabled him to capture the nomination in July.

Casey and Meese Take Over

Both Sears and his cautious strategy were dumped. The strategy was the first to go, as Reagan embarked on a whirlwind, 21-day campaign tour through New England. He appeared at two debates and "won" them both. In the first, he came out on top simply by being there.

In the second, in Nashua, N.H., Reagan scored points by trying to include other GOP candidates in a debate that the sponsor, *The Nashua Telegraph*, wanted to limit to just Reagan and Bush. When the debate's moderator, Jon Breen, tried to keep Reagan from speaking on behalf of the other candidates, the usually mild-mannered Californian snapped, "I paid for this microphone, Mr. Green [sic]."

Even though in the end the others did not participate, Reagan's efforts won over the crowd. In a quick reversal from the perceptions gained in Iowa, Reagan was now seen as the one seeking a full and open dialogue, while Bush was viewed as the imperious candidate trying to shut out the other contenders.

Three days later, on Feb. 26, Reagan won the New Hampshire primary by more than a 2-1 margin over Bush and regained the momentum he had lost in Iowa. The same day, Sears was officially dropped from the campaign. Brought in to replace him was an old Reagan friend, William J. Casey, a New York lawyer and former chairman of the Securities and Exchange Commission.

Along with chief of staff Edwin Meese III — one old-time aide Sears had been unable to purge — Casey rebuilt the Reagan campaign, focusing special attention on the financial side.

During the early months, spending had gotten out of hand. And, long before the last round of crucial primaries, Reagan was in danger of going over the $14.7 million federally imposed ceiling on the amount candidates could spend during the primaries. In March, Reagan's monthly payroll of more than a half-million dollars was cut in half. Efforts were drastically curtailed in many primary states where Reagan expected to do well.

With a new team and with the candidate out of his straitjacket, Reagan methodically gathered in the 998 delegates needed to win the GOP nomination.

Primary Sweepstakes to Reagan

During the 15-week primary season, beginning with New Hampshire, Reagan lost only four of the state preference primaries he entered — Massachusetts, Connecticut, Pennsylvania and Michigan.

In states that chose their delegates in caucuses, Reagan was even more impressive. He won just under 400 of the 478 delegates picked by caucuses. In state after state, Reagan's efforts since 1976 paid off handsomely. With his organization still intact and with many of his supporters in important party positions, Reagan swept all the delegates in such states as Arizona, Oklahoma, Colorado and Virginia.

But it was in the early primaries that Reagan was able to pare the field from a half dozen major candidates to just two.

In South Carolina March 8, Reagan knocked former Texas Gov. John B. Connally out of the race. Connally had skipped the earlier New England primaries, concentrating all his efforts on the Palmetto State. He finished a distant second there, with less than 30 percent, to Reagan's 54.7 percent.

Ten days later Reagan deflated John B. Anderson's surging campaign with a solid victory in the congressman's home state of Illinois. Anderson was banking on his ability to attract crossover voters from the Democratic side, but the results showed that Reagan's appeal with independents and Democrats was as strong as Anderson's. A similar result two weeks later in Wisconsin forced Anderson out of the GOP contest and into his unsuccessful independent bid for the White House.

By April the GOP contest was reduced to Bush's frantic efforts to catch Reagan in a few major states. Connally and Anderson were vanquished. Senate Minority Leader Howard H. Baker Jr. of Tennessee had dropped out after four quick defeats. Neither Rep. Philip M. Crane of Illinois nor Sen. Robert Dole of Kansas had ever caught the voters' attention. And on March 15 Ford put to rest growing speculation that he might jump into the race in an effort to stop Reagan.

Bush topped Reagan in Pennsylvania on April 22 and in Michigan four weeks later. But it was too little too late to catch the one-time movie star. Bush, Reagan's last rival for the nomination, withdrew from the presidential race May 26, 1980.

GOP National Convention

Having outdistanced all the opposition, Reagan easily won his party's 1980 nomination at the Republican National Convention, held in Detroit July 14-17.

The long-awaited moment of glory for the former California governor nearly was overshadowed by an unusual flap over the selection of the vice presidential candidate, which provided the only suspense at the GOP convention.

Who would be the party's choice for president had been determined long before when Reagan won 28 out of the 34 Republican presidential primaries and eliminated all of his major rivals. The last to withdraw — George Bush — was tapped by Reagan late on the night of July 16 and then announced during a dramatic, post-midnight appearance by the Californian at the convention.

The selection of Bush came only after an effort to get Ford on the ticket fell through. With the former president out of the picture, Reagan turned quickly to Bush. The pairing of Reagan and Bush on the ticket combined two candidates who had garnered nearly 85 percent of the GOP primary vote in 1980.

Reagan's acceptance of Bush, the favorite of the party's moderate wing, was viewed as one of a series of actions during the convention that showed Reagan to be more interested in winning the election than on insisting on ideological purity at all costs. Rather than follow a hard line on the right, as GOP presidential candidate Barry Goldwater and his supporters did in 1964, Reagan avoided appearing extreme.

Other actions that demonstrated Reagan's pragmatism included:

● The party's 1980 platform, written under the aegis of Reagan's allies and advisers, which muted internal party differences and stressed agreement, particularly in opposing Carter administration policies. The document remained, however, a basically conservative statement.

● Restraint in the treatment of Reagan's opponents in the 1980 primaries. Unlike 1964, when Goldwater's backers booed New York Gov. Nelson A. Rockefeller in San Francisco, Reagan embraced his one-time challengers for the nomination, and unity was the byword of the convention.

The convention concluded with former President Ford joining Reagan and Bush on the podium in a scene of party unity. It was a reversal of the ending four years earlier in Kansas City, when a victorious Ford called Reagan to the platform for a unity picture.

The Party Platform

When the GOP opened its 32nd national convention July 14, the emphasis was on party unity and on assailing the alleged incompetence of the Carter administration.

Speaker after speaker directed tough rhetoric at President Carter, accusing him of spurring rampant inflation, unemployment, a weak national defense and diminished U.S. prestige abroad. The solutions, nearly everyone asserted, lay with the election of Reagan as president.

Several of the day's speakers brought the delegates to their feet, but Ford was clearly the favorite. "We cannot stand four more years of soaring inflation, sky-high interest rates, rising unemployment and shrinking take-home pay," Ford said. "We cannot stake our survival on four more years of weak and wavering leadership and lagging defenses."

The Republicans chose Detroit as their convention site to emphasize their desire to attract new party supporters such as Democrats, labor, blacks and the poor — groups found in abundance in the host city.

The convention harmony was seen early in the proceedings, particularly in the nearly unanimous adoption July 15 of the party platform, which generally followed Reagan's wishes. Four years earlier, platform deliberations were marked by discord between the Reagan and Ford factions. The delegates' credentials and party rules also were approved without opposition.

The sole public note of dissent on the platform came when a delegate from Hawaii tried to suspend the convention rules in a bid to criticize the section of the platform dealing with abortion. But the request was not supported by any other state delegation.

In addition to calling for a constitutional amendment opposing abortions, the platform advocated the appointment of federal judges who "respect traditional family values and the sanctity of innocent human life," a phrase that annoyed party moderates.

As crafted by the convention's platform committee, the party's 1980 program offered something to practically every party faction, but pleased none completely.

Though it took a hard line on abortion, for instance, the platform took no position at all on ratification of the Equal Rights Amendment. Instead, it stated that this was an issue best left to the state legislatures. Reagan said he personally opposed the ERA, but as a concession to party moderates he indicated he could live with a platform that remained neutral on the issue.

In most respects, the platform was a traditional Republican document. It called for major tax cuts for individuals as well as businesses, a renewed effort to reduce inflation, elimination of much federal regulation, an end to the Democrats' alleged reliance on government to solve social ills and a significant buildup of the nation's defenses.

With barely a whisper of dissent, the convention July 15 also quickly approved by voice vote the report of the convention's rules committee. There was little that was controversial in the report, although the committee took several important actions. One was to delete the "justice resolution," a rule binding delegates in most primary states. It had been added in 1976 by Ford supporters, who feared a defection of "closet" delegates to Reagan.

Reagan's Nomination

Reagan won the Republican presidential nomination July 16 on the first ballot. He received 1,939 of the 1,994 delegate votes, 97 percent of the total. Independent candidate Anderson drew 37 votes. Reagan's nomination then was made unanimous.

Reagan received unanimous support from all but seven state delegations, a reflection of the overwhelming consensus on the choice for president that pervaded the convention. Bush delegates from every state except Michigan cast their votes for Reagan, but most of the delegates Anderson won in the primaries remained firmly in his corner.

Having eliminated his rivals in the primaries, Reagan was the only campaigner whose name was placed in nomination. Laxalt, his close friend and campaign chairman, gave the nominating speech, citing Reagan's accomplishments as a two-term governor of California.

Hailing Reagan as a "citizen politician," Laxalt declared that "unlike one Jimmy Carter, he proved he can govern as well as he can campaign."

Acceptance Speech

Except for his opening comments, the presidential nominee's acceptance speech July 17 was vintage Reagan. He combined sharp jabs at the alleged shortcomings of the Carter administration with a reaffirmation of his own conservative credo. *(Text, p. 99)*

Reagan began by trying to soothe the dissatisfaction of many Republicans over the absence of a pro-Equal Rights Amendment (ERA) plank in the party platform. He pledged if elected to establish a liaison with the states to eliminate discrimination against women.

Support of the ERA had been a staple of Republican platforms since 1940, but its omission from the 1980 document had been approved overwhelmingly by the platform committee.

The decision to adopt language that merely "acknowledged" efforts of ERA supporters and opponents alike prompted cries of protest that the party had turned its back on women's rights.

Reagan also underscored the new Republican bid for urban votes by contending that minorities were the prime victims of the Democrats' economic failures. He pledged that a Reagan administration would not ignore urban minorities and would help find new skills and job opportunities for them.

The remainder of the speech reflected Reagan's rock-ribbed conservatism, which was anathema to many voters when he mounted his first bid for the Republican nomination in 1968. In 1980, though, Reagan was confident his basic themes reflected the American political mainstream.

Reagan cited three grave threats to the nation's existence — "a disintegrating economy, a weakened defense and an energy policy based on the sharing of scarcity."

The culprits, Reagan contended, were President Carter and the Democratic Congress, which preached that the American people had to lower their expectations and tighten their belts. "I utterly reject that view," he declared. Reagan claimed the solution was not in the "trust me" government of the Carter administration, but in a new "compact" that placed ultimate trust in the people.

He saw little virtue in extensive use of federal power. "Government is never more dangerous," he warned, "than when our desire to have it help us blinds us to its great power to harm us."

It was time, Reagan declared, "for the government to go on a diet." And he pledged his first action as president would be to institute a federal hiring freeze, followed by a detailed review of government spending. Programs that could be administered more effectively at the state and local levels would be transferred, Reagan promised, along with their funding sources.

'Economic Stew'

After lambasting Carter's economic policies, which he contended had produced "an economic stew that has turned the national stomach," Reagan reasserted his support for a 30 percent reduction in the federal income tax rate over the next three years, beginning with a 10 percent tax cut in 1981. The Californian also pledged to step up business depreciation tax write-offs to stimulate investment and cut government costs as a percentage of the gross national product.

Reagan's energy policy was unabashedly pro-growth, as he called for unleashing American industry to mine more coal, explore for oil and natural gas deposits and build more nuclear power plants. Conservation should be encouraged, he declared, but as a secondary goal to economic prosperity.

Reagan ridiculed the Carter administration's conduct of foreign policy, calling it weak, vacillating and transparently hypocritical. He voiced his opposition to a peacetime draft or even to Carter's draft registration plan, but pledged his support for higher military pay. "We know only too well that war comes not when the forces of freedom are strong, but it is when they are weak that tyrants are tempted."

Choosing Bush

For most of the evening of July 16, it looked as though Ford would occupy the second spot on the ticket, which would have made him the first former president to run for vice president.

Private opinion polls reportedly had shown that Ford was the only Republican who would enhance Reagan's chances in the November election against Jimmy Carter.

Fewer Reagan 'Misstatements' Dotted 1980 Campaign Trail

During the 1980 presidential primaries, Ronald Reagan's occasional verbal slip-ups seemed to have little impact on the campaign, unlike the reaction they caused during his 1976 campaign for the presidency.

That year, Reagan earned a reputation for loose talk and poorly thought-out proposals. Speaking from his now-famous note cards, he often repeated attention-getting statistics that later proved to have little basis in fact. His ad-libbed one-liners had always been an effective part of his speaking style, but they were rarely carefully researched because his aides never knew they were coming.

At one point, Reagan's 1976 campaign had been set back for several weeks while he tried, with little success, to explain how he had arrived at a $90 billion figure for the amount of money he would save by transferring federal domestic programs to state and local governments.

During the 1980 primary season, several news organizations reported that Reagan's standard speech was replete with factual errors, but they appeared to have little influence on the outcome of the primaries.

Reagan never documented his assertions that 23,300 General Motors employees were hired just "to comply with government-required paper work," and that there were more oil reserves in Alaska than in Saudi Arabia. But, gradually, such references were deleted from the standard stump speech.

The former California governor managed to overcome several other embarrassments as well during the early primaries. In an unguarded moment with the press on Feb. 16 in New Hampshire, Reagan told an ethnic joke about Italians and Poles that was widely reported, much to Reagan's chagrin. Five weeks later, on March 23 in Kansas, he admitted that he did not know enough about agricultural parity to comment on a farmer's question. But neither event had a lasting impact.

After he won the nomination, Reagan's faux pas had widespread, if only temporary, impact on the general election campaign.

At an Aug. 16 press conference, Reagan suggested that the United States should have "governmental" relations with Taiwan. Then he spent several days trying to explain that he was not advocating the resumption of diplomatic relations with Taiwan or the "two China" policy of the early 1970s. It was just "a matter of semantics," Reagan said.

Reagan also may have raised eyebrows by discussing his views on evolution, in which he said he still had questions about the validity of the theory, and on the Vietnam War. He told the Veterans of Foreign Wars at their Aug. 18 Chicago convention that America's involvement in that conflict was "a noble cause."

In the early phase of the election campaign against Carter, the most embarrassing moment for the GOP nominee came at the Michigan State Fair outside Detroit. At a Labor Day rally, Reagan pointed out that while he was opening his campaign for the presidency in an economically distressed industrial state, Carter was opening his campaign at a picnic in Tuscumbia, Ala. — "the city that gave birth to and is the parent body of the Ku Klux Klan."

Not only was the statement inaccurate, it also was considered by many Southern governors to be an insult to the region. The next day, Reagan issued a written apology.

The result of those events was to focus the campaign on him, not on President Carter, which had been at the heart of the Reagan strategy. Rather than being in a position to attack Carter's economic programs, Reagan temporarily had to defend himself from attacks such as those made by Carter's Transportation Secretary Neil Goldschmidt, who charged Reagan with "filling the air with misstatements, half-truths and twin positions."

And a number of Republicans had described the combination as a "dream ticket." Groups described as "friends of Ronald Reagan" and "friends of Gerald Ford" had met four times earlier during the convention to discuss the possibility of forging a Reagan-Ford ticket.

Rumors began to circulate on the convention floor that Ford was being tapped for the second spot. Ford himself had encouraged this speculation. In two televised interviews during the week he strongly hinted he would agree to be Reagan's running mate if certain conditions were met.

Ford declined to spell out in detail what his conditions were, but in listing his requirements for taking the job it became clear he wanted responsibilities that would have made him, in effect, co-president with Reagan. The discussions reportedly centered around providing a role for Ford somewhat akin to the position of White House chief of staff. In such a post he would have had responsibility for such

agencies as the Office of Management and Budget, the National Security Council, the domestic policy staff and the Council of Economic Advisers.

But late on July 16 the Reagan-Ford arrangement fell apart. Ford went to Reagan's suite in the Detroit Plaza Hotel, and the two men agreed that it would be better for Ford to campaign for the GOP ticket rather than be a member of it.

The speculation prompted Reagan to visit the convention hall at about 12:15 a.m. July 17 to quell "rumors and gossip" and to announce his choice of Bush. "It is necessary to break with tradition just as in this campaign we're going to break with tradition," Reagan told the cheering delegates.

He added: "It is true we've gone over this and over this and he and I have come to the conclusion that he believes he can be of more value campaigning his heart out as former president, as he has promised to do, than as a member of the ticket." He then asked the delegates to support Bush.

The Reagan camp refused to acknowledge that Bush was the second choice, even though it was widely perceived that way. "There was everybody else and then the Ford option," Edwin Meese, Reagan's chief of staff, said later.

Bush's Assets

Bush was one of the vice presidential possibilities favored by those in the party who believed Reagan had to reach outside the GOP's conservative wing if he were to have broad appeal in the general election. Bush supporters said his background would balance the ticket geographically and that his extensive government service would overcome criticism that Reagan did not have any Washington experience.

Bush's first appearance at the convention earlier on the evening of July 16 produced a rousing demonstration from supporters throughout the hall. His strongest support came from the Northeastern and Midwestern delegations and in the other states where he won primary victories. Six Southern state GOP chairmen also had supported him. Ford, too, had been quoted earlier as supporting Bush, although he declined to comment on a favorite in interviews during the convention.

Reagan and Bush held their first joint press conference on the morning of July 17 and downplayed their differences. Repeatedly questioned about his criticism of Reagan's policies during the primaries, Bush finally said, "What difference does it make? It's irrelevant."

"The old days of separating Republicans into two camps are over," said Reagan.

Reagan aide Meese later commented on what the Reagan camp considered Bush's strong points:

"I think he ran an outstanding campaign, did very well in at least two industrial states, has a good deal of experience in Washington and in federal matters, was a congressman, so understands congressional relations, and has a great deal of experience in foreign affairs. All these things are pluses.

"Politically, he's a good campaigner, has the support of people throughout the country that you might say are marginally committed to Ronald Reagan, so this extends our scope as far as the electorate is concerned."

Bush Nominated

Bush was formally elected Reagan's vice presidential nominee at the final convention session July 17.

Sen. Robert Dole of Kansas, Ford's running mate four years earlier, nominated Bush with a plea for party unity. "This man has your philosophy," he told the delegates. "This is not the time to stress our differences but to stress the unity in our party."

Bush was an easy winner, receiving 1,832 votes on the first roll call. Bush's nomination then was made unanimous.

Bush began his brief acceptance speech by announcing his wholehearted support of the conservative party platform. He followed by warning the delegates against overconfidence. *(Text, p. 102)*

"He [Carter] is a formidable campaigner who can be expected to use the power of his office to suit his own political ends," Bush asserted. "The stakes for America and the free world are too great to allow ourselves to become complacent."

General Election Campaign

Highlights of the fall election campaign included two nationally televised presidential debates. The first, held on Sept. 21, was boycotted by President Carter because he said it would be unfair for him to debate two Republicans — Reagan and independent candidate John B. Anderson.

The second debate, which almost did not take place because of objections of one kind or another by both sides, pitted Reagan against Carter and was held Oct. 28. It covered both foreign and domestic issues.

Several other developments during the campaign gave indications of Reagan's positions and attitudes on major controversies. A fracas arose over the Carter administration's disclosure in August that the United States was developing a new, supposedly radar-resistant warplane called "Stealth."

Reagan on Sept. 4 labeled the administration's announcement a "serious breach of national security" and said it was designed to offset Carter's 1977 cancellation of the B-1 bomber. Carter replied Sept. 9 that the public admission was made only after news of the project's existence had been leaked. And he argued that no technological details were publicized.

On Sept. 5 the Carter organization released four Reagan quotations — dating from 1964, 1965, 1966 and 1976 — in which the Republican seemed to call for making Social Security voluntary. Reagan advisers, aware that the statements could alarm elderly voters, said the former California governor had changed his position and now favored keeping the existing system. *(Reagan campaign gaffes, box, p. 81)*

Reagan advocated scrapping Carter's entire energy program. Among other things, he called for repeal of the windfall profits tax, an end to the Department of Energy and repeal of the federally imposed 55 mph speed limit that was passed in 1974.

As an energy conservation measure, Carter had ordered the gradual phase-out, between June 1979 and September 1981, of price controls on domestically produced oil, an action that contributed to higher prices of gasoline and heating fuel. (Soon after taking office, Reagan issued an executive order immediately ending all remaining controls on oil prices Jan. 28 rather than waiting for complete decontrol on Sept. 30.)

During the campaign, Carter had labeled as "outrageous" Reagan's contention that the oil companies could produce an abundance of energy within the United States if freed from federal interference. Another key element of Carter's energy policy opposed by Reagan was a $20 billion program of subsidies for private development of synthetic fuels, which won congressional approval late in the 96th Congress.

Aware of the president's ability to manipulate events, Reagan's advisers late in the campaign feared an "October surprise" from the White House, possibly in foreign affairs. But as it turned out, the "surprise," of which there were two, apparently bolstered Reagan rather than Carter.

The first was the much ballyhooed debate between the two major candidates. Although Carter expected to score well in the debate by demonstrating his detailed knowledge of the issues and his grasp of the presidency, Reagan appeared to have impressed voters more by his debating presence and responses to Carter's attacks.

The second "surprise" was the 11th-hour injection of the American hostage crisis into the campaign and the Iranian leaders' miscalculation that Carter would accept

Presidential Voting by Regions, 1976-1980

	1976			1980				Net Change in Carter % 1976-80
	Turnout (in millions)	Carter	Ford	Turnout (in millions)	Carter	Reagan	Anderson	
East	22.1	51%	47%	21.9	43%	47%	9%	− 9%
South	20.6	54	45	23.1	44	52	3	−10
Midwest	24.2	48	50	25.2	41	51	7	− 7
West	14.7	46	51	16.3	34	54	9	−11
TOTAL	81.6	50%	48%	86.5	41%	51%	7%	− 9%

SOURCE: Official election results from the 50 states and the District of Columbia.

their demands for the release of the hostages before Election Day. Although Carter tried to keep the negotiations — which reached a peak during the weekend before the Nov. 4 election — out of the campaign, the publicity given them so close to the election apparently worked against the president.

Reagan-Anderson Debate

The League of Women Voters, which planned to sponsor three debates among the major presidential contenders, decided Sept. 9 to include Anderson after he achieved a 15 percent standing in the national polls. Carter refused to participate unless he could have a one-on-one debate with Reagan first. Reagan, however, insisted that Anderson take part in the first meeting. Polls had shown that Anderson would take more votes away from Carter than from Reagan. The Anderson threat took on added significance Sept. 6 when the policy committee of New York's Liberal Party voted to put him on their ballot line.

Most political analysts felt that Reagan and Anderson were able to appeal to their basic constituencies in the debate, which was staged in Baltimore. In addition, the familiar public personae of the two men were on view — Reagan, the smooth and easygoing television performer who dispensed optimistic visions; Anderson, the stern and articulate schoolmaster who called for sacrifices.

Reagan, showing his gift for conveying ideas in easily understood sentences, reiterated his call for decreasing the size of government and the need for greater military spending. He plugged his proposal for massive tax cuts to stimulate the economy and advocated a reduction in federal regulations, which he said stifled initiative.

With his good-humored, avuncular style, Reagan also attempted to undercut Carter's accusations that he was a racist and a warmonger. The president's non-appearance gave Reagan and Anderson a chance to capitalize on the unpopularity of his decision by trying to paint him as arrogant. A Sept. 16 Gallup Poll, taken five days before the debate, showed 61 percent disapproving of the president's action and 25 percent approving. Privately, Carter's aides admitted that the president did not want to enhance the stature of Rep. Anderson by having him appear as an equal in a debate with the president.

The candidates covered five issues, but did not touch on foreign policy:

Economy and Taxes. Decrying election year tax cuts, Anderson said he would slice government spending before reducing taxes. He proposed $11.3 billion in specific cuts, including paying federal retirement benefits once instead of twice a year. He characterized Reagan's proposed tax cut as inflationary and maintained that an Anderson tax reduction plan would spur production, not consumption.

Reagan said his plan to cut personal income tax rates by 30 percent over three years would lead to a balanced budget in 1983 because of the greater revenues it would stimulate through enhanced economic activity.

Energy. "We will have to change ... some of the lifestyles we now enjoy," said Anderson, as he plugged his 50-cent-per-gallon gasoline tax, which would be used to offset scheduled Social Security tax hikes and discourage fuel consumption. Auto use should be cut down and replaced by mass transit, he declared.

Reagan gently ridiculed the Anderson gas tax. "Why take it in the first place if you're going to give it back?" he asked. According to Reagan, the nation had ample energy resources of its own. The task, he maintained, was to free producers from the regulatory burdens that he said had hindered energy exploration.

Defense. Both candidates were against conscription in peacetime and for boosts in military pay to solve the services' manpower shortage. As an extra incentive, Reagan called for a return to the GI Bill, which had been eliminated in 1975 for new servicemen and women. It provided educational benefits.

But Anderson said that, unlike Reagan, he saw no need for the MX missile, which he labeled a "boondoggle." Reagan replied that the weapon was necessary to maintain the nation's strategic balance with the Soviet Union and asserted that it could be built for less than the $54 billion cost cited by Anderson.

Cities. To salvage the nation's deteriorating urban areas, Reagan advocated imposing tax moratoriums to lure business into the cities. Boarded up, government-held homes should be sold for $1 each to homesteaders who would live in them and refurbish them, he said. A program nearly identical to the one Reagan proposed had been in existence since 1974.

Anderson's solution relied on public expenditures. He called for a $4 billion federal fund, financed by alcohol and tobacco taxes, to rebuild streets and water systems, and for a $1 billion youth employment program dedicated to energy conservation projects.

Abortion. On this emotional topic, Anderson said it was a mother's right to choose whether to end her pregnancy, without interference from the state. Reagan was against abortion and noted that "everybody who is for abortion has already been born."

Reagan-Carter Debate

The long-awaited, major-party presidential debate, which had been discussed ever since the two candidates were nominated during the summer, finally was held Oct. 28.

The 90-minute, nationally televised confrontation, put on in Cleveland by the League of Women Voters, was billed as the pivotal event of a close campaign. Neither candidate knocked the other out rhetorically or committed a fatal gaffe in the opinion of most analysts. *(Text, p. 103)*

The debate featured attempts by Carter to paint Reagan as "dangerous" to world peace and charges by Reagan that the president had mismanaged the economy. The debaters sought to capitalize on each other's weak points. For Reagan, one task was to appear "presidential." And even some Carter aides conceded that the Republican's stage presence had been superior to Carter's. To offset questions about his experience, Reagan often referred to his tenure as governor of California (1967-75), which he said "would be the seventh ranking economic power in the world" if it were a nation.

Carter's goal, apart from feeding doubts about the capabilities of his adversary, was to appeal to elements of the Democratic coalition, which he needed to win. With liberals and women in mind, he cited his support for the Equal Rights Amendment, which Reagan opposed. For minority viewers, he mentioned his record level of appointments of blacks to judgeships and executive branch posts. And he pointed to his regional ties by stating at one point, "I'm a Southerner."

Reagan found himself on the defensive more often than Carter, primarily because three of the eight questions dealt with national security, which allowed the president to decry hard-line Reagan positions. Carter said Reagan's desire to scrap the Strategic Arms Limitation Treaty (SALT II) would lead to an arms race that could threaten world peace.

Trying to shuck this warmonger label, Reagan retorted that his "first priority must be world peace, and that use of force is always, and only, a last resort when everything else has failed." Saying Carter had been out-negotiated on SALT, he proposed that the treaty be renegotiated to mandate actual arms cuts.

Carter also took the offensive on economic issues, charging that Reagan's three-year, 30 percent tax reduction plan was inflationary. Reagan shot back that the inflation rate had soared under Carter. Reagan sought to deflect Carter's attacks by contending five times that his stands had been distorted.

Summary of Arguments

Here is a sampling of the candidates' reponses:

Military Forces. Reagan charged Carter with increasing the danger of war by weakening the nation's defenses through canceling or delaying production of weapons systems.

Carter declared that Reagan advocated "simple answers" and had favored the use of U.S. military force in the past during international disputes, such as a fishing rights disagreement with Ecuador.

Inflation. Carter quoted Reagan's running mate, George Bush, as describing the Reagan tax cut proposal as "voodoo economics."

Reagan said the scheme would not stimulate inflation, as Carter contended. "Why is it inflationary to let the people keep more of their money and spend it the way they'd like...?" he asked.

Cities. Reagan reiterated his plan to create "development zones" in blighted urban areas, using tax incentives to entice business. But he angered some black viewers by saying, "[W]hen I was young ... this country didn't even know it had a racial problem."

Carter said money from the oil windfall profits tax, which he proposed, would help revitalize urban mass transit systems.

Terrorism. The president declared that Reagan opposed efforts to stem the proliferation of nuclear weapons, which could fall into terrorists' hands.

The Republican denied that and castigated Carter for permitting the taking of the hostages in Iran. "[W]e could have ... either strengthened our security there or removed our personnel before the kidnap," he said.

Energy. Reagan, Carter said, wanted "to put all our eggs in one basket and give that basket to the major oil companies." But Reagan charged that the administration had hindered energy production through over-regulation.

Impact on Election

A CBS News poll found that 44 percent of those surveyed thought Reagan had won, compared with 36 percent who gave the debate to Carter and 20 percent who said it was a tie or did not know.

Some political analysts felt that Reagan had gained not so much on "debaters' points" as on his success in appearing calm and reasonable while Carter was trying to depict him as someone quick to anger and likely to lead the country into a nuclear war. This had been Carter's strategy in the closing days of the campaign, and Reagan's restraint in the debate effectively defused it. Thus the debate was seen as contributing to Reagan's Nov. 4 landslide by bringing to his camp hundreds of thousands of voters who, according to the polls, had been wavering right up to the last minute.

Other Factors in Victory

Carter officials claimed their campaign began to unravel during the weekend before the election, when the Iranian government publicized its conditions for the release of the American hostages. The Americans had been taken captive Nov. 4, 1979, exactly one year before the 1980 election. Presidential aides contended that Iran's demands focused voter frustration on a major national concern and triggered a late surge to Reagan.

But Carter's prospects had appeared tenuous long before that. Through most of his term, he had a low voter approval rating. To many voters, he appeared to be a man

Official 1980 Presidential Election Results

Total Popular Vote: 86,513,296   Reagan's Plurality: 8,417,992

	RONALD REAGAN (Republican)		JIMMY CARTER (Democrat)		JOHN B. ANDERSON (Independent)		ED CLARK (Libertarian)		BARRY COMMONER (Citizens)		OTHER[1]	
	Votes	%	Votes	%	Votes	%	Votes	%	Votes	%	Votes	%
Alabama	654,192	48.8	636,730	47.5	16,481	1.2	13,318	1.0	517	0.0	20,721	1.5
Alaska	86,112	54.4	41,842	26.4	11,156	7.0	18,479	11.7			805	0.5
Arizona	529,688	60.6	246,843	28.2	76,952	8.8	18,784	2.2	551[2]	0.1	1,127	0.1
Arkansas	403,164	48.1	398,041	47.5	22,468	2.7	8,970	1.1	2,345	0.3	2,594	0.3
California	4,524,835	52.7	3,083,652	35.9	739,832	8.6	148,434	1.7	61,063	0.7	29,214	0.4
Colorado	652,264	55.0	368,009	31.1	130,633	11.0	25,744	2.2	5,614	0.5	2,186	0.2
Connecticut	677,210	48.2	541,732	38.5	171,807	12.2	8,570	0.6	6,130	0.4	836	0.1
Delaware	111,252	47.2	105,754	44.8	16,288	6.9	1,974	0.9	103[2]	0.0	529	0.2
District of Columbia	23,313	13.4	130,231	74.9	16,131	9.3	1,104	0.6	1,826	1.1	1,284	0.7
Florida	2,046,951	55.5	1,419,475	38.5	189,692	5.2	30,524	0.8			285	0.0
Georgia	654,168	41.0	890,955	55.8	36,055	2.2	15,627	1.0	104[2]	0.0	8	0.0
Hawaii	130,112	42.9	135,879	44.8	32,021	10.6	3,269	1.1	1,548	0.5	458	0.1
Idaho	290,699	66.4	110,192	25.2	27,058	6.2	8,425	1.9			1,470	0.3
Illinois	2,358,094	49.7	1,981,413	41.7	346,754	7.3	38,939	0.8	10,692	0.2	13,874	0.3
Indiana	1,255,656	56.0	844,197	37.6	111,639	5.0	19,627	0.9	4,852	0.2	6,062	0.3
Iowa	676,026	51.3	508,672	38.6	115,633	8.8	13,123	1.0	2,273	0.2	1,934	0.1
Kansas	566,812	57.8	326,150	33.3	68,231	7.0	14,470	1.5			4,132	0.4
Kentucky	635,274	49.0	617,417	47.7	31,127	2.4	5,531	0.4	1,304	0.1	4,974	0.4
Louisiana	792,853	51.2	708,453	45.8	26,345	1.7	8,240	0.5	1,584	0.1	11,116	0.7
Maine	238,522	45.6	220,974	42.3	53,327	10.2	5,119	1.0	4,394	0.8	675	0.1
Maryland	680,606	44.2	726,161	47.1	119,537	7.8	14,192	0.9				
Massachusetts	1,056,223	41.8	1,053,800	41.7	382,539	15.2	22,038	0.9	2,056[2]	0.1	7,972	0.3
Michigan	1,915,225	49.0	1,661,532	42.5	275,223	7.0	41,597	1.1	11,930	0.3	4,218	0.1
Minnesota	873,268	42.6	954,173	46.5	174,997	8.5	31,593	1.5	8,406	0.4	9,479	0.5
Mississippi	441,089	49.4	429,281	48.1	12,036	1.4	5,465	0.6			4,749	0.5
Missouri	1,074,181	51.2	931,182	44.3	77,920	3.7	14,422	0.7	573[2]	0.0	1,546	0.1
Montana	206,814	56.8	118,032	32.4	29,281	8.1	9,825	2.7				
Nebraska	419,214	65.6	166,424	26.0	44,854	7.0	9,041	1.4				
Nevada	155,017	62.5	66,666	26.9	17,651	7.1	4,358	1.8			4,193	1.7
New Hampshire	221,705	57.7	108,864	28.4	49,693	12.9	2,064	0.5	1,320	0.4	344	0.1
New Jersey	1,546,557	52.0	1,147,364	38.6	234,632	7.9	20,652	0.6	8,203	0.3	18,276	0.6
New Mexico	250,779	55.0	167,826	36.8	29,459	6.5	4,365	0.9	2,202	0.5	1,606	0.3
New York	2,893,831	46.7	2,728,372	44.0	467,801	7.5	52,648	0.8	23,186	0.4	36,121	0.6
North Carolina	915,018	49.3	875,635	47.2	52,800	2.9	9,677	0.5	2,287	0.1	416	0.0
North Dakota	193,695	64.2	79,189	26.3	23,640	7.8	3,743	1.2	429	0.2	849	0.3
Ohio	2,206,545	51.5	1,752,414	40.9	254,472	5.9	49,033	1.2	8,564	0.2	12,575	0.3
Oklahoma	695,570	60.5	402,026	35.0	38,284	3.3	13,828	1.2				
Oregon	571,044	48.3	456,890	38.7	112,389	9.5	25,838	2.2	13,642	1.2	1,713	0.1
Pennsylvania	2,261,872	49.6	1,937,540	42.5	292,921	6.4	33,263	0.7	10,430	0.2	25,475	0.6
Rhode Island	154,793	37.2	198,342	47.7	59,819	14.4	2,458	0.6	67[2]	0.0	593	0.1
South Carolina	441,841	49.4	430,385	48.2	14,153	1.6	5,139	0.6			2,177	0.2
South Dakota	198,343	60.5	103,855	31.7	21,431	6.5	3,824	1.2			250	0.1
Tennessee	787,761	48.7	783,051	48.4	35,991	2.2	7,116	0.4	1,112	0.1	2,585	0.2
Texas	2,510,705	55.3	1,881,147	41.4	111,613	2.5	37,643	0.8	453[2]	0.0	75	0.0
Utah	439,687	72.8	124,266	20.6	30,284	5.0	7,156	1.2	1,009	0.1	1,750	0.3
Vermont	94,628	44.4	81,952	38.4	31,761	14.9	1,900	0.9	2,316	1.1	742	0.3
Virginia	989,609	53.0	752,174	40.3	95,418	5.1	12,821	0.7	14,024	0.8	1,986	0.1
Washington	865,244	49.7	650,193	37.3	185,073	10.6	29,213	1.7	9,403	0.5	3,268	0.2
West Virginia	334,206	45.3	367,462	49.8	31,691	4.3	4,356	0.6				
Wisconsin	1,088,845	47.9	981,584	43.2	160,657	7.1	29,135	1.3	7,767	0.3	5,233	0.2
Wyoming	110,700	62.6	49,427	28.0	12,072	6.8	4,514	2.6				
	43,901,812	50.7	35,483,820	41.0	5,719,722	6.6	921,188	1.1	234,279	0.3	252,475	0.3

NOTE: Based on official returns from all 50 states and the District of Columbia. In Mississippi and South Carolina, voters balloted for individual electors. The total used is for the candidate's elector receiving the highest number of votes.

1 Others receiving votes: Hall (Communist), 44,954; Rarick (American Independent), 41,268; DeBerry (Socialist Workers), 40,145; McCormack (Right to Life), 32,327; Smith (Peace and Freedom), 18,116; Griswold (Workers World), 13,300; Bubar (National Statesman), 7,212; McReynolds (Socialist), 6,895; Greaves (American), 6,647; Pulley (Socialist Workers), 6,271; American Party line (no candidate), 6,136; None of the Above, 4,193; Congress (Socialist Workers), 4,029; Lynen ("Middle Class"), 3,694; Gahres ("Down with Lawyers"), 1,718; Shelton (American), 1,555; Wendelken (Independent), 923; McLain (Natural People's League), 296; Scattered write-ins, 12,796.

2 Write-in vote.

of integrity but a leader lacking the ability to communicate his vision of the future.

Throughout the fall Reagan had pounded away at Carter's failures in dealing with the economy, successfully courting a large share of the traditionally Democratic, blue-collar vote. He promised more forceful leadership in confronting economic problems and alleged U.S. military weakness.

Carter complained that Reagan was offering simplistic solutions to complex problems. But his frequent allusions to Reagan as a right-winger and a threat to world peace seemed to backfire. Carter's attacks undermined one of the president's strongest assets — his reputation as a politician with a high sense of decency.

While the charges appeared to succeed temporarily in raising voter fear of a Reagan presidency, the Californian's affable performance in the nationally televised debate Oct. 28 seemed to take much of the steam out of the Carter assault. After the debate, Reagan began to pull ahead.

But no one publicly forecast the rout that developed on election day. In most of the states that were expected to be close or were considered to be in the Carter column, Reagan won, frequently by comfortable margins. In states Reagan was expected to carry, he won overwhelmingly.

Carter's percentage of the vote dropped below his 1976 share in every state by at least two percentage points. In nearly half the states it declined by at least 10 percentage points.

A variety of public opinion polls showed an unusually large number of undecided voters in the final weeks of the campaign. Possibly as a result of the Oct. 28 debate, many of them became reconciled to Reagan and voted for him in large numbers on Nov. 4.

But many others may not have voted. A long-standing assumption was that the larger the turnout, the better the chances for Democratic candidates because of the larger number of registered Democratic voters. But the turnout Nov. 4 was bad news for Carter.

Only about 53 percent of the nation's voting age population of 160.5 million went to the polls, marking the fifth consecutive election that the presidential turnout had declined. The 1980 figure was a full percentage point below the 1976 turnout rate of 54.4 percent and the lowest turnout since 1948.

The decline was particularly severe in the East, a region where Carter needed to do well, but didn't. In New York alone, about a half million fewer voters cast ballots than in 1976.

That year Carter won the presidency by reconstructing in varying proportions Roosevelt's New Deal coalition. It included the South, the industrial Northeast, organized labor, minorities and the liberal community. With his roots in rural Georgia and discontent over Ford's farm policy, Carter was also able to make a better-than-usual showing in rural areas for a Democratic candidate.

But it was quickly apparent on Election Night that Carter's victorious coalition of 1976 had fallen apart. Only minority groups — Hispanics and blacks — continued to give the lion's share of their vote to the Democratic candidate. Reagan made deep inroads into all other segments of the Carter coalition.

An ABC News exit poll of voters Nov. 4 found Carter ran only narrowly ahead of Reagan among several key traditionally Democratic constituencies. Among labor union families, for instance, Carter led by only 8 percentage points. Among Jewish voters, he led by only 7 percentage points.

A variety of surveys showed that Carter drew more than 80 percent of the black vote. But even among this loyal Democratic voting bloc there were problems. A survey of urban black precincts by the Joint Center for Political Studies indicated that the turnout of blacks throughout the country had declined from 1976.

By portraying Reagan as an ultraconservative outside the political mainstream, Carter had hoped to offset his losses among other groups by wooing the support of moderate Republican suburban voters. But Reagan matched or exceeded Ford's margins in suburbs from coast to coast.

Reagan's Regional Sweep

Reagan easily carried every region of the country, including the keystones of Carter's 1976 triumph — the industrial Northeast and the president's native South.

In 1976 Carter won 51 percent of the popular vote in the East and 108 of the region's 144 electoral votes. He did even better in the South, garnering 54 percent of the popular vote and 127 out of 147 electoral votes.

In 1980 he won only 43 percent of the popular vote in the East and just 23 electoral votes — from Maryland, Rhode Island, West Virginia and the District of Columbia. In the South he received 44 percent of the vote and 12 electoral votes, all from his home state of Georgia. *(Regional vote, box, p. 83)*

Anderson made his greatest impact in the East, enabling Reagan to sweep the region even though he was barely able to match Ford's share of the popular vote four years earlier. If Anderson had not been on the ballot, Carter probably could have carried several more Eastern states, including vote-rich New York (41 electoral votes) and Massachusetts (14).

But the problem for Carter in the East was more than Anderson. Probably in no other region was the president plagued more by a low Democratic turnout. A lack of voter enthusiasm for Carter was obvious across the country throughout the campaign. In New York alone, Carter's total vote was about 750,000 below his winning total in 1976.

In the South, Carter's problem was a defection of many white voters to Reagan. The Georgian had scored a virtual sweep of his home region four years earlier by building a coalition of blacks and rural whites.

Blacks held for Carter in 1980, although apparently voting in reduced numbers. But many whites defected to Reagan, who had long been popular in the South. Reagan's victory in many states was narrow — seven of his victories in this region were won by 5 percentage points or fewer. But his inroads were enough to reverse the 1976 election map and swing virtually the whole region back into the GOP column.

The results were even worse for Carter in the rest of the country. The Midwest had been a major battleground in 1976. Ford won the regional popular vote by only 2 percentage points, with Carter picking up the electoral votes of Minnesota (10), Missouri (12), Ohio (25) and Wisconsin (11), which enabled him to win the election.

In 1980 Reagan won the Midwest by 10 percentage points. Only Vice President Walter F. Mondale's home state of Minnesota voted Democratic. Illinois, Michigan and Ohio — all closely contested and considered pivotal — went decisively to Reagan by margins of at least 8 percentage points.

Ohio mirrored Carter's problems nationally. He carried it narrowly in 1976 by rolling up a lead of nearly 100,000 votes in the state's major urban center, Cuyahoga County

1980 Electoral Votes by States

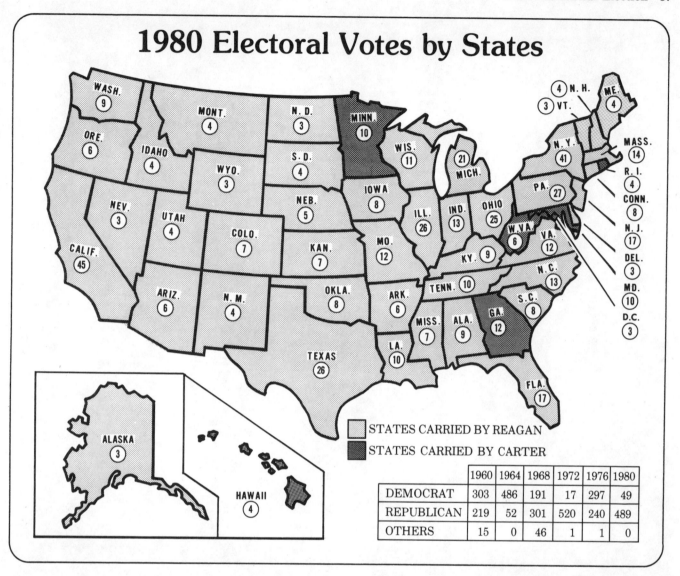

	1960	1964	1968	1972	1976	1980
DEMOCRAT	303	486	191	17	297	49
REPUBLICAN	219	52	301	520	240	489
OTHERS	15	0	46	1	1	0

STATES CARRIED BY REAGAN

STATES CARRIED BY CARTER

(Cleveland), sweeping the other traditionally Democratic industrial centers of northern Ohio and making deep inroads into the normally Republican rural vote. In 1980 his pluralities in Cuyahoga County and economically depressed industrial centers such as Mahoning County (Youngstown) were trimmed in half, and the rural appeal that he had displayed in 1976 evaporated. As a result, Reagan carried Ohio by more than 450,000 votes.

The defection of many Democratic blue-collar voters to Reagan was one of the keys to the Republican landslide. As a Baptist from the rural South, Carter never had been particularly popular among urban Catholic ethnic voters, many of them blue-collar workers.

Reagan's strength in the nation's agricultural heartland padded his margin. By exploiting his own agrar-

ian background and the unpopularity of Ford's 1975 grain embargo, Carter nearly captured several Midwestern farm states in 1976. In his re-election campaign he had to defend a grain embargo of his own, and the vote there was not even close. Reagan ran far ahead in the agricultural Midwest.

That was also the story in the West. Carter carried only Hawaii in 1976. But he finished only 5 percentage points behind Ford in the regional popular vote by running well in several other states, including California.

But in 1980, Carter's appeal to Western voters was diminished. He won Hawaii again, but in few other states did he even come close to Reagan.

Reagan carried his home region by nearly 20 percentage points. In six Western states, he crushed the president by more than a 2-1 margin.

Election Chronology, 1979-81

1979

Jan. 24. John B. Connally, former Texas governor and secretary of the Treasury during the Nixon administration, declares his candidacy for the Republican presidential nomination. He is the second announced Republican candidate. Rep. Philip M. Crane (Ill.) declared on Aug. 2, 1978.

March 4. A Gallup Poll of Republican voters on prospective presidential candidates shows former California Gov. Ronald Reagan with 31 percent, former President Gerald R. Ford with 26 percent, Connally with 12 percent and Sen. Howard H. Baker Jr. of Tennessee with 8 percent. A similar poll released on Dec. 28, 1978, showed Reagan with 40 percent, Ford 24 percent, Baker 9 percent and Connally 6 percent.

March 10. Connally is favored by Midwest GOP officials meeting in Indianapolis, according to a CBS News poll. Connally receives the support of 28 percent of those polled, compared with Reagan's 21 percent and Bush's 17 percent.

March 12. Sen. Lowell P. Weicker Jr. (Conn.) declares his candidacy for the Republican presidential nomination.

May 1. George Bush, former director of the CIA, GOP national chairman and U. S. representative from Texas, announces his candidacy for the Republican presidential nomination.

May 14. Sen. Robert Dole (Kan.) announces his candidacy for the Republican presidential nomination.

May 16. Sen. Weicker drops out of the race for the Republican nomination after nine weeks, citing his third-place standing in his home state of Connecticut.

May 25. Ford announces he has no intention of seeking the Republican presidential nomination, yet says he "learned a long time ago never to say never."

June 8. Rep. John B. Anderson (Ill.) announces his candidacy for the Republican presidential nomination.

July 26. Reagan's campaign committee reports having raised more than $1.4 million for the still-undeclared candidate.

Aug. 2. A Larry Pressler for President Committee is announced, but a formal declaration by the South Dakota senator is withheld pending demonstration of sufficient financial and political support.

Sept. 10. A Draft Haig Committee is formed to promote the candidacy of retired Gen. Alexander M. Haig Jr.

Sept. 16. Forces loyal to Reagan defeat a proposal to modify California's winner-take-all Republican primary at a meeting of the GOP State Central Committee.

Sept. 20. The New Hampshire Primary Committee to Draft President Ford in 1980 is launched following a *Boston Globe* poll showing Ford leading Reagan 38 percent to 34 percent in New Hampshire.

Sept. 25. Sen. Pressler formally announces his candidacy for the Republican presidential nomination.

Oct. 12. Gov. Richard A. Snelling, R-Vt., announces plans to spend between $4,000 and $6,000 of his own money for a national mail campaign to urge a candidacy for former President Ford.

Nov. 3. Bush is the surprise victor in a straw poll of Maine Republicans attending an informal convention in Portland. Bush polls 35 percent, Baker 33 percent and Connally 18 percent. Reagan, who did not attend the affair, polls 7 percent.

Nov. 4. U.S. Embassy personnel in Tehran, Iran, are taken hostage by "student" militants protesting the entry of the former shah of Iran into the United States for medical treatment.

Nov. 7. A straw poll taken at the Florida Republican Convention in Orlando shows Reagan the choice of 36 percent of the delegates compared with 27 percent for Connally and 26 percent for Bush.

Nov. 13. Reagan formally announces his candidacy for the Republican presidential nomination.

Nov. 14. Reagan rules out joint appearances or debates with his Republican rivals.

Nov. 25. A Gallup Poll conducted between Nov. 2-5 shows Republicans favoring Reagan over Ford 33 percent to 22 percent, with Baker receiving 14 percent. Without Ford, the results are Reagan 41 percent, Baker 18 percent and Connally 13 percent. An ABC News/Harris Survey of Republicans and independents conducted Nov. 7-10 gives Reagan 38 percent, Baker 21 percent and Connally 15 percent.

Dec. 11. A Gallup Poll completed Dec. 9 indicates that either President Carter or Sen. Edward M. Kennedy, D-Mass., would defeat Reagan in a general election. Carter leads Reagan 60 percent to 36 percent, up from his 53-47 lead of mid-October. Kennedy's margin of 5 percent over Reagan is down 11 percent from his lead in the mid-October poll.

Dec. 22. Haig announces his decision not to seek the Republican presidential nomination.

Dec. 27. Soviet troops enter Afghanistan to quell the growing insurgency. Coupled with the situation in Iran, the invasion leads to heightened debate over U.S. foreign and defense policy.

1980

Jan. 5. Six of the seven Republican presidential candidates debate in Des Moines, Iowa. Reagan does not participate.

Jan. 21. Bush upsets Reagan in the Iowa precinct caucuses. Mindful of the importance of Iowa to Carter's 1976 presidential bid, Bush's 32-29 percent victory over the front-running Reagan receives extensive media coverage.

Jan. 22. Reagan reconsiders his decision not to debate his Republican rivals.

Feb. 2. In the campaign's first delegate distribution, Reagan wins six delegates in Arkansas' district caucuses to Baker's four and Bush's one.

Feb. 17. Bush wins the Puerto Rican primary with Baker a distant second. Reagan is not entered.

Feb. 18. Reagan apologizes for an ethnic joke told two days earlier, saying the joke was meant to illustrate the type of humor he deplores.

Feb. 20. Reagan participates in his first debate of the campaign, joining the other six Republican candidates in New Hampshire.

Feb. 23. What was scheduled as a two-man debate between Reagan and Bush in Nashua, N.H., attains national significance when Anderson, Baker, Crane and Dole, invited by Reagan, also show up and try to participate. Though the debate's sponsor, *The Nashua Telegraph,* enforces the original two-man format, the pre-debate controversy receives more national attention than the debate itself, which is televised only locally. Reagan's support of an open debate seems to contrast favorably with Bush's position supporting the sponsor for a one-on-one event.

Feb. 26. Reagan grabs 50 percent of the New Hampshire primary vote and defeats runner-up Bush by better than two-to-one. In the aftermath, John Sears, Reagan's campaign chief, along with two other high-ranking campaign aides are dismissed, reportedly for advising Reagan to remain above the political fray. This had cost Reagan dearly in the Iowa caucuses.

An old Reagan friend, William J. Casey, former chairman of the Securities and Exchange Commission, and veteran Reagan aide Edwin Meese III are placed in charge of rebuilding the campaign.

March 4. In a close three-way race, Bush edges out Reagan and Anderson in the Massachusetts primary. Bush and Anderson both receive 31 percent of the vote while Reagan gets 29 percent.

Reagan wins the Vermont primary, edging Anderson in another very close race 31 percent to 30 percent.

March 5. After finishing fourth in both Massachusetts and Vermont, Sen. Baker withdraws his bid for the Republican presidential nomination.

March 8. Reagan easily turns back a determined challenge by Connally in the South Carolina primary. Reagan polls 54 percent to Connally's 30 percent and Bush's 15 percent.

March 9. Saying Reagan is "still the champ," Connally quits the race for the Republican nomination.

March 11. Reagan sweeps to victory in the Alabama, Florida and Georgia primaries. Bush's last-minute drive in Florida, and token efforts in Alabama and Georgia, are not enough to keep Reagan from compiling impressive victories by margins of 70 percent to 26 percent in Alabama, 57-30 percent in Florida and 73-13 percent in Georgia.

March 15. Ford announces his decision not to enter the Republican primary race.

Dole, saying he lacks the "five M's" — money, management, manpower, media and momentum — withdraws his bid for the Republican nomination.

March 18. Native-son Anderson is easily defeated in the Illinois primary by Reagan, 48 percent to 37 percent. Bush is a distant third with 11 percent.

March 25. Reagan dominates the New York delegate primary, amassing 75 delegates to six for Bush and 35 listed as uncommitted.

Bush is victorious in Connecticut, the state where he grew up and which his father served as a U.S. senator, by defeating Reagan and Anderson in the primary. Bush receives 39 percent of the vote, to 34 percent for Reagan and 22 percent for Anderson.

Connally endorses Reagan, citing his "unprecedented" support "among middle Americans."

April 1. Reagan wins the Kansas and Wisconsin primaries and has one-third of the delegates needed for nomination, according to *The New York Times.* Reagan dominates the Kansas vote, polling 63 percent to Anderson's 18 percent and Bush's 13 percent.

In a closer race, Reagan takes Wisconsin over Bush 40 percent to 31 percent. Anderson wins 28 percent of the Wisconsin vote.

A Gallup Poll made available April 1 shows Carter's lead over Reagan fell 20 points since the end of February when a similar study was completed. The new figures show Carter in front 48 percent to 43 percent, compared with the earlier margin of 58 percent to 33 percent. With Anderson included, the results are Carter 39 percent, Reagan 34 percent and Anderson 21 percent.

April 22. Bush defeats Reagan in the Pennsylvania primary popular vote, their first one-on-one primary contest. Reagan, concentrating on the separate delegate-selection process, wins two-thirds of Pennsylvania's Republican delegates.

April 24. Rep. Anderson, conceding the Republican nomination to Reagan, withdraws from that contest and announces an independent presidential bid to offer "a choice . . . for the nation."

The attempted rescue of the American hostages held in Iran fails, leaving eight servicemen dead.

May 3. In a hard-fought contest, Reagan defeats Bush in the Texas primary, 51 percent to 47 percent. Texas is Bush's adopted home, but also a state where Reagan has always been popular, having carried the state's entire delegation against President Ford in the 1976 Republican presidential primary.

Reagan picks up additional strength by dominating the delegate selection in four states and Guam. Reagan gains all 28 delegates in the Arizona caucus, 16 in Minnesota and 12 in the Missouri congressional district meetings. In Oklahoma, Reagan wins 18 delegates and is assured of the other 16 to be chosen later in May at a state party convention. Guam gives Reagan its four delegates.

May 4. Illinois Gov. James R. Thompson endorses Reagan, calling him the "overwhelming choice of my party." Thompson is an important figure among Republican moderates.

May 6. Primary contests afford Reagan three more easy victories. He outpolls Bush 74 percent to 16 percent in Indiana, 67-22 percent in North Carolina and 74-18 percent in Tennessee. Bush's consolation is the District of Columbia, which he carries with 71 percent of the vote.

May 13. Maryland voters prefer Reagan over Bush by 48 percent to 41 percent in that state's Republican presidential primary. In another contest, Reagan coasts to victory in Nebraska with 78 percent of the vote.

May 20. Bush surprises Reagan by handily winning the Michigan primary, 57 percent to Reagan's 32 percent. Reagan counters by taking the Oregon vote, 54 percent to 35 percent.

According to reports by ABC and CBS News, Reagan has acquired more than the 998 delegates needed to ensure his nomination by the Republican National Convention.

May 26. George Bush ends his bid for the Republican presidential nomination, citing financial difficulties and the "perception that the campaign is over." Bush's move, technically a suspension rather than a termination, will keep alive the flow of federal funds to his indebted campaign.

May 27. Reagan sweeps to barely contested victories in the Idaho, Kentucky and Nevada primaries.

June 3. The final round of presidential primaries is anticlimactic as Reagan amasses victories in California, Montana, New Jersey, Ohio, Rhode Island, South Dakota and West Virginia.

June 23. Polls available in mid-June show Reagan edging in front of Carter for the first time. In a three-way contest, Gallup gives Reagan 36 percent, Carter 35 percent and Anderson 23 percent. A *Newsweek* poll has Reagan leading Carter 40 percent to 36 percent, with 19 percent for Anderson. The Roper organization's findings show Reagan with 34 percent, leading Carter (29 percent) and Anderson (20 percent).

July 14—17. The Republican National Convention is held in Detroit. Former President Ford sets off a wild spree of speculation by seriously flirting with the vice presidential nomination. Negotiations between the Ford and Reagan camps fail to produce an acceptable working arrangement, prompting Reagan to make an appearance prior to his acceptance of the presidential nomination to calm the convention and announce his selection of Bush as his running mate. The Republican Party emerges from the convention more unified than it has been in years.

July 30. Bill Wilkinson, leader of the Invisible Empire, Knights of the Ku Klux Klan, one of the nation's largest Klan factions, endorses Reagan for president. Though Reagan repudiates the Klan support, he is also endorsed by Don Black, grand wizard of the Knights of the Ku Klux Klan, on Sept. 2.

Aug. 11—14. The Democratic National Convention is held in New York City. Sen. Kennedy withdraws after losing a rules fight to open the convention's nominating process. This assures President Carter's renomination. After much speculation, Kennedy joins Carter and Mondale on the convention platform in a strained show of party unity.

Sept. 1. Reagan officially kicks off his presidential campaign with a speech in Jersey City, N.J. Carter is in Tuscumbia, Ala.

Sept. 4. The Federal Election Commission rules that independent candidate John B. Anderson will be eligible for retroactive federal campaign funds if he receives more than 5 percent of the vote in the general election.

Sept. 21. Reagan and Anderson participate in a nationally televised debate sponsored by the U.S. League of Women Voters in Baltimore. Carter refuses to participate in a three-way debate, wanting instead to meet Reagan one-on-one. Reagan insists on including Anderson in any debate. The league determines that Anderson may participate in the debate only if he maintains a 15 percent standing in the national polls.

Sept. 28. Polls taken before and after the debate by *The New York Times*/CBS News show Reagan reversing a 40-to-36 percent deficit to take a 40-to-35 percent lead over Carter. Anderson is supported by 9 percent of the voters. An ABC News/Harris Survey released Sept. 23 indicates that 60 percent of the respondents think Carter's refusal to participate in the debate is wrong.

Oct. 16. Black civil rights leaders the Rev. Ralph David Abernathy and Hosea Williams endorse the Reagan/Bush ticket. According to Abernathy, "we don't need this doctor anymore, because we as the patients are getting sicker. We need to change doctors." Charles Evers, black mayor of Fayette, Miss., follows with his endorsement on Oct. 22. Former Sen. Eugene J. McCarthy, D-Minn., adds his support the following day saying among other things that Reagan "has run a more dignified campaign."

Oct. 27. Polls indicate a virtual toss-up in the presidential race. The Gallup and ABC News/Harris surveys give Carter a 45-to-42 percent lead. The Associated Press/NBC News poll has Carter ahead 42 to 36 percent while several organizations, including *Time, Newsweek* and *The New York Times*/CBS News indicate a one-point Carter margin.

Oct. 28. Reagan and Carter meet in their only debate, just six days before the election. The 1-1/2-hour event is televised nationally from the Cleveland Convention Center Music Hall. Neither candidate makes a damaging gaffe, and Reagan closes by asking, "Are you better off than you were four years ago?"

Nov. 4. Ronald Reagan is elected the 40th president of the United States in a landslide victory. Reagan carries 44 states with 489 electoral votes to Carter's six states and the District of Columbia with 49 electoral votes. The popular vote margin is 43,901,812 or 50.7 percent for Reagan and 35,483,820 or 41 percent for Carter. Carter's concession at 9:50 p.m. (EST) is the earliest since Alton D. Parker bowed to Theodore Roosevelt in 1904. There is some speculation that the early concession, coupled with the 8:15 p.m. (EST) prediction by NBC News of Reagan's win, cuts into Democratic votes in state and local races in the West where polls are still open. The massive shift away from Carter, undetected by any published poll in the last few days of the race, is attributed to the lingering hostage crisis and the state of the economy. *(See box, p. 85, for earlier results.)*

Nov. 11. In his first news conference as president-elect, Reagan says he is "not going to intrude" on the waning Carter administration.

Nov. 14. Reagan fills two key White House staff positions, naming Edwin Meese III as counselor to the president and James A. Baker III as White House chief of staff.

Nov. 17. Reagan arrives in Washington, D.C., for a series of meetings with transition, government and labor leaders. The president-elect generally is lauded for his efforts and is joined by Bush on Nov. 18.

Nov. 20. With his wife Nancy, Reagan visits the White House for his first meeting with Carter since the debate. Reagan terms the 90-minute meeting a "very enjoyable, very productive hour or so." Later, Reagan meets with West German Chancellor Helmut Schmidt. Reagan leaves for Los Angeles on Nov. 21.

Dec. 11. Eight Cabinet-level appointments are announced, pending Senate confirmation. They are: Donald T. Regan as secretary of the Treasury, Caspar W. Weinberger as secretary of defense, Malcolm Baldrige as secretary of commerce, Rep. Dave A. Stockman, R-Mich, as director of the Office of Management and Budget, former Sen. Richard S. Schweiker, R-Pa., as secretary of health and human services, Andrew L. "Drew" Lewis Jr. as secretary of transportation, William French Smith as attorney general and William J. Casey as director of Central Intelligence.

Dec. 16. Retired Gen. Alexander M. Haig Jr. is nominated secretary of state and Raymond J. Donovan secretary of labor.

Dec. 22. Five more Cabinet officers are named: Samuel R. Pierce Jr. as secretary of housing and urban development, Jeane J. Kirkpatrick as United Nations ambassador, James G. Watt as secretary of the interior, former Gov.

James B. Edwards, R-S.C., as secretary of energy and John R. Block as secretary of agriculture.

1981

Jan. 6. A joint session of Congress officially counts and certifies the votes of the Electoral College. The results give Reagan 489 votes to Carter's 49.

Jan. 7. The nomination of Terrel H. Bell to head the Department of Education is announced.

Jan. 16. William E. Brock III is named to the Cabinet-level position of U.S. trade representative.

Jan. 20. Ronald Wilson Reagan is sworn in as the 40th president of the United States at noon (EST). For the first time the ceremonies are held on the West Front of the U.S. Capitol. The president stresses economic themes in his inaugural address.

The 52 American hostages leave Iran bound for Algiers after 444 days of captivity and less than one hour after the end of Jimmy Carter's presidency.

Reagan on the Issues: 1979-81

The following are excerpts from Ronald Reagan's statements on various issues made during the primary and general election campaigns, as well as during the first month of his administration. The excerpts were compiled from Reagan's candidacy announcement, his debates with Jimmy Carter and John B. Anderson, and assorted statements and interviews given during this period. Spelling, punctuation and capitalization of the original quoted material have been retained.

Domestic Policy

Abortion

Interview, Boston Globe, *Jan. 13, 1980:*

I talked to people in the medical profession. I talked to those in religious circles. I talked to lawyers and I, finally, my own study and research came to the conclusion that interrupting a pregnancy is the taking of a human life. Now I also recognize that we, in our Judea-Christian tradition, have permitted that in self defense. Therefore, I recognize the right of a mother to protect her life against even that of her own unborn child if its necessary to save her life.

Debate with Anderson, Sept. 21, 1980

With regard to the freedom of the individual for choice with regard to abortion, there's one individual who's not being considered at all. That's the one who's being aborted. And I've noticed that everybody that is for abortion has already been born. I think that technically, I know this is a difficult and an emotional problem and many people sincerely feel on both sides of this, but I do believe that maybe we could find the answer, through medical evidence, if we would determine once and for all, is an unborn child a human being? I happen to believe it is.

Budget Cuts

News Conference, Jan. 29, 1981:

They'll be made every place. What we meant by — maybe across-the-board was the wrong decision although it describes it. What I meant was that no one is exempt from being looked at for areas in which we can make cuts in spending. And yes, they probably are going to be bigger than anyone has ever attempted because this administration did not come here to be a caretaker government and just hope we could go along the same way and maybe do it a little better. We think the time has come where there

has to be a change of direction of this country and it's going to begin with reducing government spending.

Economic Address, Feb. 18, 1981:

It is important to note that we are only reducing the rate of increase in taxing and spending. We are not attempting to cut either spending or taxing levels below that which we presently have. This plan will get our economy moving again, increase productivity growth, and thus create the jobs our people must have.

And I am asking that you join me in reducing direct Federal spending by $41.4 billion in fiscal year 1982, along with another $7.7 billion in user fees and off-budget savings for a total savings of $49.1 billion.

This will still allow an increase of $40.8 billion over 1981 spending.

I know that exaggerated and inaccurate stories about these cuts have disturbed many people, particularly those dependent on grant and benefit programs for their basic needs.... We will continue to fulfill the obligations that spring from our national conscience.

Chrysler

Interview, U.S. News & World Report, *Jan. 19, 1981:*

This is something I have to look into, not only for Chrysler but for the whole automobile industry. I want to determine how much of the trouble that industry is in has been due to government intervention. I'm not one who wants to see us get into a situation where we automatically bail out businesses that fail. Many of them may fail because of their own management problems.

There is a reason to believe that government mandates have had something to do with troubles in the auto industry. If so, government has two responsibilities: The first is to bail out or help bail out a company that's suffered because of that. The second is to do away with the mandates and the regulations that cause the trouble in the first place.

Cities

Debate with Anderson, Sept. 21, 1980:

The mayors that I've talked to in some of our leading cities tell me that the federal grants that come for a specific cause or a specific objective come with such red tape, such priorities established by a bureaucracy in Washington, that the local governments' hands are tied with regard to using that money as they feel it could best be used and for what they think might be the top priority.

If they had that money without those government restrictions, everyone of them has told me they could make great savings and make far greater use of the money.

Debate With Carter, Oct. 29, 1980:

I have been talking to a number of Congressmen who have much the same idea that I have. And that is that in the inner-city areas, that in cooperation with local government and with national government and using tax incentives and with cooperation with the private sector, that we have development zones. Let the local entity, the city, declare this particular area based on the standards of the percentage of people on welfare, unemployed and so forth in that area. And then, through tax incentives, induce the creation of business providing jobs and so forth in those areas. The elements of government, through these tax incentives, for example, a business that would not have for a period of time an increase in the property tax reflecting its development of the unused property that it was making, wouldn't be any loss to the city, because the city isn't getting any tax from that now. And there would simply be a delay and on the other hand many of the people that would then be given jobs are presently wards of the government and it wouldn't hurt to give them a tax incentive because that wouldn't be costing government either.

Church and State

Debate With Anderson, Sept. 21, 1980:

Well, whether I agree or disagree with some individual, or what he may say or how he may say it, I don't think there's any way that we can suggest that because people believe in God and go to church that they should not want reflected in those people and those causes that they support their own belief in morality and in the high traditions and standards that we've abandoned so much in this country.

Going around this country I think that I have felt a great hunger in America for a spiritual revival, for a belief that a law must be based on a higher law for a return to traditions and values that we once had....

Civil Rights

Debate With Carter, Oct. 29, 1980:

I believe in it. I am eternally optimistic. And I happen to believe that we've made great progress from the days when I was young and when this country didn't even know it had a racial problem.

I know those things can grow out of despair in an inner city when there's hopelessness at home, lack of work and so forth. But I believe that all of us together — and I believe the Presidency is what Teddy Roosevelt said it was: It's a bully pulpit.

And I think that something can be done from there, because the goal for all of us should be that one day things will be done neither because of, nor in spite of, any of the differences between us — ethnic differences or racial differences, whatever they may be. That we will have total equal opportunity for all people.

News Conference, Jan. 29, 1981:

No, there will be no retreat. This administration is going to be dedicated to equality. I think we've made great progress in the civil rights field. I think there are some things, however, that have but may not be as useful as they once were, or that may even be distorted in the practice, such as some affirmative action programs becoming quota systems and I'm old enough to remember when quotas existed in the United States for the purpose of discrimination. And I don't want to see that happen again.

Draft Registration

Debate With Anderson, Sept. 21, 1980:

I, too, believe in the voluntary military. As a matter of fact, today the shortage of non-commissioned officers that John mentioned are such that if we tried to have a draft today, we wouldn't have the non-commissioned officers to train the draftees.

I believe the answer lies in first recognizing human nature and how we make everything else work in this country.... Forty-six percent of the people who enlisted in voluntary military up until

1977 said they did so for one particular reason — the GI Bill of Rights.... In 1977, we took that away from the military. That meant immediately, 46 percent of your people who were signing had no reason for signing up. So I think it is a case of pay scale....

News Conference, Jan. 29, 1981:

...I just didn't feel that the advance registration, on all the evidence we could get, would materially speed up the process if an emergency required the draft. It did create bureaucracy. It caused, certainly, some unrest and dissatisfaction, and we were told that it would only be a matter of several days if we had to call up a draft that we could do that several days earlier with the registration than we would be able if there was no registration at all.

This is one that's something to be looked at further down. I've only been here nine days....

Economic Policy

Announcement of Candidacy, Nov. 13, 1979:

The people have not created this disaster in our economy; the federal government has. It has overspent, overestimated, and over-regulated. It has failed to deliver services within the revenues it should be allowed to raise from taxes. In the thirty-four years since the end of World War II, it has spent 448 billion dollars more than it has collected in taxes — 448 billion dollars of printing-press money, which has made every dollar you earn worth less and less. At the same time, the federal government has cynically told us that high taxes on business will in some way "solve" the problem and allow the average taxpayer to pay less. Well, business is not a taxpayer; it is a tax collector. Business has to pass its tax burden on to the customer as part of the cost of doing business. You and I pay the taxes imposed on business every time we go to the store. Only people pay taxes and it is political demagoguery or economic illiteracy to try and tell us otherwise.

The key to restoring the health of the economy lies in cutting taxes. At the same time, we need to get the waste out of federal spending. This does not mean sacrificing essential services....

By reducing federal tax rates where they discourage individual initiative — especially personal income tax rates — we can restore incentives, invite greater economic growth and at the same time help give us better government instead of bigger government. Proposals such as the Kemp-Roth bill would bring about this kind of realistic reductions in tax rates.

Economic Address, Feb. 18, 1981:

...I am proposing a comprehensive four-point program.... This plan is aimed at reducing the growth in Government spending and taxing, reforming and eliminating regulations which are unnecessary and unproductive or counterproductive, and encouraging a consistent monetary policy aimed at maintaining the value of the currency.

Energy

Announcement of Candidacy, Nov. 13, 1979:

Solving the energy crisis will not be easy, but it can be done. First we must decide that "less" is not enough. Next, we must remove government obstacles to energy production. And, we must make use of those technological advantages we still possess.

It is no program simply to say "use less energy." Of course waste must be eliminated and efficiency promoted, but for the government simply to tell the people to conserve is not an energy policy. At best it means we will run out of energy a little more slowly. But a day will come when the lights will dim and the wheels of industry will turn more slowly and finally stop. As President I will not endorse any course which has this as its principal objective.

Debate With Carter, Oct. 29, 1980:

I'm not so sure that it means steadily higher fuel costs, but I do believe that this nation has been portrayed for too long a time to the people as being energy poor when it is energy rich....

With our modern technolgy, yes we can burn our coal within the limits of the Clean Air Act. I think as technology improves, we'll be able to do even better with that.

The other thing is that we have only leased out and begun to explore 2 percent of our outer continental shelf for oil, where it is believed by everyone familiar with that fuel and that source of energy, that there are vast supplies yet to be found. Our government has, in the last year or so, taken out of multiple use millions of acres of public land that once were, while they were public lands, subject to multiple use exploration for minerals, and so forth. It is believed that probably 70 percent of the potential oil in the United States is probably hidden in those lands. And no one is allowed to even go and explore to find out if it is there. This is particularly true of the recent efforts to shut down part of Alaska.

Nuclear power — there were 36 power plants planned in this country. And let me add the word safety: It must be done with the utmost of safety. But 32 of those have given up and canceled their plans to build and, again, because Government regulations and permits and so forth — make it take — more than twice as long to build a nuclear plant in the United States as it does to build one in Japan or in Western Europe.

We have the sources here. We are energy rich. And coal is one of the great potentials we have.

Announcement, Jan. 28, 1981:

I am ordering — effective immediately — the elimination of remaining Federal controls on U.S. oil production and marketing.

For more than nine years, restrictive price controls have held U.S. oil production below its potential, artificially boosted energy consumption, aggravated our balance of payments problems and stifled technological breakthroughs. Price controls have also made us more energy-dependent on the OPEC nations — a development that has jeopardized our economic security and undermined price stability at home....

This step will also stimulate energy conservation. At the same time, the elimination of price controls will end the entitlements system, which has been, in reality, a subsidy for the importation of foreign oil.

Federalism

Announcement of Candidacy, Nov. 13, 1979:

The 10th article of the Bill of Rights is explicit in pointing out that the federal government should do only those things specifically called for in the Constitution. All others shall remain with states or the people. We haven't been observing that 10th article of late. The federal government has taken on functions it was never intended to perform and which it does not perform well. There should be a planned, orderly transfer of such functions to states and communities and a transfer with them of the sources of taxation to pay for them.

Inflation

Interview, Detroit News, Jan. 13, 1980:

Well, government causes inflation. Therefore, government is the only one who can stop it. When this administration tells the people of this country they are responsible for inflation and we've got to have less people working, have unemployment, buy less, and so forth; if we're to lick inflation, that's foolishness. If inflation was the answer to unemployment, we would just double inflation and cut employment by two.

Debate With Carter, Oct. 29, 1980:

I think this idea that has been spawned here in our country that inflation somehow came upon us like a plague and therefore it's uncontrollable and no one can do anything about it, is entirely spurious and it's dangerous to say this to the people....

We don't have inflation because the people are living too well. We have inflation because the Government is living too well....

...Yes, you can lick inflation by increasing productivity and by decreasing the cost of Government to the place that we have balanced budgets and are no longer running — grinding out printing-press money, flooding the market with it because the Government is spending more than it takes in.

National Health Insurance

Interview, Detroit News, Jan. 13, 1980:

Well, I am opposed to nationalized health service. And I am opposed to it on a simple basis: Every place that they are trying it in the world today, they have found it doesn't work as well as what we have. Now I know there will always be people who cannot afford medical care, and we have always taken care of them — probably not as well as we should....

...Suppose we turn to the private health insurance industry ... and the government said ... those people who cannot afford to provide for themselves ... can choose whichever one of these is best for their purposes: Give them a tax credit (or), at least, a tax deduction (for their premiums).

Social Security

Debate With Carter, Oct. 29, 1980:

The Social Security System was based on a false premise with regard to how fast the number of workers would increase and how fast the number of retirees would increase.

It is actuarily out of balance. And this first became evident about 16 years ago. And some of us were voicing warnings then. Now it is trillions of dollars out of balance.

And the only answer that has come so far is the biggest single tax increase in our nation's history, the payroll tax increase for Social Security, which will only put a Band-Aid on this and postpone the day of reckoning by a few years at most.

What is needed is a study that I have proposed by a task force of experts to look into this entire problem as to how it can be reformed and made actuarily sound, but with the premise that no one presently dependent on Social Security is going to have the rug pulled out from under them and not get their check.

Wage and Price Controls

Interview, Detroit News, Jan. 13, 1980:

I wouldn't do it for the simple reason that they didn't work 2,000 years ago. They didn't work in ancient Babylon. They never have worked. I don't believe they are the answer to our problems. Wages and prices — and this applies to the President's voluntary guidelines — are not the cause of inflation. They are the result. No, I wouldn't use them.

News Conference, Jan. 29, 1981:

...I'm taking major steps toward the elimination of the Council on Wage and Price Stability. This council has been a failure. It has been totally ineffective in controlling inflation and it's imposed unnecessary burdens on labor and business. Therefore, I am now ending the Wage and Price program of the Council. I am eliminating a staff that carries out its wage-price activities and I'm asking Congress to rescind its budget, saving the taxpayers some $1-1/2 million a year.

Welfare

Interview, Detroit News, Jan 13, 1980:

I think one of the big things wrong with welfare today — and there is much wrong with it — (is that) if welfare were truly successful, (government) would be boasting each year of how much it has reduced the welfare rolls, how many less people there were in need of assistance. Now remember ... we're not talking about those people who are invalid and through no fault of their own cannot provide for themselves. We have always taken care of those people — and always will. We're talking about those people who are able-bodied and who, for whatever reason — it may be lack of skill or whatever — have not been able to make their way out there in the competitive world. So the idea of welfare should be to put those people back on their feet, make them self-supporting and independent.

And I believe we've got a better chance for that if we transfer welfare back to the states ... they can't possibly make those regulations in Washington to fit this whole diversified country: Montana, Mississippi, Los Angeles, New York. It won't work.

Foreign and Defense Policy

Africa

Message to the 11th African-American Conference, Jan. 11, 1981:

We believe it is important to strengthen our African ties, and we recognize that in advancing this mutual interest, American investment, trade, economic assistance and security-related support can play an important role.

China

Interview, Detroit News, *Jan. 13, 1980:*

With regard to mainland China, while it would be fine to have good relations with them, I don't think we ever should have had those relations to the extent of throwing Taiwan overboard. And I think we should always keep an eye on the mainland Chinese, because of the fact that they are Communist and right now they are in Moscow trying to repair their fences.

Interview, U.S. News & World Report, *Jan. 19, 1981:*

I've said repeatedly I believe in maintaining and developing those relations. Actually, I don't think ever since the abandonment of Taiwan and the arrangement that this administration made with the People's Republic of China — I don't think you can point to anything substantial that resulted. There wasn't any real expansion of our relationship, to speak of. And I think we paid something of a price for it.

I believe we should go forward. At the same time, I don't think that we should throw aside Taiwan, a longtime friend and ally. I don't think we have to.

Middle East

Interview, Detroit News, *Jan. 13, 1980:*

...Palestine, as a British mandate, was divided basically into Jordan and Israel. Jordan was 80 percent of Palestine. Israel was a little less than 20 percent. The Palestinians are Arabs, they speak that language. I think that they have a heritage in a number of countries and I know that the Palestinians' problem must be solved. I don't think it is a 100 percent Israeli problem. I think that if you wanted to divide it, it's 80 percent Jordan's problem.

Interview, Politics Today, *January/February 1980:*

...I don't believe this country should be imposing a settlement in the Middle East. I think we should be in the position we were in a few years ago where we agreed to help negotiate — and won the confidence of both sides.... I believe that the United States has a moral commitment, that Israel has the right to exist as a nation. And beyond that we must recognize that it is a two-way street, not just a one-way road for us. They are the last stable democracy there in the Middle East. They have the last military combat experience. They stand as a deterrent to further Soviet moves in that direction. Without them we would probably have to have military forces there. So let's recognize their contributions to our own welfare. Treat them as an ally, and make sure to consult with them.

...I draw a line between the Palestinians and the PLO — Palestinians, a million and a half refugees: and PLO, not an elected body, representing in fact only themselves, and purely terrorists. I don't understand how you ever can reconcile negotiating while you're looking down the barrel of a terrorist's gun.

Joint Interview, The New York Times *and others, Feb. 3, 1981:*

What I have called for, and what I think is needed as we refurbish our capability, is a presence in the Middle East. And I think this is something we ought to also take up with our own allies in Europe, because there would be total disaster to the European economy if there was an interference with the energy supply; they're far more dependent on it than we are....

What is meant by a presence is that we're there enough to know and for the Soviets to know that if they made a reckless move, they would be risking a confrontation with the United States.

Military Strength

Interview, Wall Street Journal, *May 6, 1980:*

The Soviet Union has opened a gap; it is a widening gap between us. We need a fast on-line deterrent that would prevent them from reaching some place here in the near future in which their margin of superiority would be great enough for them to think in terms of an ultimatum. Now I don't know what that deterrent could be. It might be a new offensive weapon that would give us apparently a second-strike capacity, which the Soviets could not afford. Many of the other weapons that we suggest, like reinstituting the B-1 bomber, might well be necessary, but I don't think we can get it on line quickly enough to fill that gap.

Interview, Boston Globe, *Jan. 13, 1980:*

...What I have said is that our defenses must be whatever is necessary to ensure that the potential enemy will never dare attack you. Now if that is equivalence or if that is superiority, you must have the degree to know that you are safe. I could see if you really strive for an obvious superiority then you may tempt the other side into being afraid and you continue escalating on both sides....

North American Accord

Announcement of Candidacy, Nov. 13, 1979:

We live on a continent whose three countries possess the assets to make it the strongest, most prosperous and self-sufficient area on earth. Within the borders of this North American continent are the food, resources, technology and undeveloped territory which, properly managed, could dramatically improve the quality of life of all its inhabitants.

It is no accident that this unmatched potential for progress and prosperity exists in three countries with such long-standing heritages of free government. A developing closeness among Canada, Mexico and the United States — a North American accord — would permit achievement of that potential in each country beyond that which I believe any of them — strong as they are — could accomplish in the absence of such cooperation. In fact, the key to our own future security may lie in both Mexico and Canada becoming much stronger countries than they are today.

Puerto Rico

Announcement of Candidacy, Nov. 13, 1979:

I favor statehood for Puerto Rico and if the people of Puerto Rico vote for statehood in their coming referendum I would, as President, initiate the enabling legislation to make this a reality.

SALT II

Interview, U.S. News & World Report, *Jan. 19, 1981:*

I've made it plain that I would enter into discussions with the Soviets regarding legitimate disarmament, but it would have to be legitimate. In any talks, there has to be linkage. I don't think we can sit there and talk about some agreement on weapons and ignore what they're doing with regard to intervening in other countries, taking over other countries. It has all got to be a part of the same package. If we're going to have good relations, then it must be based on conduct different from what they've done in the past.

News Conference, Jan. 29, 1981:

I don't think that a treaty — SALT means strategic arms limitation, but actually permits a buildup on both sides of strategic nuclear weapons — can properly [be] called that, and I have said that when we can, and I am willing for our people to go into negotiations — or let me say discussions leading to negotiations — that we should start negotiating on the basis of trying to effect an actual reduction in the numbers of nuclear weapons. That would then be real strategic arms limitations....

Interview, The New York Times *and others, Feb. 2, 1981:*

I've told the State Department that I have no timetable with regard to discussions that might lead toward future negotiations; because, as I said all through the campaign, anytime they want to sit down and discuss a legitimate reduction of nuclear weapons, I'm willing to get into such negotiations.

Soviet Union

News Conference, Jan. 29, 1981:

Well, so far détente's been a one-way street that the Soviet Union has used to pursue its own aims. I don't have to think of an answer as to what I think their intentions are. They have repeated it. I know of no leader of the Soviet Union since the revolution and including the present leadership that has not more than once repeated in the various communist congresses they hold, their determination that their goal must be the promotion of world revolution and a one world socialist or communist state, whichever word you want to use.

Now, as long as they do that and as long as they at the same time have openly and publicly declared that the only morality they recognize is what will further their cause, meaning they reserve unto themselves the right to commit any crime, to lie, to cheat, in order to attain that, and that is moral, not immoral, and we operate on a different set of standards. I think when you do business with them even as a détente, you keep that in mind.

Terrorism

Remarks, White House Ceremony Welcoming Home From Iran Former U.S. Hostages, Jan. 27, 1981:

Let terrorists be aware that when the rules of international behavior are violated, our policy will be one of swift and effective retribution. We hear it said that we live in an era of limits to our power. Well, let it also be understood there are limits to our patience.

Vietnam War

Speech, St. Paul, Minn., Jan. 25, 1980:

Now it's true Vietnam was not a war fought according to MacArthur's dictum, "There is no substitute for victory." It may also be true that Vietnam was the wrong war, in the wrong place at the wrong time. But 50,000 Americans died in Southeast Asia. They were not engaged in some racist enterprise as candidate Carter charged in 1976. And when 50,000 Americans make the ultimate sacrifice to defend the people of a small, defenseless country in Southeast Asia from Communist tyranny, that, my friends, is a collective act of moral courage, not an example of moral poverty.

War and Peace

Debate With Carter, Oct. 29, 1980:

And I'm only here to tell you that I believe with all my heart that first priority must be world peace, and that use of force is always, and only, a last resort when everything else has failed. And then only with regard to our national security.

Now I believe also that meeting this mission, this responsibilty for preserving the peace, which I believe is a responsibility peculiar to our country, that we cannot shirk our responsibility as the leader of the free world because we're the only one that can do it. And therefore, the burden of maintaining the peace falls on us. And to maintain the peace requires strength.

America has never gotten in a war because we were too strong. We can get into a war by letting events get out of hand, as they have in the last three and a half years, under the foreign policies of this administration of Mr. Carter's, until we're faced each time with a crisis. And good management in preserving the peace requires that we control the events and try to intercept before they become a crisis.

But I have seen four wars in my lifetime. I'm a father of sons, I have a grandson. I don't ever want to see another generation of young Americans bleed their lives into sandy beachheads in the Pacific or rice paddies and jungles in Asia or the muddy, bloody battlefields of Europe.

Speeches, Debate Texts

Among the more notable public speeches made by Ronald Reagan during the 1980 campaign was his address to the delegates at the Republican National Convention, accepting their nomination to the presidency. In his speech, Reagan put forth his party's plan for returning the country to economic health.

George Bush, selected by Reagan as his running mate, spoke briefly to the delegates in accepting the vice presidential nomination. Bush thanked the convention for its support and tried to placate GOP members who may have preferred a more conservative candidate. Bush then introduced Reagan. The texts of both speeches follow.

Also included in this section is the text of the nationally televised debate between Reagan and President Carter. After Reagan's landslide victory in the Nov. 4 election, polls showed that the debate had been a major factor in a massive shift of votes away from Carter in the final days of the campaign.

Reagan's inaugural address, his first speech as president, also is recorded here, as is his Feb. 18 address to Congress outlining his economic proposals.

RONALD REAGAN ACCEPTANCE SPEECH

Following is the text of the speech given at the Republican National Convention in Detroit, Mich., by Ronald Reagan, accepting his party's nomination for president, on July 17, 1980.

Mr. Chairman, Mr. Vice President-to-be, this convention, my fellow citizens of this great Nation:

With a deep awareness of the responsibility conferred by your trust, I accept your nomination for the Presidency of the United States. I do so with deep gratitude, and I think also I might interject, on behalf of all of us, our thanks to Detroit and the people of Michigan and to this city for the warm hospitality.

And I thank you for your wholehearted response to my recommendation in regard to George Bush as a candidate for Vice President.

I am very proud of our Party tonight. This convention has shown to all America a party united, with positive programs for solving the nation's problems; a party ready to build a new consensus with all those across the land who share a community of values embodied in these words: family, work, neighborhood, peace and freedom.

Now, I know that we have had a quarrel or two, but only as to the method of attaining a goal. There was no argument about the goal. As President, I will establish a liaison with the fifty Governors to encourage them to eliminate, wherever it exists, discrimination against women. I will monitor federal laws to ensure their implementation and to add statutes if they are needed.

More than anything else, I want my candidacy to unify our country, to renew the American spirit and sense of purpose. I want to carry our message to every American, regardless of party affiliation, who is a member of this community of shared values.

Never before in our history have Americans been called upon to face three grave threats to our very existence, any one of which could destroy us. We face a disintegrating economy, a weakened defense and an energy policy based on the sharing of scarcity.

Unprecedented Calamity

The major issue of this campaign is the direct political, personal and moral responsibility of Democratic Party leadership — in the White House and in the Congress — for this unprecedented calamity which has befallen us. They tell us they have done the most that humanly could be done. They say that the United States has had its day in the sun; that our nation has passed its zenith. They expect you to tell your children that the American people no longer have the will to cope with their problems; that the future will be one of sacrifice and few opportunities.

My fellow citizens, I utterly reject that view.

The American people, the most generous on earth, who created the highest standard of living, are not going to accept the notion that we can only make a better world for others by moving backwards ourselves. Those who believe we can have no business leading the nation.

I will not stand by and watch this great country destroy itself under mediocre leadership that drifts from one crisis to the next, eroding our national will and purpose. We have come together here because the American people deserve better from those to whom they entrust our nation's highest offices — we stand united in our resolve to do something about it.

Rebirth of Leadership

We need a rebirth of the American tradition of leadership at *every* level of government and in *private* life as well. The

United States of America is unique in world history because it has a genius for leaders — many leaders — on many levels. But, back in 1976, Mr. Carter said, "Trust *me*." And a lot of people did. Now, many of those people are out of work. Many have seen their savings eaten away by inflation. Many others on fixed incomes, especially the elderly, have watched helplessly as the cruel tax of inflation wasted away their purchasing power. And, today, a great many who trusted Mr. Carter wonder if we can survive the Carter policies of national defense.

"Trust me" government asks that we concentrate our hopes and dreams on one man; that we trust him to do what is best for us. Well, my view of government places trust not in one person or one party, but in those values that transcend persons and parties. The trust is where it belongs — in the people. The responsibility to live up to that trust is where *it* belongs, in their elected leaders. That kind of relationship, between the people and their elected leaders, is a special kind of compact.

Three hundred and sixty years ago, in 1620, a group of families dared to cross a mighty ocean to build a future for themselves in a new world. When they arrived at Plymouth, Massachusetts, they formed what they called a "compact," an agreement among themselves to build a community and abide by its laws.

The single act — the voluntary binding together of free people to live under the law — set the pattern for what was to come.

A century and a half later, the descendants of those people pledged their lives, their fortunes and their sacred honor to found this nation. Some forfeited their fortunes and their lives; none sacrificed honor.

Four score and seven years later, Abraham Lincoln called upon the people of all America to renew their dedication and their commitment to a government of, for and by the people.

Isn't it once again time to renew our compact of freedom; to pledge to each other all that is best in our lives; all that gives meaning to them, for the sake of this, our beloved and blessed land?

New Beginning

Together, let us make this a new beginning. Let us make a commitment to care for the needy; to teach our children the virtues handed down to us by our families; to have the courage to defend those values and virtues and the willingness to sacrifice for them.

Let us pledge to restore, in our time, the American spirit of voluntary service, of cooperation, of private and community initiative; a spirit that flows like a deep and mighty river through the history of our nation.

As your nominee, I pledge to you to restore to the federal government the capacity to do the people's work without dominating their lives. I pledge to you a government that will not only work well, but wisely; its ability to act tempered by prudence, and its willingness to do good balanced by the knowledge that government is never more dangerous than when our desire to have it help us blinds us to its great power to harm us.

The first Republican President once said, "While the people retain their virtue and their vigilance, no administration by any extreme of wickedness or folly can seriously injure the government in the short space of four years."

If Mr. Lincoln could see what has happened in the last three and a half years, he might hedge a little on that statement. But, with the virtues that are our legacy as a free people and with the vigilance that sustains liberty, we still have time to use our renewed compact to overcome the injuries that have been done to America these three and a half years.

First, we must overcome something the present administration has cooked up: a new and altogether indigestible economic stew, one part inflation, one part high unemployment, one part recession, one part runaway taxes, one part deficit spending, seasoned by an energy crisis. It's an economic stew that has turned the national stomach!

Ours are not problems of abstract economic theory. These are problems of flesh and blood; problems that cause pain and destroy the moral fiber of real people who should not suffer the further indignity of being told by the government that it is all somehow their fault. We do not have inflation because, as Mr. Carter says, we have lived too well.

The head of the government which has utterly refused to live within its means and which has, in the last few days, told us that this coming year's deficit will be $60 billion, dares to point the finger of blame at business and labor, both of which have been engaged in a losing struggle just trying to stay even.

High taxes, we are told, are somehow good for us, as if, when government spends our money it isn't inflationary, but when we spend it, it is.

Those who preside over the worst energy shortage in our history tell us to use less, so that we will run out of oil, gasoline and natural gas a little more slowly. Conservation is desirable, of course, for we must not waste energy. But conservation is not the sole answer to our energy needs.

America must get to work producing more energy. The Republican program for solving economic problems is based on growth and productivity.

Large amounts of oil and natural gas lay beneath our land and off our shores, untouched because the present administration seems to believe the American people would rather see more regulation, taxes and controls than more energy.

Coal offers great potential. So does nuclear energy produced under rigorous safety standards. It could supply electricity for thousands of industries and millions of jobs and homes. It must not be thwarted by a tiny minority opposed to economic growth which often finds friendly ears in regulatory agencies for its obstructionist campaigns.

Now, make no mistake. We will not permit the safety of our people or our environmental heritage to be jeopardized, but we are going to reaffirm that the economic prosperity of our people is a fundamental part of our environemnt.

Our problems are both acute and chronic, yet all we hear from those in positions of leadership are the same tired proposals for more government tinkering, more meddling and more control — all of which led us to this state in the first place.

Record of Carter Administration

Can anyone look at the record of this administration and say, "Well done?" Can anyone compare the state of our economy when the Carter administration took office with where we are today and say, "Keep up the good work?" Can anyone look at our reduced standing in the world today and say, "Let's have four more years of this?"

I believe the American people are going to answer these questions as you answered them in the first week of this November and their answer will be: "No — we have had enough!" And, then it will be up to us beginning next January 20th to offer an administration and Congressional leadership of competence and more than a little courage.

We must have the clarity of vision to see the difference between what is essential and what is merely desirable; and then the courage to bring our government back under control.

It is essential that we maintain both the forward momentum of economic growth and the strength of the safety net beneath those in society who need help. We also believe it is essential that the integrity of all aspects of Social Security be preserved.

Beyond these essentials, I believe it is clear our federal government is overgrown and overweight. Indeed, it is time for our government to go on a diet. Therefore, my first act as Chief Executive will be to impose an immediate and thorough freeze on federal hiring.

Then, we are going to enlist the very best minds from business, labor and whatever quarter to conduct a detailed review of every department, bureau and agency that lives by federal appropriation. We are going to enlist the help and ideas of many dedicated and hard-working government employees at all levels who want a more efficient government just as much as the rest of us do. I know that many are demoralized by the confusion and waste they confront in their world as a result of failed and failing policies.

Our instructions to the groups we enlist will be simple and direct. We will remind them that government programs exist at the sufferance of the American taxpayer and are paid for with money earned by working men and women. Any programs that represent a waste of their money — a theft from their pocketbooks — must have that waste eliminated or that program must go. It must be by Executive Order where possible, by Congressional action where necessary. Everything that can be run more effectively by state and local government we shall turn over to state and local government, along with the funding sources to pay for it. We are going to put an end to the money merry-go-round where our money becomes Washington's money, to be spent by the states and cities exactly the way the federal bureaucrats tell them to.

I will not accept the excuse that the federal government has grown so big and powerful that it is beyond the control of any President, any administration or Congress. We are going to put an end to the notion that the American taxpayer exists to fund the federal government. The federal government exists to serve the American people. On January 20th, we are going to reestablish that truth.

Work and Family

Also on that date we are going to initiate action to get substantial relief for our taxpaying citizens and action to put people back to work. None of this will be based on any new form of monetary tinkering or fiscal sleight-of-hand. We will simply apply to government the common sense we all use in our daily lives.

Work and family are at the center of our lives, the foundation of our dignity as a free people. When we deprive people of what they have earned, or take away their jobs, we destroy their dignity and undermine their families. We can't support our families unless there are jobs; and we can't have jobs unless people have both money to invest and the faith to invest it.

These are concepts that stem from an economic system that for more than 200 years has helped us master a continent, create a previously undreamed-of prosperity for our people and has fed millions of others around the globe. That system will continue to serve us in the future if our government will stop ignoring the basic values on which it was built and stop betraying the trust and goodwill of the American workers who keep it going.

The American people are carrying the heaviest peacetime tax burden in our nation's history — and it will grow even heavier, under present law, next January. We are taxing ourselves into economic exhaustion and stagnation, crushing our ability and incentive to save, invest and produce.

This must stop! We must halt this fiscal self-destruction and restore sanity to our economic system. I have long advocated a 30 percent reduction in income tax rates over a period of three years. This phased tax reduction would begin with a 10 percent "down payment" tax cut in 1981, which the Republicans in Congress and I have already proposed. A phased reduction of tax rates would go a long way toward easing the heavy burden on the American people. But, we should not stop there.

Within the context of economic conditions and appropriate budget priorities during each fiscal year of my Presidency, I would strive to go further. This would include improvement in business depreciation taxes so we can stimulate investment in order to get plants and equipment replaced, put more Americans back to work and put our nation back on the road to being competitive in world commerce. We will also work to reduce the cost of government as a percentage of our Gross National Product.

The first task of national leadership is to set realistic and honest priorities in our policies and our budget, and I pledge that my administration will do that.

When I talk of tax cuts, I am reminded that every major tax cut in this century has strengthened the economy, generated renewed productivity and ended up yielding new revenues for the government by creating new investment, new jobs and more commerce among our people.

The present administration has been forced by us Republicans to play follow-the-leader with regard to a tax cut. But, in this election year we must take with the proverbial "grain of salt" any tax cut proposed by those who have already given us the greatest single tax increase in our nation's history.

When those in leadership give us tax increases and tell us

we must also do with less, have they thought about those who have always had less — especially the minorities? This is like telling them that just as they step on that first rung of the ladder of opportunity, the ladder is being pulled up from under them. That may be the Democratic leadership's message to the minorities, but it won't be ours.

Ours will be: we have to move ahead, but we are not going to leave *anyone* behind.

Thanks to the economic policies of the Democratic Party, millions of Americans find themselves out of work. Millions more have never even had a fair chance to learn new skills, hold a decent job, or secure for themselves and their families a share in the prosperity of this nation.

It is time to put America back to work, to make our cities and towns resound with the confident voices of men and women of all races, nationalities and faiths bringing home to their families a paycheck they can cash for honest money.

For those without skills, we will find a way to help them get new skills.

For those without job opportunities, we will stimulate new opportunities, particularly in the inner cities where they live.

For those who have abandoned hope, we will restore hope and we will welcome them into a great national crusade to make America great again.

Foreign Affairs

When we move from domestic affairs and cast our eyes abroad, we see an equally sorry chapter on the record of the present administration.

—A Soviet combat brigade trains in Cuba, just 90 miles from our shores.

—A Soviet army of invasion occupies Afghanistan, further threatening our vital interests in the Middle East.

—America's defense strength is at its lowest ebb in a generation, while the Soviet Union is vastly outspending us in both strategic and conventional arms.

—Our European allies, looking nervously at the growing menace from the East, turn to us for leadership and fail to find it.

—And, incredibly, more than 50 . . . of our fellow Americans have been held captive for over eight months by a dictatorial foreign power that holds us up to ridicule before the world.

Adversaries large and small test our will and seek to confound our resolve, but we are given weakness when we need strength; vacillation when the times demand firmness.

The Carter administration lives in the world of make-believe. Every day it dreams up a response to that day's troubles, regardless of what happened yesterday and what will happen tomorrow. But you and I live in a real world where disasters are overtaking our nation without any real response from Washington.

I condemn this make-believe, its self-deceit and, above all, its transparent hypocrisy.

For example, Mr. Carter says he supports the volunteer army, but he lets military pay and benefits slip so low that many of our enlisted personnel are actually eligible for food stamps. Reenlistment rates drop and just recently, after he fought all week against a proposed pay increase for men and women in the military, he then helicoptered out to the carrier, the *U.S.S. Nimitz,* which was returning from long months of duty in the Indian Ocean, and told the crew of that ship that he advocated better pay for them and their comrades! Where does he stand now that he is back on shore?

I will tell you where *I* stand. I do not favor a peacetime draft or registration, but I do favor pay and benefit levels that will attract and keep highly motivated men and women in our volunteer forces and an active reserve trained and ready for an instant call in case of an emergency.

You know, there may be a sailor at the helm of the ship of state, but the ship has no rudder. Critical decisions are made at times almost in comic fashion, but who can laugh? Who was not embarrassed when the administration handed a major propaganda victory in the United Nations to the enemies of Israel, our staunch Middle East allies [sic] for three decades, and then claimed that the American vote was a "mistake," the result of a "failure of communication" between the President, his Secretary of State and his U.N. Ambassador?

Who does not feel a growing sense of unease as our allies, facing repeated instances of an amateurish and confused administration, reluctantly conclude that America is unwilling or unable to fulfill its obligation as leader of the free world?

Who does not feel rising alarm when the question in any discussion of foreign policy is no longer, "Should we do something?", but "Do we have the capacity to do anything?"

Four More Years of Weakness

The administration which has brought us to this state is seeking your endorsement for four more years of weakness, indecision, mediocrity and incompetence. No American should vote until he or she has asked, is the United States stronger and more respected now than it was three and a half years ago? Is the world today a safer place in which to live?

It is the responsibility of the President of the United States, in working for peace, to ensure that the safety of our people cannot successfully be threatened by a hostile foreign power. As President, fulfilling that responsibility will be my number one priority.

We are not a warlike people. Quite the opposite. We always seek to live in peace. We resort to force infrequently and with great reluctance — and only after we have determined that it is absolutely necessary. We are awed, and rightly so, by the forces of destruction at loose in the world in this nuclear era. But neither can we be naive or foolish. Four times in my lifetime America has gone to war, bleeding the lives of its young men into the sands of beachheads, the fields of Europe and the jungles and rice paddies of Asia. We know only too well that war comes not when the forces of freedom are strong. It is when they are weak that tyrants are tempted.

We simply cannot learn these lessons the hard way again without risking our destruction.

Of all the objectives we seek, first and foremost is the establishment of lasting world peace. We must always stand ready to negotiate in good faith, ready to pursue any reasonable avenue that holds forth the promise of lessening tensions and furthering the prospects of peace. But let our friends and those who may wish us ill take note: the United States has an obligation to its citizens and to the people of the world never to let those who would destroy freedom dictate the future course of human life on this planet. I would regard my election as proof that we have renewed our resolve to preserve world peace and freedom. This nation will once again be strong enough to do that.

This evening marks the last step, save one, of a campaign that has taken Nancy and me from one end of this great land to the other, over many months and thousands of miles. There are those who question the way we choose a President; who say that our process imposes difficult and exhausting burdens on those who seek the office. I have not found it so.

It is impossible to capture in words the splendor of this vast continent which God has granted as our portion of his creation. There are no words to express the extraordinary strength and character of this breed of people we call Americans.

Everywhere we have met thousands of Democrats, Independents and Republicans who come from all economic conditions, all walks of life, bound together in that community of shared values of family, work, neighborhood, peace and freedom. They are concerned, yes, but they are not frightened. They are disturbed, but not dismayed. They are the kind of men and women Tom Paine had in mind when he wrote — during the darkest days of the American Revolution — "We have it in our power to begin the world over again."

Nearly 150 years after Tom Paine wrote those words, an American President told the generation of the Great Depression that it had a "rendezvous with destiny." I believe this generation of Americans today has a rendezvous with destiny.

Tonight, let us dedicate ourselves to renewing the American compact. I ask you not simply to "Trust me," but to trust your values — our values — and to hold me responsible for living up to them. I ask you to trust that American spirit which knows no ethnic, religious, social, political, regional or economic boundaries; the spirit that burned with zeal in the hearts of millions of immigrants from every corner of the earth who came here in search of freedom.

Some say that spirit no longer exists. But I have seen it — I have felt it — all across the land; in the big cities, the small towns and in rural America. It is still there, ready to blaze into life if you and I are willing to do what has to be done. We have to do the practical things, the down-to-earth things such as creating policies that will stimulate our economy, increase productivity and put America back to work.

The Time Is Now

The time is *now* to limit federal spending; to insist on a stable monetary reform and to free ourselves from imported oil.

The time is *now* to resolve that the basis of a firm and principled foreign policy is one that takes the world as it is and seeks to change it by leadership and example; not by harangue, harassment or wishful thinking.

The time is *now* to say that while we shall seek new friendships and expand and improve others, we shall not do so by breaking our word or casting aside old friends and allies.

And, the time is *now* to redeem promises once made to the American people by another candidate, in another time and another place.

He said, "...For three long years I have been going up and down this country preaching that government — federal, state and local — costs too much. I shall not stop that preaching. As an immediate program of action, we must abolish useless offices. We must eliminate unnecessary functions of government....

"...we must consolidate subdivisions of government and, like the private citizen, give up luxuries which we can no longer afford."

And then he said, "I propose to you, my friends, and through you that government of all kinds, big and little, be made solvent and that the example be set by the President of the United States and his Cabinet."

Those were Franklin Delano Roosevelt's words as he accepted the nomination for President in 1932.

The time is *now*, my fellow Americans, to recapture our destiny, to take it into our own hands. To do this it will take many of us working together. I ask you tonight all over this land to volunteer your help in this cause so that we can carry our message throughout the land.

Isn't it time that we, the people, carried out these unkept promises? That we pledge to each other and to all America on this July day 48 years later, we intend to do just that!

I have thought of something that is not part of my speech, and I worry over whether I should do it. Can we doubt that only a Divine Providence placed this land, this island of freedom, here as a refuge for all those people in the world who yearn to breathe free — Jews and Christians enduring persecution behind the Iron Curtain, the boat people of Southeast Asia, of Cuba and of Haiti, the victims of drought and famine in Africa, the Freedom Fighters of Afghanistan, and our own countrymen held in savage captivity.

I will confess that I have been a little afraid to suggest what I am going to suggest. I am more afraid not to.

Can we begin our crusade joined together in a moment of silent prayer.

God bless America.

GEORGE BUSH ACCEPTANCE SPEECH

Following is the speech given by George Herbert Walker Bush as he accepted the Republican Party's nomi-

nation for vice president on July 17, 1980, at the Republican National Convention held in Detroit.

Thank you very much ladies and gentlemen. Mr. Chairman, my fellow Republicans and fellow Americans, let me express my heartfelt thanks for the honor you have given me; the opportunity to run on our party's national ticket with a great leader like Ronald Reagan. On behalf of Barbara and the rest of the Bush family, all I can say is that we are overwhelmed and grateful for your expression of confidence.

With a deep sense of commitment, I accept your nomination to serve as our party's candidate for Vice President on a ticket headed by the leader of our party and the next President of the United States, Ronald Reagan. I accept.

I enthusiastically support our platform. I pledge to you my total dedication and energies in a united effort to see to it that next January 20th, Ronald Reagan becomes our Nation's 40th President and that a great new era will begin for America in the decade of these '80's. We need change.

Because of Ronald Reagan's leadership, we Republicans emerge from this convention as a strong, united party rededicated to the principles that made our country great. There has been a spirit of victory in the air this past week in Detroit but if that spirit is to be translated into reality, it is up to each and every one of us to help carry Ronald Reagan's message of a strong, free America the length and the breadth of this land.

Let there be no mistake, though. Jimmy Carter, though he may in the past four years been a failed President, he is a formidable campaigner who can be expected to use the power of his office to suit his own political ends. And so, my fellow Republicans, I say to you, let's forget the pollsters and forget the pundits and remember only that political victories are hard; dedicated things come about only by tough work and that in this crucial election year, the stakes for America and the free world are too great to allow ourselves to become complacent.

We have a great mission not unlike that great mission undertaken by our party 28 summers ago, when another great Republican leader, Dwight Eisenhower, began his campaign to restore the faith of the American people in their government. Dwight Eisenhower, a man of decency, compassion and strength, led America three decades ago into a new era of peace and prosperity. And so, Ronald Reagan, a man of decency, compassion and strength, will lead America into a new era of greatness in this decade of the 1980's. This is the mission, the great mission, all of us working together, joined by millions of disillusioned Democrats and disappointed Independents, must undertake in the campaign ahead.

My fellow Republicans, this is Ronald Reagan's night. He is the man whom you and the American people are waiting to hear. Let me then conclude these words of acceptance by paraphrasing what I told this convention last evening, just moments before you nominated our party's standard-bearer for the presidency.

I said and I repeat tonight, let us, united in spirit and purpose, go forward from this convention city to make 1980 one of victory not only for Ronald Reagan and our party, but for the United States of America and the cause of freedom throughout the world.

CARTER-REAGAN PRESIDENTIAL DEBATE

Following is the official League of Women Voters Education Fund transcript of the debate between presidential candidates Jimmy Carter and Ronald Reagan. The debate was held in Cleveland, Ohio, on Oct. 28, 1980. The journalists on the panel were Marvin Stone, editor of U.S.

News & World Report; Harry Ellis of The Christian Science Monitor; William Hilliard, assistant managing editor of The Oregonian [Portland]; and Barbara Walters of ABC News. The moderator was Howard K. Smith, also of ABC News. Ruth Hinerfeld of the League of Women Voters Education Fund introduced the debate.

Hinerfeld: Good evening. I'm Ruth Hinerfeld of the League of Women Voters Education Fund. Next Tuesday is Election Day. Before going to the polls, voters want to understand the issues and know the candidates' positions. Tonight, voters will have an opportunity to see and hear the major party candidates for the Presidency state their views on issues that affect us all. The League of Women Voters is proud to present this Presidential Debate. Our moderator is Howard K. Smith.

Smith: Thank you, Mrs. Hinerfeld. The League of Women Voters is pleased to welcome to the Cleveland Ohio Convention Center Music Hall President Jimmy Carter, the Democratic Party's candidate for reelection to the Presidency, and Governor Ronald Reagan of California, the Republican Party's candidate for the Presidency. The candidates will debate questions on domestic, economic, foreign policy, and national security issues.

The questions are going to be posed by a panel of distinguished journalists who are here with me. They are: Marvin Stone, the editor of *U.S. News & World Report*; Harry Ellis, national correspondent of the *Christian Science Monitor*; William Hilliard, assistant managing editor of the *Portland Oregonian*; Barbara Walters, correspondent, ABC News.

The ground rules for this, as agreed by you gentlemen, are these: Each panelist down here will ask a question, the same question, to each of the two candidates. After the two candidates have answered, a panelist will ask follow-up questions to try to sharpen the answers. The candidates will then have an opportunity each to make a rebuttal. That will constitute the first half of the debate, and I will state the rules for the second half later on.

Some other rules: The candidates are not permitted to bring prepared notes to the podium, but are permitted to make notes during the debate. If the candidates exceed the allotted time agreed on, I will reluctantly but certainly interrupt. We ask the Convention Center audience here to abide by one ground rule. Please do not applaud or express approval or disapproval during the debate.

Now, based on the toss of the coin, Governor Reagan will respond to the first question from Marvin Stone.

Use of Military Power

Stone: Governor, as you're well aware, the question of war and peace has emerged as a central issue in this campaign in the give and take of recent weeks. President Carter has been criticized for responding late to aggressive Soviet impulses, for insufficient build-up of our armed forces, and a paralysis in dealing with Afghanistan and Iran. You have been criticized for being all too quick to advocate the use of lots of muscle — military action — to deal with foreign crises. Specifically, what are the differences between the two of you on the uses of American military power?

Reagan: I don't know what the differences might be, because I don't know what Mr. Carter's policies are. I do know what he has said about mine. And I'm only here to tell you that I believe with all my heart that our first priority must be world peace, and that use of force is always and only a last resort, when everything else has failed, and then only with regard to our national security.

Now, I believe, also, that this meeting . . . this mission, this responsibility for preserving the peace, which I believe is a responsibility peculiar to our country, and that we cannot shirk our responsibility as a leader of the Free World because we're the only ones that can do it. Therefore, the burden of maintaining the peace falls on us. And to maintain that peace requires strength. America has never gotten in a war because we were too strong. We can get into a war by letting events get out of hand, as they have in the last three and a half years under the foreign policies of this Administration of Mr. Carter's, until we're faced each time with a crisis. And good management in preserving the peace requires that we control the events and try to intercept before they become a crisis.

I have seen four wars in my lifetime. I'm a father of sons; I have a grandson. I don't ever want to see another generation of young Americans bleed their lives into sandy beachheads in the Pacific, or rice paddies and jungles in the . . . in Asia or the muddy battlefields of Europe.

Smith: Mr. Stone, do you have a follow-up question for the Governor?

Stone: Yes. Governor, we've been hearing that the defense build-up that you would associate yourself with would cost tens of billions of dollars more than is now contemplated. Assuming that the American people are ready to bear this cost, they nevertheless keep asking the following question: How do you reconcile huge increases in military outlays with your promise of substantial tax cuts and of balancing the budget, which in this fiscal year, the one that just ended, ran more than $60 billion in the red?

Reagan: Mr. Stone, I have submitted an economic plan that I have worked out in concert with a number of fine economists in this country, all of whom approve it, and believe that over a five year projection, this plan can permit the extra spending for needed refurbishing of our defensive posture, that it can provide for a balanced budget by 1983 if not earlier, and that we can afford — along with the cuts that I have proposed in Government spending — we can afford the tax cuts I have proposed and probably mainly because Mr. Carter's economic policy has built into the next five years, and on beyond that, a tax increase that will be taking $86 billion more out of the people's pockets than was taken this year. And my tax cut does not come close to eliminating that $86 billion increase. I'm only reducing the amount of the increase. In other words, what I'm talking about is not putting government back to getting less money than government's been getting, but simply cutting the increase in . . . in spending.

Smith: The same question now goes to President Carter. President Carter, would you like to have the question repeated?

Stone: Yes, President Carter, the question of war and peace, a central issue in this campaign. You've been criticized for, in the give and take, for responding late to aggressive Soviet impulses, for an insufficient build-up of our armed forces, and a paralysis in dealing with Afghanistan and Iran. Governor Reagan, on the other hand, has been criticized for being all too quick to advocate the use of lots of muscle — military action — to deal with foreign crises such as I have mentioned. Specifically, what are the differences between the two of you on the uses of American military power?

Carter: Mr. Stone, I've had to make thousands of decisions since I've been President, serving in the Oval Office. And with each one of those decisions that affect the future of my country, I have learned in the process. I think I'm a much wiser and more experienced man than I was when I debated four years ago against President Ford. I've also learned that there are no simple answers to complicated questions. H. L. Mencken said that for every problem there's a simple answer. It would be neat and plausible and wrong.

The fact is that this nation, in the eight years before I became President, had its own military strength decreased. Seven out of eight years, the budget commitments for defense went down, 37% in all. Since I've been in office, we've had a steady, carefully planned, methodical but very effective increase in our commitment for defense.

But what we've done is use that enormous power and prestige and military strength of the United States to preserve the peace. We've not only kept peace for our own country, but we've been able to extend the benefits of peace to others. In the Middle East, we've worked for a peace treaty between Israel and Egypt, successfully, and have tied ourselves together with Israel and Egypt in a common defense capability. This is a very good step forward for our nation's security, and we'll continue to do as we have done in the past.

I might also add that there are decisions that are made in the Oval Office by every President which are profound in nature. There are always trouble spots in the world, and how those troubled areas are addressed by a President alone in that Oval Office affects our nation directly, the involvement of the United States and also our American interests. That is a basic decision that has to be made so frequently, by every President who serves. That is what I have tried to do successfully by keeping our country at peace.

Smith: Mr. Stone, do you have a follow-up for. . . ?

Stone: Yes. I would like to be a little more specific on the use of military power, and let's talk about one area for a moment. Under what circumstances would you use military forces to deal with, for example, a shut-off of the Persian Oil Gulf [*sic*], if that should occur, or to counter Russian expansion beyond Afghanistan into either Iran or Pakistan? I ask this question in view of charges that we are woefully unprepared to project sustained — and I emphasize the word sustained — power in that part of the world.

Carter: Mr. Stone, in my State of the Union address earlier this year, I pointed out that any threat to the stability or security of the Persian Gulf would be a threat to the security of our own country. In the past, we have not had an adequate military presence in that region. Now we have two major carrier task forces. We have access to facilities in five different areas of that region. And we've made it clear that working with our allies and others, that we are prepared to address any foreseeable eventuality which might interrupt commerce with that crucial area of the world.

But in doing this, we have made sure that we address this question peacefully, not injecting American military forces into combat, but letting the strength of our nation be felt in a beneficial way. This, I believe, has assured that our interests will be protected in the Persian Gulf region, as we have done in the Middle East and throughout the world.

Smith: Governor Reagan, you have a minute to comment or rebut.

Reagan: Well yes, I question the figure about the decline in defense spending under the two previous Administrations in the preceding eight years to this Administration. I would call to your attention that we were in a war that wound down during those eight years, which of course made a change in military spending because of turning from war to peace. I also would like to point out that Republican presidents in those years, faced with a Democratic majority in both houses of the Congress, found that their requests for defense budgets were very often cut.

Now, Gerald Ford left a five-year projected plan for a military build-up to restore our defenses, and President Carter's Administration reduced that by 38%, cut 60 ships out of the Navy building program that had been proposed, and stopped the . . . the B-1, delayed the Cruise missile, stopped the production line for the Minuteman missile, stopped the Trident or delayed the Trident submarine, and now is planning a mobile military force that can be delivered to various spots in the world, which does make me question his assaults on whether I am the one who is quick to look for use of force.

Smith: President Carter, you have the last word on this question.

Carter: Well, there are various elements of defense. One is to control nuclear weapons, which I hope we'll get to later on because that is the most important single issue in this campaign. Another one is how to address troubled areas of the world. I think, habitually, Governor Reagan has advocated the injection of military forces into troubled areas, when I and my predecessors — both Democrats and Republicans — have advocated resolving those troubles in those difficult areas of the world peacefully, diplomatically, and through negotiation. In addition to that, the build-up of military forces is good for our country because we've got to have military strength to preserve the peace. But I'll always remember that the best weapons are the ones that are never fired in combat, and the best soldier is one who never has to lay his life down on the field of battle. Strength is imperative for peace, but the two must go hand in hand.

Smith: Thank you gentlemen. The next question is from Harry Ellis to President Carter.

Inflation and Government Spending

Ellis: Mr. President, when you were elected in 1976, the Consumer Price Index stood at 4.8%. It now stands at more than 12%. Perhaps more significantly, the nation's broader, underlying inflation rate has gone up from 7% to 9%. Now, a part of that was due to external factors beyond U.S. control, notably the more than doubling of oil prices by OPEC last year. Because the United States remains vulnerable to such external shocks, can inflation in fact be controlled? If so, what measures would you pursue in a second term?

Carter: Again it's important to put the situation in perspective. In 1974, we had a so-called oil shock, wherein the price of OPEC oil was raised to an extraordinary degree. We had an even worse oil shock in 1979. In 1974, we had the worst recession, the deepest and most penetrating recession since the Second World War. The recession that resulted this time was the briefest since the Second World War.

In addition, we've brought down inflation. Earlier this year, in the first quarter, we did have a very severe inflation pressure brought about by the OPEC price increase. It averaged about 18% in the first quarter of this year. In the second quarter, we had dropped it down to about 13%. The most recent figures, the last three months, on the third quarter of this year, the inflation rate is 7% — still too high, but it illustrates very vividly that in addition to providing an enormous number of jobs — nine million new jobs in the last three and a half years — that the inflationary threat is still urgent on us.

I notice that Governor Reagan recently mentioned the Reagan-Kemp-Roth proposal, which his own running mate, George Bush, described as voodoo economics, and said that it would result in a 30% inflation rate. And Business Week, which is not a Democratic publication, said that this Reagan-Kemp-Roth proposal — and I quote them, I think — was completely irresponsible and would result in inflationary pressures which would destroy this nation.

So our proposals are very sound and very carefully considered to stimulate jobs, to improve the industrial complex of this country, to create tools for American workers, and at the same time would be anti-inflationary in nature. So to add nine million new jobs, to control inflation, and to plan for the future with an energy policy now intact as a foundation is our plan for the years ahead.

Smith: Mr. Ellis, do you have a follow-up question for Mr. Carter?

Ellis: Yes. Mr. President, you have mentioned the creation of nine million new jobs. At the same time, the unemployment rate still hangs high, as does the inflation rate. Now, I wonder, can you tell us what additional policies you would pursue in a second administration in order to try to bring down that inflation rate? And would it be an act of leadership to tell the American people they are going to have to sacrifice to adopt a leaner lifestyle for some time to come?

Carter: Yes. We have demanded that the American people sacrifice, and they have done very well. As a matter of fact, we're importing today about one-third less oil from overseas than we did just a year ago. We've had a 25% reduction since the first year I was in office. At the same time, as I have said earlier, we have added about nine million net new jobs in that period of time — a record never before achieved.

Also, the new energy policy has been predicated on two factors: One is conservation, which requires sacrifice, and the other one, increase in production of American energy, which is going along very well — more coal this year than ever before in American history, more oil and gas wells drilled this year than ever before in history.

The new economic revitalization program that we have in mind, which will be implemented next year, would result in tax credits which would let business invest in new tools and new factories to create even more new jobs — about one million in the next two years. And we also have planned a youth employment program which would encompass 600,000 jobs for young people. This has already passed the House, and it has an excellent prospect to pass the Senate.

Smith: Now, the same question goes to Governor Reagan. Governor Reagan, would you like to have the question repeated?

Ellis: Governor Reagan, during the past four years, the Consumer Price Index has risen from 4.8% to currently over 12%. And perhaps more significantly, the nation's broader, underlying rate of inflation has gone up from 7% to 9%. Now, a part of that has been due to external factors beyond U.S. control, notably the more than doubling of OPEC oil prices last year, which leads me to ask you whether, since the United States remains vulnerable to such external shocks, can inflation in fact be controlled? If so, specifically what measures would you pursue?

Reagan: Mr. Ellis, I think this idea that has been spawned here in our country that inflation somehow came upon us like a plague and therefore it's uncontrollable and no one can do anything about it, is entirely spurious and it's dangerous to say this to the people. When Mr. Carter became President, inflation was 4.8%, as you said. It had been cut in two by President Gerald Ford. It is now running at 12.7%.

President Carter also has spoken of the new jobs created. Well, we always, with the normal growth in our country and increase in population, increase the number of jobs. But that can't hide the fact that there are 8 million men and women out of work in America today, and 2 million of those lost their jobs in just the last few months. Mr. Carter had also promised that he would not use unemployment as a tool to fight against inflation. And yet, his 1980 economic message stated that we would reduce productivity and gross national product and increase unemployment in order to get a handle on inflation, because in January, at the beginning of the year, it was more than 18%. Since then, he has blamed the people for inflation, OPEC, he has blamed the Federal Reserve system, he has blamed the lack of productivity of the American people, he has then accused the people of living too well and that we must share in scarcity, we must sacrifice and get used to doing with less. We don't have inflation because the people are living too well. We have inflation because the Government is living too well. And the last statement, just a few days ago, was a speech to the effect that we have inflation because Government revenues have not kept pace with Government spending.

I see my time is running out here. I'll have to get this out very fast. Yes, you can lick inflation by increasing productivity and by decreasing the cost of government to the place that we have balanced budgets, and are no longer grinding out printing press money, flooding the market with it because the Government is spending more than it takes in. And my economic plan calls for that. The President's economic plan calls for increasing the taxes to the point that we finally take so much money away from the people that we can balance the budget in that way. But we will have a very poor nation and a very unsound economy if we follow that path.

Smith: A follow-up, Mr. Ellis?

Ellis: Yes. You have centered on cutting Government spending in what you have just said about your own policies. You have also said that you would increase defense spending. Specifically, where would you cut Government spending if you were to increase defense spending and also cut taxes, so that, presumably, Federal revenues would shrink?

Reagan: Well, most people, when they think about cutting Government spending, they think in terms of eliminating necessary programs or wiping out something, some service that Government is supposed to perform. I believe that there is enough extravagance and fat in government. As a matter of fact, one of the secretaries of HEW under Mr. Carter testified that he thought there was $7 billion worth of fraud and waste in welfare and in the medical programs associated with it. We've had the General Accounting Office estimate that there is probably tens of billions of dollars that is lost in fraud alone, and they have added that waste adds even more to that.

We have a program for a gradual reduction of Government spending based on these theories, and I have a task force now that has been working on where those cuts could be made. I'm confident that it can be done and that it will reduce inflation because I did it in California. And inflation went down below the national average in California when we returned the money to the people and reduced Government spending.

Smith: President Carter.

Carter: Governor Reagan's proposal, the Reagan-Kemp-Roth proposal, is one of the most highly inflationary ideas that ever has been presented to the American public. He would actually have to cut Government spending by at least $130 billion in order to balance the budget under this ridiculous proposal. I notice that his task force that is working for his future plans had some of their ideas revealed in The Wall Street Journal this week. One of those ideas was to repeal the minimum wage, and several times this year, Governor Reagan has said that the major cause of unemployment is the minimum wage. This is a heartless kind of approach to the working families of our country, which is typical of many Republican leaders of the past, but, I think, has been accentuated under Governor Reagan.

In California — I'm surprised Governor Reagan brought this up — he had the three largest tax increases in the history of that state under his administration. He more than doubled state spending while he was Governor — 122% increase — and had between a 20% and 30% increase in the number of employees...

Smith: Sorry to interrupt, Mr. Carter.

Carter: ...in California. Thank you, sir.

Smith: Governor Reagan has the last word on this question.

Reagan: Yes. The figures that the President has just used about California is a distortion of the situation there, because while I was Governor of California, our spending in California increased less per capita than the spending in Georgia while Mr. Carter was Governor of Georgia in the same four years. The size of government increased only one-sixth in California of what it increased in proportion to the population in Georgia.

And the idea that my tax-cut proposal is inflationary: I would like to ask the President why is it inflationary to let the people keep more of their money and spend it the way that they like, and it isn't inflationary to let him take that money and spend it the way he wants?

Smith: I wish that question need not be rhetorical, but it must be because we've run out of time on that. Now, the third question to Governor Reagan from William Hilliard.

Urban Decay

Hilliard: Yes. Governor Reagan, the decline of our cities has been hastened by the continual rise in crime, strained race relations, the fall in the quality of public education, persistence of abnormal poverty in a rich nation, and a decline in the services to the public. The signs seem to point toward a deterioration that could lead to the establishment of a permanent underclass in the cities. What, specifically, would you do in the next four years to reverse this trend?

Reagan: I have been talking to a number of Congressmen who have much the same idea that I have, and that is that in the inner city areas, that in cooperation with the local government and the national Government, and using tax incentives and with cooperating with the private sector, that we have development zones. Let the local entity, the city, declare this particular area, based on the standards of the percentage of people on welfare, unemployed, and so forth, in that area. And then, through tax incentives, induce the creation of businesses providing jobs and so forth in those areas. The elements of government through these tax incentives.... For example, a business that would not have, for a period of time, an increase in the property tax reflecting its development of the unused property that it was making wouldn't be any loss to the city because the city isn't getting any tax from that now. And there would simply be a delay, and on the other hand, many of the people who would then be given jobs are presently wards of the Government, and it wouldn't hurt to give them a tax incentive, because they ... that wouldn't be costing Government anything either.

I think there are things to do in this regard. I stood in the South Bronx on the exact spot that President Carter stood on in 1977. You have to see it to believe it. It looks like a bombed-out city — great, gaunt skeletons of buildings, windows smashed out, painted on one of them "Unkept promises;" on another,

"Despair." And this was the spot at which President Carter had promised that he was going to bring in a vast program to rebuild this department. There are whole ... or this area ... there are whole blocks of land that are left bare, just bulldozed down flat. And nothing has been done, and they are now charging to take tourists there to see this terrible desolation. I talked to a man just briefly there who asked me one simple question: "Do I have reason to hope that I can someday take care of my family again? Nothing has been done."

Smith: Follow-up, Mr. Hilliard?

Racial Inequities

Hilliard: Yes, Governor Reagan. Blacks and other non-whites are increasing in numbers in our cities. Many of them feel that they are facing a hostility from whites that prevents them from joining the economic mainstream of our society. There is racial confrontation in the schools, on jobs, and in housing, as non-whites seek to reap the benefits of a free society. What do you think is the nation's future as a multi-racial society?

Reagan: I believe in it. I am eternally optimistic, and I happen to believe that we've made great progress from the days when I was young and when this country didn't even know it had a racial problem. I know those things can grow out of despair in an inner city, when there's hopelessness at home, lack of work, and so forth. But I believe that all of us together, and I believe the Presidency is what Teddy Roosevelt said it was. It's a bully pulpit. And I think that something can be done from there, because a goal for all of us should be that one day, things will be done neither because of nor in spite of any of the differences between us — ethnic differences or racial differences, whatever they may be — that we will have total equal opportunity for all people. And I would do everything I could in my power to bring that about.

Smith: Mr. Hilliard, would you repeat your question for President Carter?

Hilliard: President Carter, the decline of our cities has been hastened by the continual rise in crime, strained race relations, the fall in the quality of public education, persistence of abnormal poverty in a rich nation, and a decline in services to the public. The signs seem to point toward a deterioration that could lead to the establishment of a permanent underclass in the cities. What, specifically, would you do in the next four years to reverse this trend?

Carter: Thank you, Mr. Hilliard. When I was campaigning in 1976, everywhere I went, the mayors and local officials were in despair about the rapidly deteriorating central cities of our nation. We initiated a very fine urban renewal program, working with the mayors, the governors, and other interested officials. This has been a very successful effort. That's one of the main reasons that we've had such an increase in the number of people employed. Of the nine million people put to work in new jobs since I've been in office, 1.3 million of those has been among black Americans, and another million among those who speak Spanish.

We now are planning to continue the revitalization program with increased commitments of rapid transit, mass transit. Under the windfall profits tax, we expect to spend about $43 billion in the next 10 years to rebuild the transportation systems of our country. We also are pursuing housing programs. We've had a 73% increase in the allotment of Federal funds for improved education. These are the kinds of efforts worked on a joint basis with community leaders, particularly in the minority areas of the central cities that have been deteriorating so rapidly in the past.

It's very important to us that this be done with the full involvement of minority citizens. I have brought into the top level, top levels of government, into the White House, into administrative offices of the Executive branch, into the judicial system, highly qualified black and Spanish citizens and women who in the past had been excluded.

I noticed that Governor Reagan said that when he was a young man that there was no knowledge of a racial problem in this country. Those who suffered from discrimination because of race or sex certainly knew we had a racial problem. We have gone a long way toward correcting these problems, but we still have a long way to go.

Smith: Follow-up question?

Hilliard: Yes. President Carter, I would like to repeat the same follow-up to you. Blacks and other non-whites are increasing in numbers in our cities. Many of them feel that they are facing a hostility from whites that prevents them from joining the economic mainstream of our society. There is racial confrontation in the schools, on jobs, and in housing, as non-whites seek to reap the benefits of a free society. What is your assessment of the nation's future as a multi-racial society?

Carter: Ours is a nation of refugees, a nation of immigrants. Almost all of our citizens came here from other lands and now have hopes, which are being realized, for a better life, preserving their ethnic commitments, their family structures, their religious beliefs, preserving their relationships with their relatives in foreign countries, but still holding themselves together in a very coherent society, which gives our nation its strength.

In the past, those minority groups have often been excluded from participation in the affairs of government. Since I've been President, I've appointed, for instance, more than twice as many black Federal judges as all previous presidents in the history of this country. I've done the same thing in the appointment of women, and also Spanish-speaking Americans. To involve them in the administration of government and the feeling that they belong to the societal structure that makes decisions in the judiciary and in the executive branch is a very important commitment which I am trying to realize and will continue to do so in the future.

Smith: Governor Reagan, you have a minute for rebuttal.

Reagan: Yes. The President talks of Government programs, and they have their place. But as governor, when I was at that end of the line and receiving some of these grants for Government programs, I saw that so many of them were dead-end. They were public employment for these people who really want to get out into the private job market where there are jobs with a future.

Now, the President spoke a moment ago about . . . that I was against the minimum wage. I wish he could have been with me when I sat with a group of teenagers who were black, and who were telling me about their unemployment problems, and that it was the minimum wage that had done away with the jobs that they once could get. And indeed, every time it has increased you will find there is an increase in minority unemployment among young people. And therefore, I have been in favor of a separate minimum for them.

With regard to the great progress that has been made with this Government spending, the rate of black unemployment in Detroit, Michigan is 56%.

Smith: President Carter, you have the last word on this question.

Carter: It's obvious that we still have a long way to go in fully incorporating the minority groups into the mainstream of American life. We have made good progress, and there is no doubt in my mind that the commitment to unemployment compensation, the minimum wage, welfare, national health insurance, those kinds of commitments that have typified the Democratic party since ancient history in this country's political life are a very important element of the future. In all those elements, Governor Reagan has repeatedly spoken out against them, which, to me, shows a very great insensitivity to giving deprived families a better chance in life. This, to me, is a very important difference between him and me in this election, and I believe the American people will judge accordingly.

There is no doubt in my mind that in the downtown central cities, with the, with the new commitment on an energy policy, with a chance to revitalize homes and to make them more fuel efficient, with a chance for our synthetic fuels program, solar power, this will give us an additional opportunity for jobs which will pay rich dividends.

Terrorism Policy

Smith: Now, a question from Barbara Walters.

Walters: Mr. President, the eyes of the country tonight are on the hostages in Iran. I realize this is a sensitive area, but the question of how we respond to acts of terrorism goes beyond this current crisis. Other countries have policies that determine how they will respond. Israel, for example, considers hostages like soldiers and will not negotiate with terrorists. For the future, Mr. President, the country has a right to know, do you have a policy for dealing with terrorism wherever it might happen, and, what have we learned from this experience in Iran that might cause us to do things differently if this, or something similar, happens again?

Carter: Barbara, one of the blights on this world is the threat and the activities of terrorists. At one of the recent economic summit conferences between myself and the other leaders of the Western world, we committed ourselves to take strong action against terrorism. Airplane hijacking was one of the elements of that commitment. There is no doubt that we have seen in recent years — in recent months — additional acts of violence against Jews in France and, of course, against those who live in Israel, by the PLO and other terrorist organizations.

Ultimately, the most serious terrorist threat is if one of those radical nations, who believe in terrorism as a policy, should have atomic weapons. Both I and all my predecessors have had a deep commitment to controlling the proliferation of nuclear weapons. In countries like Libya or Iraq, we have even alienated some of our closest trade partners because we have insisted upon the control of the spread of nuclear weapons to those potentially terrorist countries.

When Governor Reagan has been asked about that, he makes the very disturbing comment that non-proliferation, or the control of the spread of nuclear weapons, is none of our business. And recently when he was asked specifically about Iraq, he said there is nothing we can do about it.

This ultimate terrorist threat is the most fearsome of all, and it's part of a pattern where our country must stand firm to control terrorism of all kinds.

Smith: Ms. Walters, a follow up?

Walters: While we are discussing policy, had Iran not taken American hostages, I assume that, in order to preserve our neutrality, we would have stopped the flow of spare parts and vital war materials once war broke out between Iraq and Iran. Now we're offering to lift the ban on such goods if they let our people come home. Doesn't this reward terrorism, compromise our neutrality, and possibly antagonize nations now friendly to us in the Middle East?

Carter: We will maintain our position of neutrality in the Iran and Iraq war. We have no plans to sell additional material or goods to Iran, that might be of a warlike nature. When I made my decision to stop all trade with Iran as a result of the taking of our hostages, I announced then, and have consistently maintained since then, that if the hostages are released safely, we would make delivery on those items which Iran owns — which they have bought and paid for — also, that the frozen Iranian assets would be released. That's been a consistent policy, one I intend to carry out.

Smith: Would you repeat the question now for Governor Reagan, please, Ms. Walters?

Walters: Yes. Governor, the eyes of the country tonight remain on the hostages in Iran, but the question of how we respond to acts of terrorism goes beyond this current crisis. There are other countries that have policies that determine how they will respond. Israel, for example, considers hostages like soldiers and will not negotiate with terrorists.

For the future, the country has the right to know, do you have a policy for dealing with terrorism wherever it might happen, and what have we learned from this experience in Iran that might cause us to do things differently if this, or something similar, should happen again?

Reagan: Barbara, you've asked that question twice. I think you ought to have at least one answer to it. I have been accused lately of having a secret plan with regard to the hostages. Now, this comes from an answer that I've made at least 50 times during this campaign to the press, when I am asked have you any ideas of what you would do if you were there? And I said, well, yes. And I think that anyone that's seeking this position, as well as other people, probably, have thought to themselves, what about this, what about that? These are just ideas of what I would think of if I were in that position and had access to the information, and which I would know all the options that were open to me.

I have never answered the question, however; second, the one that says, well, tell me, what are some of those ideas? First of all, I would be fearful that I might say something that was presently under way or in negotiations, and thus expose it and endanger the hostages, and sometimes, I think some of my ideas might require quiet diplomacy where you don't say in advance, or say to anyone, what it is you're thinking of doing.

Your question is difficult to answer, because, in the situation right now, no one wants to say anything that would inadvertently delay, in any way, the return of those hostages if there . . . if there is a chance that they're coming home soon, or that might cause them harm. What I do think should be done, once they are safely here with their families, and that tragedy is over — we've endured this humiliation for just lacking one week of a year now — then, I think, it is time for us to have a complete investigation as to the diplomatic efforts that were made in the beginning, why they have been there so long, and when they come home, what did we have to do in order to bring that about — what arrangements were made? And I would suggest that Congress should hold such an investigation. In the meantime, I'm going to continue praying that they'll come home.

Smith: Follow up question.

Walters: I would like to say that neither candidate answered specifically the question of a specific policy for dealing with terrorism, but I will ask Governor Reagan a different follow-up question. You have suggested that there would be no Iranian crisis had you been President, because we would have given firmer support to the Shah. But Iran is a country of 37 million people who are resisting a government that they regarded as dictatorial.

My question is not whether the Shah's regime was preferable to the Ayatollah's, but whether the United States has the power or the right to try to determine what form of government any country will have, and do we back unpopular regimes whose major merit is that they are friendly to the United States?

Reagan: The degree of unpopularity of a regime when the choice is total authoritarianism . . . totalitarianism, I should say, in the alternative government, makes one wonder whether you are being helpful to the people. And we've been guilty of that. Because someone didn't meet exactly our standards of human rights, even though they were an ally of ours, instead of trying patiently to persuade them to change their ways, we have, in a number of instances, aided a revolutionary overthrow which results in complete totalitarianism, instead, for those people. I think that this is a kind of a hypocritical policy when, at the same time, we're maintaining a detente with the one nation in the world where there are no human rights at all — the Soviet Union.

Now, there was a second phase in the Iranian affair in which we had something to do with that. And that was, we had adequate warning that there was a threat to our embassy, and we could have done what other embassies did — either strengthen our security there, or remove our personnel before the kidnap and the takeover took place.

Smith: Governor, I'm sorry, I must interrupt. President Carter, you have a minute for rebuttal.

Carter: I didn't hear any comment from Governor Reagan about what he would do to stop or reduce terrorism in the future. What the Western allies did decide to do is to stop all air flights — commercial air flights — to any nation involved in terrorism or the hijacking of airplanes, or the harboring of hijackers. Secondly, we all committed ourselves, as have all my predecessors in the Oval Office, not to permit the spread of nuclear weapons to a terrorist nation, or to any other nation that does not presently have those weapons or capabilities for explosives. Third, not to make any sales of materiel or weapons to a nation which is involved in terrorist activities. And, lastly, not to deal with the PLO until and unless the PLO recognizes Israel's right to exist and recognizes U.N. Resolution 242 as a basis for Middle East peace.

These are a few of the things to which our nation is committed, and we will continue with these commitments.

Smith: Governor Reagan, you have the last word on that question.

Reagan: Yes. I have no quarrel whatsoever with the things that have been done, because I believe it is high time that the civilized countries of the world made it plain that there is no room worldwide for terrorism; there will be no negotiation with terrorists of any kind. And while I have a last word here, I would like to correct a misstatement of fact by the President. I have never made the statement that he suggested about nuclear pro- liferation and nuclear proliferation, or the trying to halt it, would be a major part of a foreign policy of mine.

Smith: Thank you gentlemen. That is the first half of the debate. Now, the rules for the second half are quite simple. They're only complicated when I explain them. In the second half, the panelists with me will have no follow-up questions. Instead, after the panelists have asked a question, and the candidates have answered, each of the candidates will have two opportunities to follow up, to question, to rebut, or just to comment on his op- ponent's statement.

Governor Reagan will respond, in this section, to the first question from Marvin Stone.

SALT II Treaty

Stone: Governor Reagan — arms control: The President said it was the single most important issue. Both of you have expressed the desire to end the nuclear arms race with Russia, but by methods that are vastly different. You suggest that we scrap the Salt II treaty already negotiated, and intensify the build- up of American power to induce the Soviets to sign a new treaty — one more favorable to us. President Carter, on the other hand, says he will again try to convince a reluctant Congress to ratify the present treaty on the grounds it's the best we can hope to get.

Now, both of you cannot be right. Will you tell us why you think, you are?

Reagan: Yes. I think I'm right because I believe that we must have a consistent foreign policy, a strong America, and a strong economy. And then, as we build up our national security, to restore our margin of safety, we at the same time try to restrain the Soviet build-up, which has been going forward at a rapid pace, and for quite some time.

The Salt II treaty was the result of negotiations that Mr. Carter's team entered into after he had asked the Soviet Union for a discussion of actual reduction of nuclear strategic weapons. And his emissary, I think, came home in 12 hours having heard a very definite nyet. But taking that one no from the Soviet Union, we then went back into negotiations on their terms, because Mr. Carter had cancelled the B-1 bomber, delayed the MX, de- layed the Trident submarine, delayed the Cruise missile, shut down the Missile Man — the three — the Minute Man missile production line, and whatever other things that might have been done. The Soviet Union sat at the table knowing that we had gone forward with unilateral concessions without any reciprocation from them whatsoever.

Now, I have not blocked the Salt II treaty, as Mr. Carter and Mr. Mondale suggest I have. It has been blocked by a Senate in which there is a Democratic majority. Indeed, the Senate Armed Services Committee voted 10 to 0, with seven abstentions, against the Salt II treaty, and declared that it was not in the national security interests of the United States. Besides which, it is illegal, because the law of the land, passed by Congress, says that we cannot accept a treaty in which we are not equal. And we are not equal in this treaty for one reason alone — our B-52 bombers are considered to be strategic weapons; their Backfire bombers are not.

Smith: Governor, I have to interrupt you at that point. The time is up for that. But the same question now to President Carter.

Stone: Yes. President Carter, both of you have expressed the desire to end the nuclear arms race with Russia, but through vastly different methods. The Governor suggests we scrap the

Salt II treaty which you negotiated in Vienna ... or signed in Vienna, intensify the build-up of American power to induce the Soviets to sign a new treaty, one more favorable to us. You, on the other hand, say you will again try to convince a reluctant Congress to ratify the present treaty on the grounds it is the best we can hope to get from the Russians.

You cannot both be right. Will you tell us why you think you are?

Carter: Yes, I'd be glad to. Inflation, unemployment, the cities are all very important issues, but they pale into insignificance in the life and duties of a President when compared with the control of nuclear weapons. Every President who has served in the Oval Office since Harry Truman has been dedicated to the proposition of controlling nuclear weapons.

To negotiate with the Soviet Union a balanced, controlled, observable, and then reducing levels of atomic weaponry, there is a disturbing pattern in the attitude of Governor Reagan. He has never supported any of those arms control agreements — the limited test ban, Salt I, nor the Antiballistic Missile Treaty, nor the Vladivostok Treaty negotiated with the Soviet Union by President Ford — and now he wants to throw into the wastebasket a treaty to control nuclear weapons on a balanced and equal basis between ourselves and the Soviet Union, negotiated over a seven-year period, by myself and my two Republican predecessors.

The Senate has not voted yet on the Strategic Arms Limitation Treaty. There have been preliminary skirmishings in the committees of the Senate, but the Treaty has never come to the floor of the Senate for either a debate or a vote. It's understandable that a Senator in the preliminary debates can make an irresponsible statement, or, maybe, an ill-advised statement. You've got 99 other senators to correct that mistake, if it is a mistake. But when a man who hopes to be President says, take this treaty, discard it, do not vote, do not debate, do not explore the issues, do not finally capitalize on this long negotiation — that is a very dangerous and disturbing thing.

Smith: Governor Reagan, you have an opportunity to rebut that.

Reagan: Yes, I'd like to respond very much. First of all, the Soviet Union ... if I have been critical of some of the previous agreements, it's because we've been out-negotiated for quite a long time. And they have managed, in spite of all of our attempts at arms limitation, to go forward with the biggest military build-up in the history of man.

Now, to suggest that because two Republican presidents tried to pass the Salt treaty — that puts them on its side — I would like to say that President Ford, who was within 90% of a treaty that we could be in agreement with when he left office, is emphatically against this Salt treaty. I would like to point out also that senators like Henry Jackson and Hollings of South Carolina — they are taking the lead in the fight against this particular treaty.

I am not talking of scrapping. I am talking of taking the treaty back, and going back into negotiations. And I would say to the Soviet Union, we will sit and negotiate with you as long as it takes, to have not only legitimate arms limitation, but to have a reduction of these nuclear weapons to the point that neither one of us represents a threat to the other. That is hardly throwing away a treaty and being opposed to arms limitation.

Smith: President Carter?

Carter: Yes. Governor Reagan is making some very misleading and disturbing statements. He not only advocates the scrapping of this treaty — and I don't know what these men that he quotes are against the treaty in its final form — but he also advocates the possibility, he said it's been a missing element, of playing a trump card against the Soviet Union of a nuclear arms race, and is insisting upon nuclear superiority by our own nation, as a predication for negotiation in the future with the Soviet Union.

If President Brezhnev said, we will scrap this treaty, negotiated under three American Presidents over a seven-year period of time, we insist upon nuclear superiority as a basis for future negotiations, and we believe that the launching of a nuclear arms race is a good basis for future negotiations, it's obvious that I, as President, and all Americans, would reject such a proposition. This would mean the resumption of a very dangerous nuclear arms race. It would be very disturbing to American people. It would change the basic tone and commitment that our nation has experienced ever since the Second World War, with all Presidents, Democratic and Republican. And it would also be very disturbing to our allies, all of whom support this nuclear arms treaty. In addition to that, the adversarial relationship between ourselves and the Soviet Union would undoubtedly deteriorate very rapidly.

This attitude is extremely dangerous and belligerent in its tone, although it's said with a quiet voice.

Smith: Governor Reagan?

Reagan: I know the President's supposed to be replying to me, but sometimes, I have a hard time in connecting what he's saying, with what I have said or what my positions are. I sometimes think he's like the witch doctor that gets mad when a good doctor comes along with a cure that'll work.

My point I have made already, Mr. President, with regard to negotiating: it does not call for nuclear superiority on the part of the United States. It calls for a mutual reduction of these weapons, as I say, that neither of us can represent a threat to the other. And to suggest that the Salt II treaty that your negotiators negotiated was just a continuation, and based on all of the preceding efforts by two previous Presidents, is just not true. It was a new negotiation because, as I say, President Ford was within about 10% of having a solution that could be acceptable. And I think our allies would be very happy to go along with a fair and verifiable Salt agreement.

Smith: President Carter, you have the last word on this question.

Carter: I think, to close out this discussion, it would be better to put into perspective what we're talking about. I had a discussion with my daughter, Amy, the other day, before I came here, to ask her what the most important issue was. She said she thought nuclear weaponry — and the control of nuclear arms.

This is a formidable force. Some of these weapons have 10 megatons of explosion. If you put 50 tons of TNT in each one of railroad cars, you would have a carload of TNT — a trainload of TNT stretching across this nation. That's one major war explosion in a warhead. We have thousands, equivalent of megaton, or million tons, of TNT warheads. The control of these weapons is the single major responsibility of a President, and to cast out this commitment of all presidents, because of some slight technicalities that can be corrected, is a very dangerous approach.

Smith: We have to go to another question now, from Harry Ellis to President Carter.

Alternative Fuels

Ellis: Mr. President, as you have said, Americans, through conservation, are importing much less oil today than we were even a year ago. Yet U.S. dependence on Arab oil as a percentage of total imports is today much higher than it was at the time of the 1973 Arab oil embargo, and for some time to come, the loss of substantial amounts of Arab oil could plunge the U.S. into depression.

This means that a bridge must be built out of this dependence. Can the United States develop synthetic fuels and other alternative energy sources without damage to the environment, and will this process mean steadily higher fuel bills for American families?

Carter: I don't think there's any doubt that, in the future, the cost of oil is going to go up. What I've had as a basic commitment since I've been President is to reduce our dependence on foreign oil. It can only be done in two ways: one, to conserve energy — to stop the waste of energy — and, secondly, to produce more American energy. We've been very successful in both cases. We've now reduced the importing of foreign oil in the last year alone by one-third. We imported today 2 million barrels of oil less than we did the same date just a year ago.

This commitment has been opening up a very bright vista for our nation in the future, because with the windfall profits tax as a base, we now have an opportunity to use American technology and American ability and American natural resources to expand rapidly the production of synthetic fuels, yes; to expand rapidly the production of solar energy, yes; and also to produce the traditional kinds of American energy. We will drill more oil and gas wells this year than any year in history. We'll produce more coal this year than any year in history. We are exporting more coal this year than any year in history.

And we have an opportunity now, with improved transportation systems and improved loading facilities in our ports, to see a very good opportunity on a world international market, to replace OPEC oil with American coal as a basic energy source. This exciting future will not only give us more energy security, but will also open up vast opportunities for Americans to live a better life and to have millions of new jobs associated with this new and very dynamic industry now in prospect because of the new energy policy that we've put into effect.

Smith: Would you repeat the question now for Governor Reagan?

Ellis: Governor Reagan, Americans, through conservation, are importing much less oil today than we were even a year ago. And yet, U.S. reliance on Arab oil as a percentage of total imports is much higher today than it was during the 1973 Arab oil embargo. And the substantial loss of Arab oil could plunge the United States into depression.

The question is whether the development of alternative energy sources, in order to reduce this dependence, can be done without damaging the environment, and will it mean for American families steadily higher fuel bills?

Reagan: I'm not so sure that it means steadily higher fuel costs, but I do believe that this nation has been portrayed for too long a time to the people as being energy-poor when it is energy-rich. The coal that the President mentioned — yes, we have it — and yet one-eighth of our total coal resources is not being utilized at all right now. The mines are closed down; there are 22,000 miners out of work. Most of this is due to regulations which either interfere with the mining of it or prevent the burning of it. With our modern technology, yes, we can burn our coal within the limits of the Clean Air Act. I think, as technology improves, we'll be able to do even better with that.

The other thing is that we have only leased out — begun to explore — 2% of our outer continental shelf for oil, where it is believed, by everyone familiar with that fuel and that source of energy, that there are vast supplies yet to be found. Our Government has, in the last year or so, taken out of multiple use millions of acres of public lands that once were — well, they were public lands subject to multiple use — exploration for minerals and so forth. It is believed that probably 70% of the potential oil in the United States is probably hidden in those lands, and no one is allowed to even go and explore to find out if it is there. This is particularly true of the recent efforts to shut down part of Alaska.

Nuclear power: There were 36 power plants planned in this country. And let me add the word safety; it must be done with the utmost of safety. But 32 of those have given up and cancelled their plans to build, and again, because Government regulations and permits, and so forth, take — make it take — more than twice as long to build a nuclear plant in the United States as it does to build one in Japan or in Western Europe.

We have the sources here. We are energy rich, and coal is one of the great potentials we have.

Smith: President Carter, your comment?

Carter: To repeat myself, we have this year the opportunity, which we'll realize, to produce 800 million tons of coal — an unequalled record in the history of our country. Governor Reagan says that this is not a good achievement, and he blames restraints on coal production on regulations — regulations that affect the life and the health and safety of miners, and also regulations that protect the purity of our air and the quality of our water and our land. We cannot cast aside those regulations. We have a chance in the next 15 years, insisting upon the health and safety of workers in the mines, and also preserving the same high air and water pollution standards, to triple the amount of coal we produce.

Governor Reagan's approach to our energy policy, which has already proven its effectiveness, is to repeal, or to change substantially, the windfall profits tax — to return a major portion of $227 billion back to the oil companies; to do away with the Department of Energy; to short-circuit our synthetic fuels program; to put a minimal emphasis on solar power; to emphasize strongly nuclear power plants as a major source of energy in the future. He wants to put all our eggs in one basket and give that basket to the major oil companies.

Smith: Governor Reagan.

Reagan: That is a misstatement, of course, of my position. I just happen to believe that free enterprise can do a better job of producing the things that people need than government can. The Department of Energy has a multi-billion-dollar budget in excess of $10 billion. It hasn't produced a quart of oil or a lump of coal, or anything else in the line of energy. And for Mr. Carter to suggest that I want to do away with the safety laws and with the laws that pertain to clean water and clean air, and so forth. As Governor of California, I took charge of passing the strictest air pollution laws in the United States — the strictest air quality law that has even been adopted in the United States. And we created an OSHA — an Occupational Safety and Health Agency — for the protection of employees before the Federal Government had one in place. And to this day, not one of its decisions or rulings has ever been challenged.

So, I think some of those charges are missing the point. I am suggesting that there are literally thousands of unnecessary regulations that invade every facet of business, and indeed, very much of our personal lives, that are unnecessary; that Government can do without; that have added $130 billion to the cost of production in this country; and that are contributing their part to inflation. And I would like to see us a little more free, as we once were.

Smith: President Carter, another crack at that?

Carter: Sure. As a matter of fact, the air pollution standard laws that were passed in California were passed over the objections of Governor Reagan, and this is a very well-known fact. Also, recently, when someone suggested that the Occupational Safety and Health Act should be abolished, Governor Reagan responded, amen.

The offshore drilling rights is a question that Governor Reagan raises often. As a matter of fact, in the proposal for the Alaska lands legislation, 100% of all the offshore lands would be open for exploration, and 95% of all the Alaska lands, where it is suspected or believed that minerals might exist. We have, with our five-year plan for the leasing of offshore lands, proposed more land to be drilled than has been opened up for drilling since this program first started in 1954. So we're not putting restraints on American exploration, we're encouraging it in every way we can.

Smith: Governor Reagan, you have the last word on this question.

Reagan: Yes. If it is a well-known fact that I opposed air pollution laws in California, the only thing I can possibly think of is that the President must be suggesting the law that the Federal Government tried to impose on the State of California — not a law, but regulations — that would have made it impossible to drive an automobile within the city limits of any California city, or to have a place to put it if you did drive it against their regulations. It would have destroyed the economy of California, and, I must say, we had the support of Congress when we pointed out how ridiculous this attempt was by the Environmental Protection Agency. We still have the strictest air control, or air pollution laws in the country.

As for offshore oiling, only 2% now is so leased and is producing oil. The rest, as to whether the lands are going to be opened in the next five years or so — we're already five years behind in what we should be doing. There is more oil now, in the wells that have been drilled, than has been taken out in 121 years that they've been drilled.

Smith: Thank you Governor. Thank you, Mr. President. The next question goes to Governor Reagan from William Hilliard.

Social Security

Hilliard: Governor Reagan, wage earners in this country — especially the young — are supporting a Social Security system that continues to affect their income drastically. The system is fostering a struggle between the young and the old, and is drifting the country toward a polarization of these two groups. How much longer can the young wage earner expect to bear the ever-increasing burden of the Social Security system?

Reagan: The Social Security system was based on a false premise, with regard to how fast the number of workers would increase and how fast the number of retirees would increase. It is actuarially out of balance, and this first became evident about 16 years ago, and some of us were voicing warnings then. Now, it is trillions of dollars out of balance, and the only answer that has come so far is the biggest single tax increase in our nation's history — the payroll tax increase for Social Security — which will only put a bandaid on this and postpone the day of reckoning by a few years at most.

What is needed is a study that I have proposed by a task force of experts to look into this entire problem as to how it can be reformed and made actuarially sound, but with the premise that no one presently dependent on Social Security is going to have the rug pulled out from under them and not get their check. We cannot frighten, as we have with the threats and the campaign rhetoric that has gone on in this campaign, our senior citizens — leave them thinking that in some way, they're endangered and they would have no place to turn. They must continue to get those checks, and I believe that the system can be put on a sound actuarial basis. But it's going to take some study and some work, and not just passing a tax increase to let the load — or the roof — fall in on the next administration.

Smith: Would you repeat that question for President Carter?

Hilliard: Yes. President Carter, wage earners in this country, especially the young, are supporting a Social Security System that continues to affect their income drastically. The system is fostering a struggle between young and old and is drifting the country toward a polarization of these two groups. How much longer can the young wage earner expect to bear the ever-increasing burden of the Social Security System?

Carter: As long as there is a Democratic president in the White House, we will have a strong and viable Social Security System, free of the threat of bankruptcy. Although Governor Reagan has changed his position lately, on four different occasions, he has advocated making Social Security a voluntary system, which would, in effect, very quickly bankrupt it. I noticed also in The Wall Street Journal early this week, that a preliminary report of his task force advocates making Social Security more sound by reducing the adjustment in Social Security for the retired people to compensate for the impact of inflation.

These kinds of approaches are very dangerous to the security, the well being and the peace of mind of the retired people of this country and those approaching retirement age. But no matter what it takes in the future to keep Social Security sound, it must be kept that way. And although there was a serious threat to the Social Security System and its integrity during the 1976 campaign and when I became President, the action of the Democratic Congress working with me has been to put Social Security back on a sound financial basis. That is the way it will stay.

Smith: Governor Reagan?

Reagan: Well, that just isn't true. It has, as I said, delayed the actuarial imbalance falling on us for just a few years with that increase in taxes, and I don't believe we can go on increasing the tax, because the problem for the young people today is that they are paying in far more than they can ever expect to get out. Now, again this statement that somehow, I wanted to destroy it and I just changed my tune, that I am for voluntary Social Security, which would mean the ruin of it.

Mr. President, the voluntary thing that I suggested many years ago was that with a young man orphaned and raised by an aunt who died, his aunt was ineligible for Social Security insurance because she was not his mother. And I suggested that if this is an insurance program, certainly the person who is paying in should be able to name his own beneficiary. That is the closest

I have every come to anything voluntary with Social Security. I, too, am pledged to a Social Security program that will reassure these senior citizens of ours that they are going to continue to get their money.

There are some changes that I would like to make. I would like to make a change in the regulation that discriminates against a wife who works and finds that she then is faced with a choice between her father's or her husband's benefits, if he dies first, or what she has paid in; but it does not recognize that she has also been paying in herself, and she is entitled to more than she presently can get. I'd like to change that.

Smith: President Carter's rebuttal now.

Carter: These constant suggestions that the basic Social Security System should be changed does call for concern and consternation among the aged of our country. It is obvious that we should have a commitment to them, that Social Security benefits should not be taxed and that there would be no peremptory change in the standards by which Social Security payments are made to retired people. We also need to continue to index Social Security payments, so that if inflation rises, the Social Security payments would rise a commensurate degree to let the buying power of a Social Security check continue intact.

In the past, the relationship between Social Security and Medicare has been very important to providing some modicum of aid for senior citizens in the retention of health benefits. Governor Reagan, as a matter of fact, began his political career campaigning around this nation against Medicare. Now, we have an opportunity to move toward national health insurance, with an emphasis on the prevention of disease, an emphasis on out-patient care, not in-patient care; an emphasis on hospital cost containment to hold down the cost of hospital care for those who are ill, an emphasis on catastrophic health insurance, so that if a family is threatened with being wiped out economically because of a very high medical bill, then the insurance would help pay for it. These are the kinds of elements of a national health insurance, important to the American people. Governor Reagan, again, typically is against such a proposal.

Smith: Governor?

Reagan: When I opposed Medicare, there was another piece of legislation meeting the same problem before the Congress. I happened to favor the other piece of legislation and thought that it would be better for the senior citizens and provide better care than the one that was finally passed. I was not opposing the principle of providing care for them. I was opposing one piece of legislation versus another.

There is something else about Social Security. Of course, it doesn't come out of the payroll tax. It comes out of a general fund, but something should be done about it. I think it is disgraceful that the Disability Insurance Fund in Social Security finds checks going every month to tens of thousands of people who are locked up in our institutions for crime or for mental illness, and they are receiving disability checks from Social Security every month while a state institution provides for all of their needs and their care.

Smith: President Carter, you have the last word on this question.

Carter: I think this debate on Social Security, Medicare, national health insurance typifies, as vividly any other subject tonight, the basic historical differences between the Democratic Party and Republican Party. The allusions to basic changes in the minimum wage is another, and the deleterious comments that Governor Reagan has made about unemployment compensation. These commitments that the Democratic Party has historically made to the working families of this nation, have been extremely important to the growth in their stature and in a better quality of life for them.

I noticed recently that Governor Reagan frequently quotes Democratic presidents in his acceptance address. I have never heard a candidate for President, who is a Republican, quote a Republican president, but when they get in office, they try to govern like Republicans. So, it is good for the American people to remember that there is a sharp basic historical difference between Governor Reagan and me on these crucial issues — also, between the two parties that we represent.

Smith: Thank you Mr. President, Governor Reagan. We now go to another question — a question to President Carter by Barbara Walters.

Opponent's Weaknesses

Walters: Thank you. You have addressed some of the major issues tonight, but the biggest issue in the minds of American voters is yourselves — your ability to lead this country. When many voters go into that booth just a week from today, they will be voting their gut instinct about you men. You have already given us your reasons why people should vote for you, now would you please tell us for this your final question, why they should not vote for your opponent, why his Presidency could be harmful to the nation and, having examined both your opponent's record and the man himself, tell us his greatest weakness.

Carter: Barbara, reluctant as I am to say anything critical about Governor Reagan, I will try to answer your question. First of all, there is the historical perspective that I just described. This is a contest between a Democrat in the mainstream of my party, as exemplified by the actions that I have taken in the Oval Office the last four years, as contrasted with Governor Reagan, who in most cases does typify his party, but in some cases, there is a radical departure by him from the heritage of Eisenhower and others. The most important crucial difference in this election campaign, in my judgment, is the approach to the control of nuclear weaponry and the inclination to control or not to control the spread of atomic weapons to other nations who don't presently have it, particularly terrorist nations.

The inclination that Governor Reagan has exemplified in many troubled times since he has been running for President — I think since 1968 — to inject American military forces in places like North Korea, to put a blockade around Cuba this year, or in some instances, to project American forces into a fishing dispute against the small nation of Ecuador on the west coast of South America. This is typical of his longstanding inclination, on the use of American power, not to resolve disputes diplomatically and peacefully, but to show that the exercise of military power is best proven by the actual use of it.

Obviously, no president wants war, and I certainly do not believe that Governor Reagan, if he were President, would want war, but a President in the Oval Office has to make a judgment on almost a daily basis about how to exercise the enormous power of our country for peace, through diplomacy, or in a careless way in a belligerent attitude which has exemplified his attitudes in the past.

Smith: Barbara, would you repeat the question for Governor Reagan?

Walters: Yes, thank you. Realizing that you may be equally reluctant to speak ill of your opponent, may I ask why people should not vote for your opponent, why his Presidency could be harmful to the nation, and having examined both your opponent's record and the man himself, could you tell us his greatest weakness?

Reagan: Well, Barbara, I believe that there is a fundamental difference — and I think it has been evident in most of the answers that Mr. Carter has given tonight — that he seeks the solution to anything as another opportunity for a Federal Government program. I happen to believe that the Federal Government has usurped powers of autonomy and authority that belong back at the state and local level. It has imposed on the individual freedoms of the people, and there are more of these things that could be solved by the people themselves, if they were given a chance, or by the levels of government that were closer to them.

Now, as to why I should be and he shouldn't be, when he was a candidate in 1976, President Carter invented a thing he called the misery index. He added the rate of unemployment and the rate of inflation, and it came, at that time, to 12.5% under President Ford. He said that no man with that size misery index has a right to seek reelection to the Presidency. Today, by his own decision, the misery index is in excess of 20%, and I think this must suggest something.

But, when I had quoted a Democratic President, as the Presi-

dent says, I was a Democrat. I said many foolish things back in those days. But the President that I quoted had made a promise, a Democrat promise, and I quoted him because it was never kept. And today, you would find that that promise is at the very heart of what Republicanism represents in this country today. That's why I believe there are going to be millions of Democrats that are going to vote with us this time around, because they too want that promise kept. It was a promise for less government and less taxes and more freedom for the people.

Smith: President Carter?

Carter: I mentioned the radical departure of Governor Reagan from the principles or ideals of historical perspective of his own party. I don't think that can be better illustrated than in the case of guaranteeing women equal rights under the Constitution of our nation. For 40 years, the Republican Party platforms called for guaranteeing women equal rights with a constitutional amendment. Six predecessors of mine who served in the Oval Office called for this guarantee of women's rights. Governor Reagan and his new Republican Party have departed from this commitment — a very severe blow to the opportunity for women to finally correct discrimination under which they have suffered.

When a man and a women do the same amount of work, a man gets paid $1.00, a women only gets paid 59 cents. And the equal rights amendment only says that equality of rights shall not be abridged for women by the Federal Government or by the state governments. That is all it says — a simple guarantee of equality of opportunity which typifies the Democratic Party, and which is a very important commitment of mine, as contrasted with Governor Reagan's radical departure from the long-standing policy of his own party.

Smith: Governor Reagan?

Reagan: Yes. Mr. President, once again, I happen to be against the amendment, because I think the amendment will take this problem out of the hands of elected legislators and put it in the hands of unelected judges. I am for equal rights, and while you have been in office for four years and not one single state — and most of them have a majority of Democratic legislators — has added to the ratification or voted to ratify the equal rights amendment. While I was Governor, more than eight years ago, I found 14 separate instances where women were discriminated against in the body of California law, and I had passed and signed into law 14 statutes that eliminated those discriminations, including the economic ones that you have just mentioned — equal pay and so forth.

I believe that if in all these years that we have spent trying to get the amendment, that we had spent as much time correcting these laws, as we did in California — and we were the first to do it. If I were President, I would also now take a look at the hundreds of Federal regulations which discriminate against women and which go right on while everyone is looking for an amendment. I would have someone ride herd on those regulations, and we would start eliminating those discriminations in the Federal Government against women.

Smith: President Carter?

Carter: Howard, I'm a Southerner, and I share the basic beliefs of my region about an excessive government intrusion into the private affairs of American citizens and also into the private affairs of the free enterprise system. One of the commitments that I made was to deregulate the major industries of this country. We've been remarkably successful, with the help of a Democratic Congress. We have deregulated the air industry, the rail industry, the trucking industry, financial institutions. We're now working on the communications industry.

In addition to that, I believe that this element of discrimination is something that the South has seen so vividly as a blight on our region of the country which has now been corrected — not only racial discrimination but discrimination against people that have to work for a living — because we have been trying to pick ourselves up by our bootstraps, since the long depression years, and lead a full and useful life in the affairs of this country. We have made remarkable success. It is part of my consciousness and of my commitment to continue this progress.

So, my heritage as a Southerner, my experience in the Oval

Office, convinces me that what I have just described is a proper course for the future.

Smith: Governor Reagan, yours is the last word.

Reagan: Well, my last word is again to say this: We were talking about this very simple amendment and women's rights. And I make it plain again: I am for women's rights. But I would like to call the attention of the people to the fact that that so-called simple amendment could be used by mischievous men to destroy discriminations that properly belong, by law, to women respecting the physical differences between the two sexes, labor laws that protect them against things that would be physically harmful to them. Those would all, could all be challenged by men. And the same would be true with regard to combat service in the military and so forth.

I thought that was the subject we were supposed to be on. But, if we're talking about how much we think about the working people and so forth, I'm the only fellow who ever ran for this job who was six times president of his own union and still has a lifetime membership in that union.

Smith: Gentlemen, each of you now has three minutes for a closing statement. President Carter, you're first.

Closing Statements

Carter: First of all, I'd like to thank the League of Women Voters for making this debate possible. I think it's been a very constructive debate and I hope it's helped to acquaint the American people with the sharp differences between myself and Governor Reagan. Also, I want to thank the people of Cleveland and Ohio for being such hospitable hosts during these last few hours in my life.

I've been President now for almost four years. I've had to make thousands of decisions, and each one of those decisions has been a learning process. I've seen the strength of my nation, and I've seen the crises it approached in a tentative way. And I've had to deal with those crises as best I could.

As I've studied the record between myself and Governor Reagan, I've been impressed with the stark differences that exist between us. I think the result of this debate indicates that that fact is true. I consider myself in the mainstream of my party. I consider myself in the mainstream even of the bipartisan list of Presidents who served before me. The United States must be a nation strong; the United States must be a nation secure. We must have a society that's just and fair. And we must extend the benefits of our own commitment to peace, to create a peaceful world.

I believe that since I've been in office, there have been six or eight areas of combat evolved in other parts of the world. In each case, I alone have had to determine the interests of my country and the degree of involvement of my country. I've done that with moderation, with care, with thoughtfulness; sometimes consulting experts. But, I've learned in this last three and a half years that when an issue is extremely difficult, when the call is very close, the chances are the experts will be divided almost 50-50. And the final judgment about the future of the nation — war, peace, involvement, reticence, thoughtfulness, care, consideration, concern — has to be made by the man in the Oval Office. It's a lonely job, but with the involvement of the American people in the process, with an open Government, the job is a very gratifying one.

The American people now are facing, next Tuesday, a lonely decision. Those listening to my voice will have to make a judgment about the future of this country. And I think they ought to remember that one vote can make a lot of difference. If one vote per precinct had changed in 1960, John Kennedy would never have been President of this nation. And if a few more people had gone to the polls and voted in 1968, Hubert Humphrey would have been President; Richard Nixon would not.

There is a partnership involved in our nation. To stay strong, to stay at peace, to raise high the banner of human rights, to set an example for the rest of the world, to let our deep beliefs and commitments be felt by others in other nations, is my plan for the future. I ask the American people to join me in this partnership.

Smith: Governor Reagan?

Reagan: Yes, I would like to add my words of thanks, too, to the ladies of the League of Women Voters for making these debates possible. I'm sorry that we couldn't persuade the bringing in of the third candidate, so that he could have been seen also in these debates. But still, it's good that at least once, all three of us were heard by the people of this country.

Next Tuesday is Election Day. Next Tuesday all of you will go to the polls, will stand there in the polling place and make a decision. I think when you make that decision, it might be well if you would ask yourself, are you better off than you were four years ago? Is it easier for you to go and buy things in the stores than it was four years ago? Is there more or less unemployment in the country than there was four years ago? Is America as respected throughout the world as it was? Do you feel that our security is as safe, that we're as strong as we were four years ago? And if you answer all of those questions yes, why then, I think your choice is very obvious as to whom you will vote for. If you don't agree, if you don't think that this course that we've been on for the last four years is what you would like to see us follow for the next four, then I could suggest another choice that you have.

This country doesn't have to be in the shape that it is in. We do not have to go on sharing in scarcity with the country getting worse off, with unemployment growing. We talk about the unemployment lines. If all of the unemployed today were in a single line allowing two feet for each of them, that line would reach from New York City to Los Angeles, California. All of this can be cured and all of it can be solved.

I have not had the experience the President has had in holding that office, but I think in being Governor of California, the most populous state in the Union — if it were a nation, it would be the seventh-ranking economic power in the world — I, too, had some lonely moments and decisions to make. I know that the economic program that I have proposed for this nation in the next few years can resolve many of the problems that trouble us today. I know because we did it there. We cut the cost — the increased cost of government — in half over the eight years. We returned $5.7 billion in tax rebates, credits and cuts to our people. We, as I have said earlier, fell below the national average in inflation when we did that. And I know that we did give back authority and autonomy to the people.

I would like to have a crusade today, and I would like to lead that crusade with your help. And it would be one to take Government off the backs of the great people of this country, and turn you loose again to do those things that I know you can do so well, because you did them and made this country great. Thank you.

Smith: Gentlemen, ladies and gentlemen, for 60 years the League of Women Voters has been committed to citizen education and effective participation of Americans in governmental and political affairs. The most critical element of all in that process is an informed citizen who goes to the polls and votes. On behalf of the League of Women Voters, now, I would like to thank President Carter and Governor Reagan for being with us in Cleveland tonight. And, ladies and gentlemen, thank you and good night.

RONALD REAGAN'S INAUGURAL ADDRESS

Following is the text of President Reagan's inaugural address as delivered from the West Front of the U.S. Capitol on Jan. 20, 1981. Immediately before the 12 noon address, the oath of office was administered by Chief Justice Warren E. Burger.

Senator Hatfield, Mr. Chief Justice, Mr. President, Vice President Bush, Vice President Mondale, Senator Baker, Speaker O'Neill, Reverend Moomaw, and my fellow citizens:

To a few of us here today this is a solemn and most momentous occasion. And, yet, in the history of our Nation it is a commonplace occurrence. The orderly transfer of authority as called for in the Constitution routinely takes place, as it has for almost two centuries, and few of us stop to think how unique we really are. In the eyes of many in the world, this every-4-year ceremony we accept as normal is nothing less than a miracle.

Mr. President, I want our fellow citizens to know how much you did to carry on this tradition. By your gracious cooperation in the transition process you have shown a watching world that we are a united people pledged to maintaining a political system which guarantees individual liberty to a greater degree than any other, and I thank you and your people for all your help in maintaining the continuity which is the hallmark of our Republic.

The business of our nation goes forward. These United States are confronted with an economic affliction of great proportions. We suffer from the longest and one of the worst sustained inflations in our national history. It distorts our economic decisions, penalizes thrift, and crushes the struggling young and the fixed-income elderly alike. It threatens to shatter the lives of millions of our people.

Idle industries have cast workers into unemployment, human misery and personal indignity. Those who do work are denied a fair return for their labor by a tax system which penalizes successful achievement and keeps us from maintaining full productivity.

But great as our tax burden is, it has not kept pace with public spending. For decades we have piled deficit upon deficit, mortgaging our future and our children's future for the temporary convenience of the present. To continue this long trend is to guarantee tremendous social, cultural, political, and economic upheavals.

You and I, as individuals, can, by borrowing, live beyond our means, but for only a limited period of time. Why, then, should we think that collectively, as a nation, we're not bound by that same limitation? We must act today in order to preserve tomorrow. And let there be no misunderstanding — we are going to begin to act beginning today.

The economic ills we suffer have come upon us over several decades. They will not go away in days, weeks, or months, but they will go away. They will go away because we as Americans have the capacity now, as we've had in the past, to do whatever needs to be done to preserve this last and greatest bastion of freedom.

In this present crisis, government is not the solution to our problem; government is the problem. From time to time we've been tempted to believe that society has become too complex to be managed by self-rule, that government by an elite group is superior to government for, by, and of the people. Well, if no one among us is capable of governing himself, then who among us has the capacity to govern someone else. All of us together — in and out of government — must bear the burden. The solutions we seek must be equitable with no one group singled out to pay a higher price.

We hear much of special interest groups. Well, our concern must be for a special interest group that has been too long neglected. It knows no sectional boundaries or ethnic and racial divisions, and it crosses political party lines. It is made up of men and women who raise our food, patrol our streets, man our mines and factories, teach our children, keep our homes, and heal us when we're sick — professionals, industrialists, shopkeepers, clerks, cabbies and truck drivers. They are, in short, "We the people," this breed called Americans.

Well, this administration's objective will be a healthy, vigorous, growing economy that provides equal opportunities for all Americans with no barriers born of bigotry or discrimination. Putting America back to work means putting all Americans back to work. Ending inflation means freeing all Americans from the terror of runaway living costs. All must share in the productive work of this "new beginning," and all must share in the bounty of a revived economy. With the idealism and fair play which are the core of our system and our strength, we can have a strong, prosperous America at peace with itself and the world.

Curbing Federal Powers

So, as we begin, let us take inventory. We are a nation that has a government — not the other way around. And this makes us special among the nations of the Earth. Our government has no power except that granted it by the people. It is time to check and reverse the growth of government which shows signs of having grown beyond the consent of the governed.

It is my intention to curb the size and influence of the Federal establishment and to demand recognition of the distinction between the powers granted to the Federal Government and those reserved to the States or to the people. All of us need to be reminded that the Federal government did not create the states; the states created the Federal Government.

Now, so there will be no misunderstanding, it's not my intention to do away with government. It is rather to make it work — work with us, not over us; to stand by our side, not ride on our back. Government can and must provide opportunity, not smother it; foster productivity, not stifle it.

If we look to the answer as to why for so many years we achieved so much, prospered as no other people on Earth, it was because here in this land we unleashed the energy and individual genius of man to a greater extent than had ever been done before. Freedom and the dignity of the individual have been more available and assured here than in any other place on Earth. The price for this freedom at times has been high. But we have never been unwilling to pay that price.

It is no coincidence that our present troubles parallel and are proportionate to the intervention and intrusion in our lives that result from unnecessary and excessive growth of government. It is time for us to realize that we are too great a nation to limit ourselves to small dreams. We're not, as some would have us believe, doomed to an inevitable decline. I do not believe in a fate that will fall on us no matter what we do. I do believe in a fate that will fall on us if we do nothing. So, with all the creative energy at our command, let us begin an era of national renewal. Let us renew our determination, our courage, and our strength. And let us renew our faith and our hope.

We have every right to dream heroic dreams. Those who say that we're in a time when there are no heroes, they just don't know where to look. You can see heroes every day going in and out of factory gates. Others, a handful in number, produce enough food to feed all of us and much of the world beyond. You meet heroes across a counter. And they're on both sides of that counter. There are entrepreneurs with faith in themselves and faith in an idea who create new jobs, new wealth and opportunity. They're individuals and families whose taxes support the government and whose voluntary gifts support church, charity, culture, art, and education. Their patriotism is quiet but deep. Their values sustain our national life.

Now, I have used the words "they" and "their" in speaking of these heroes. I could say "you" and "your," because I'm addressing the heroes of whom I speak — you, the citizens of this blessed land. Your dreams, your hopes, your goals are going to be the dreams, the hopes and the goals of this administration, so help me God.

We shall reflect the compassion that is so much a part of your makeup. How can we love our country and not love our countrymen; and loving them, reach out a hand when they fall, heal them when they're sick, and provide opportunity to make them self-sufficient so they will be equal in fact and not just in theory?

Can we solve the problems confronting us? Well, the answer is an unequivocal and emphatic yes. To paraphrase Winston Churchill, I did not take the oath I've just taken with the intention of presiding over the dissolution of the world's strongest economy.

In the days ahead I will propose removing the roadblocks that have slowed our economy and reduced productivity. Steps will be taken aimed at restoring the balance between the various levels of government. Progress may be slow, measured in inches and feet, not miles, but we will progress. It is time to reawaken this industrial giant, to get government back within its means, and to lighten our punitive tax burden. And these will be our first priorities, and on these principles there will be no compromise.

On the eve of our struggle for independence a man who might have been one of the greatest among the Founding Fathers, Dr. Joseph Warren, president of the Massachusetts Congress, said to his fellow Americans, "Our country is in danger, but not to be despaired of . . . On you depend the fortunes of America. You are to decide the important question upon which rests the happiness and the liberty of millions yet unborn. Act worthy of yourselves."

U.S.: Exemplar of Freedom

Well, I believe we, the Americans of today, are ready to act worthy of ourselves, ready to do what must be done to ensure happiness and liberty for ourselves, our children, and our children's children. And as we renew ourselves here in our own land, we will be seen as having greater strength throughout the world. We will again be the exemplar of freedom and a beacon of hope for those who do not now have freedom.

To those neighbors and allies who share our freedom, we will strengthen our historic ties and assure them of our support and firm commitment. We will match loyalty with loyalty. We will strive for mutually beneficial relations. We will not use our friendship to impose on their sovereignty, for our own sovereignty is not for sale.

As for the enemies of freedom, those who are potential adversaries, they will be reminded that peace is the highest aspiration of the American people. We will negotiate for it, sacrifice for it; we will not surrender for it now or ever.

Our forbearance should never be misunderstood. Our reluctance for conflict should not be misjudged as a failure of will. When action is required to preserve our national security, we will act. We will maintain sufficient strength to prevail if need be, knowing that if we do so we have the best chance of never having to use that strength.

Above all we must realize that no arsenal or no weapon in the arsenals of the world is so formidable as the will and moral courage of free men and women. It is a weapon our adversaries in today's world do not have. It is a weapon that we as Americans do have. Let that be understood by those who practice terrorism and prey upon their neighbors.

I'm told that tens of thousands of prayer meetings are being held on this day, and for that I am deeply grateful. We are a nation under God, and I believe God intended for us to be free. It would be fitting and good, I think, if on each Inaugural Day in future years it should be declared a day of prayer.

This is the first time in our history that this ceremony has been held, as you've been told, on this West Front of the Capitol. Standing here, one faces a magnificent vista, opening up on this city's special beauty and history. At the end of this open mall are those shrines to the giants on whose shoulders we stand.

Directly in front of me, the monument to a monumental man, George Washington, father of our country. A man of humility who came to greatness reluctantly. He led America out of revolutionary victory into infant nationhood. Off to one side, the stately memorial to Thomas Jefferson. The Declaration of Independence flames with his eloquence. And then, beyond the Reflecting Pool, the dignified columns of the Lincoln Memorial. Whoever would understand in his heart the meaning of America will find it in the life of Abraham Lincoln.

Beyond those monuments to heroism is the Potomac River, and on the far shore the sloping hills of Arlington National Cemetery with its row upon row of simple white markers bearing crosses or Stars of David. They add up to only a tiny fraction of the price that has been paid for our freedom.

Each one of those markers is a monument to the kind of hero I spoke of earlier. Their lives ended in places called Belleau Wood, The Argonne, Omaha Beach, Salerno and halfway around the world on Guadalcanal, Tarawa, Pork Chop Hill, the Chosin Reservoir, and in a hundred rice paddies and jungles of a place called Vietnam.

Under one such a marker lies a young man, Martin Treptow, who left his job in a small town barbershop in 1917 to go to France with the famed Rainbow Division. There, on the western front, he was killed trying to carry a message between battalions under heavy artillery fire.

We're told that on his body was found a diary. On the flyleaf under the heading, "My Pledge," he had written these words: "America must win this war. Therefore I will work, I will save, I will sacrifice, I will endure, I will fight cheerfully and do my utmost, as if the issue of the whole struggle depended on me alone."

The crisis we are facing today does not require of us the kind of sacrifice that Martin Treptow and so many thousands of others were called upon to make. It does require, however, our best effort and our willingness to believe in ourselves and to believe in our capacity to perform great deeds, to believe that together with God's help we can and will resolve the problems which now confront us.

And after all, why shouldn't we believe that? We are Americans.

God bless you.

PRESIDENT REAGAN'S ECONOMIC PROPOSALS TEXT

Following is the text of the address as delivered by President Reagan to a joint session of Congress on Feb. 18, 1981:

Mr. Speaker, Mr. President, distinguished Members of Congress, honored guests, and fellow citizens. Only a month ago, I was your guest in this historic building and I pledged to you my cooperation in doing what is right for this Nation that we all love so much.

I am here tonight to reaffirm that pledge and to ask that we share in restoring the promise that is offered to every citizen by this, the last, best hope of man on earth.

All of us are aware of the punishing inflation which has, for the first time in some 60 years, held to double digit figures for 2 years in a row. Interest rates have reached absurd levels of more than 20 percent and over 15 percent for those who would borrow to buy a home. All across this land one can see newly built homes standing vacant, unsold because of mortgage interest rates.

Almost eight million Americans are out of work. These are people who want to be productive. But as the months go by, despair dominates their lives. The threats of layoffs and unemployment hang over other millions, and all who work are frustrated by their inability to keep up with inflation.

One worker in a Midwest city put it to me this way: He said, "I'm bringing home more dollars than I thought I ever believed I could possibly earn, but I seem to be getting worse off." And he is. Not only have hourly earnings of the American worker, after adjusting for inflation, declined 5 percent over the past 5 years, but in these 5 years, Federal personal taxes for the average family increased 67 percent.

We can no longer procrastinate and hope that things will get better. They will not. Unless we act forcefully, and now, the economy will get worse.

National Debt

Can we who man the ship of state deny it is somewhat out of control? Our national debt is approaching $1 trillion. A few weeks ago I called such a figure — a trillion dollars — incomprehensible. I've been trying ever since to think of a way to illustrate how big a trillion is. The best I could come up with is that if you had a stack of $1,000 bills in your hand only four inches high you would be a millionaire. A trillion dollars would be a stack of $1,000 bills 67 miles high.

The interest on the public debt this year we know will be over $90 billion. And unless we change the proposed spending for the fiscal year beginning October 1, we'll add another almost $80 billion to the debt.

Adding to our troubles is a mass of regulations imposed on the shopkeeper, the farmer, the craftsman, professionals and major industry that is estimated to add $100 billion to the price of things we buy and it reduces our ability to produce. The rate of increase in American productivity, once one of the highest in the world, is among the lowest of all major industrial nations. Indeed, it has actually declined in the last 3 years.

I have painted a pretty grim picure but I think that I have painted it accurately. It is within our power to change this picture and we can act with hope. There is nothing wrong with our internal strengths. There has been no breakdown in the human, technological, and natural resources upon which the economy is built.

Four-point Proposal

Based on this confidence in a system which has never failed us — but which we have failed through a lack of confidence, and sometimes through a belief that we could fine tune the economy and get a tune to our liking — I am proposing a comprehensive four-point program. Let me outline in detail some of the principal parts of this program. You will each be provided with a completely detailed copy of the entire program.

This plan is aimed at reducing the growth in Government spending and taxing, reforming and eliminating regulations which are unnecessary and unproductive or counterproductive, and encouraging a consistent monetary policy aimed at maintaining the value of the currency.

If enacted in full, this program can help America create 13 million new jobs, nearly 3 million more than we would have without these measures. It will also help us gain control of inflation.

Tax Increase Rate Reduction

It is important to note that we are only reducing the rate of increase in taxing and spending. We are not attempting to cut either spending or taxing levels below that which we presently have. This plan will get our economy moving again, increase productivity growth, and thus create the jobs our people must have.

And I am asking that you join me in reducing direct Federal spending by $41.4 billion in fiscal year 1982, along with another $7.7 billion user fees and off-budget savings for a total savings of $49.1 billion.

This will still allow an increase of $40.8 billion over 1981 spending.

Full Funding for Truly Needy

I know that exaggerated and inaccurate stories about these cuts have disturbed many people, particularly those dependent on grant and benefit programs for their basic needs. Some of you have heard from constituents, I know, afraid that social security checks, for example, were going to be taken away from them. I regret the fear that these unfounded stories have caused and I welcome this opportunity to set things straight.

We will continue to fulfill the obligations that spring from our national conscience. Those who through no fault of their own must depend on the rest of us, the poverty stricken, the disabled, the elderly, all those with true need, can rest assured that the social safety net of programs they depend on are exempt from any cuts.

The full retirement benefits of the more than 31 million social security recipients will be continued along with an annual cost of living increase. Medicare will not be cut, nor will supplemental income for the blind, aged, and disabled, and funding will continue for veterans' pensions.

School breakfasts and lunches for the children of low income families will continue, as will nutrition and other special services for the aging. There will be no cut in Project Head Start or summer youth jobs.

All in all, nearly $216 billion worth of programs providing help for tens of millions of Americans — will be fully funded. But government will not continue to subsidize individuals or particular business interests where real need cannot be demonstrated.

And while we will reduce some subsidies to regional and local governments, we will at the same time convert a number of categorical grant programs into block grants to reduce wasteful administrative overhead and to give local government entities and States more flexibility and control. We call for an end to duplication in Federal programs and reform of those which are not cost effective.

Restore Programs to States and Private Sector

Already, some have protested that there must be no reduction in aid to schools. Let me point out that Federal aid to education amounts to only eight percent of the total educational funding. For this eight percent the Federal Government has insisted on a tremendously disproportionate share of control over our schools. Whatever reductions we've proposed in that eight percent will amount to very little in the total cost of education. They will, however, restore more authority to States and local school districts.

Historically the American people have supported by voluntary contributions more artistic and cultural activities than all the other countries in the world put together. I wholeheartedly support this approach and believe that Americans will continue their generosity. Therefore, I am proposing a savings of $85 million in the Federal subsidies now going to the arts and humanities.

There are a number of subsidies to business and industry that I believe are unnecessary. Not because the activities being subsidized aren't of value but because the marketplace contains incentives enough to warrant continuing these activities without a government subsidy. One such subsidy is the Department of Energy's synthetic fuels program. We will continue support of research leading to development of new technologies and more independence from foreign oil, but we can save at least $3.2 billion by leaving to private industry the building of plants to make liquid or gas fuels from coal.

We are asking that another major industry, business subsidy I should say, the Export-Import Bank loan authority, be reduced by one-third in 1982. We are doing this because the primary beneficiaries of tax payer funds in this case are the exporting companies themselves — most of them profitable corporations.

High Cost of Government Borrowing

This brings me to a number of other lending programs in which Government makes low-interest loans. Some of them at an interest rate as low as 2 percent. What has not been very well understood is that the Treasury Department has no money of its own. It has to go into the private capital market and borrow the money. So in this time of excessive interest rates the government finds itself borrowing at an interest rate several times as high as the interest rate it gets back from those it lends the money to. This difference, of course, is paid by your constituents, the taxpayers. They get hit again if they try to borrow because Government borrowing contributes to raising all interest rates.

By terminating the Economic Development Administration we can save hundreds of millions of dollars in 1982 and billions more over the next few years. There is a lack of consistent and convincing evidence that EDA and its Regional Commissions have been effective in creating new jobs. They have been effective in creating an array of planners, grantsmen and professional middlemen. We believe we can do better just by the expansion of the economy and the job creation which will come from our economic program.

Welfare and Unemployment Programs

The Food Stamp program will be restored to its original purpose, to assist those without resources to purchase sufficient nutritional food. We will, however, save $1.8 billion in fiscal year 1982 by removing from eligibility those who are not in real need or who are abusing the program.

Even with this reduction, the program will be budgeted for more than $10 billion.

We will tighten welfare and give more attention to outside sources of income when determining the amount of welfare an individual is allowed. This plus strong and effective work requirements will save $520 million in the next year.

I stated a moment ago our intention to keep the school breakfast and lunch programs for those in true need. But by cutting back on meals for children of families who can afford to pay, the savings will be $1.6 billion in fiscal year 1982.

Let me just touch on a few other areas which are typical of the kinds of reductions we have included in this economic package. The Trade Adjustment Assistance program provides benefits for workers who are unemployed when foreign imports reduce the market for various American products causing shutdown of plants and layoff of workers. The purpose is to help these workers find jobs in growing sectors of our economy. There is nothing wrong with that. But because these benefits are paid out on top of normal unemployment benefits, we wind up paying greater benefits to those who lose their jobs because of foreign competition than we do to their friends and neighbors who are laid off due to domestic competition. Anyone must agree that this is unfair. Putting these two programs on the same footing will save $1.15 billion in just 1 year.

Federal Regulation Burden

Earlier I made mention of changing categorical grants to States and local governments into block grants. We know, of course, that the categorical grant programs burden local and State governments with a mass of Federal regulations and Federal paperwork.

Ineffective targeting, wasteful administrative overhead — all can be eliminated by shifting the resources and decision-making authority to local and State government. This will also consolidate programs which are scattered throughout the Federal bureaucracy, bringing government closer to the people and saving $23.9 billion over the next 5 years.

Our program for economic renewal deals with a number of programs which at present are not cost-effective. An example is Medicaid. Right now Washington provides the States with unlimited matching payments for their expenditures. At the same time we here in Washington pretty much dictate how the States are going to manage these programs. We want to put a cap on how much the Federal Government will contribute but at the same time allow the States much more flexibility in managing and structuring the programs. I know from our experience in California that such flexibility could have led to far more cost-effective reforms. This will bring a savings of $1 billion next year.

Space and Postal Agencies

The space program has been and is important to America and we plan to continue it. We believe, however, that a reordering of priorities to focus on the most important and cost-effective NASA programs can result in a savings of a quarter of a billion dollars.

Coming down from space to the mailbox — the Postal Service has been consistently unable to live within its operating budget. It is still dependent on large Federal subsidies. We propose reducing those subsidies by $632 million in 1982 to press the Postal Service into becoming more effective. In subsequent years, the savings will continue to add up.

The Economic Regulatory Administration in the Department of Energy has programs to force companies to convert to specific fuels. It has the authority to administer a gas rationing plan, and prior to decontrol it ran the oil price control program. With these and other regulations gone we can save several hundreds of millions of dollars over the next few years.

Defense Spending

I'm sure there is one department you've been waiting for me to mention, the Department of Defense. It is the only department in our entire program that will actually be increased over the present budgeted figure.

But even here there was no exemption. The Department of Defense came up with a number of cuts which reduced the budget increase needed to restore our military balance. These measures will save $2.9 billion in 1982 outlays and by 1986 a total of $28.2 billion will have been saved. Perhaps I should say will have been made available for the necessary things that we must do. The aim will be to provide the most effective defense for the lowest possible cost.

I believe that my duty as President requires that I recommend increases in defense spending over the coming years.

I know that you are aware but I think it bears saying again that since 1970, the Soviet Union has invested $300 billion more in its military forces than we have. As a result of its massive military buildup, the Soviets have made a significant numerical advantage in strategic nuclear delivery systems, tactical aircraft, submarines, artillery and antiaircraft defense. To allow this imbalance to continue is a threat to our national security.

Notwithstanding our economic straits, making the financial changes beginning now is far less costly than waiting and having to attempt a crash program several years from now.

We remain committed to the goal of arms limitation through negotiation. I hope we can persuade our adversaries to come to realistic balanced and verifiable agreements.

But, as we negotiate, our security must be fully protected by a balanced and realistic defense program.

Let me say a word here about the general problem of waste and fraud in the Federal Government. One government estimate indicated that fraud alone may account for anywhere from 1 to 10 percent — as much as $25 billion — of Federal expenditures for social programs. If the tax dollars that are wasted or mismanaged are added to this fraud total, the staggering dimensions of this problem begin to emerge.

New Inspectors General

The Office of Management and Budget is now putting together an interagency task force to attack waste and fraud. We are also planning to appoint as Inspectors General highly trained professionals who will spare no effort to do this job.

No administration can promise to immediately stop a trend that has grown in recent years as quickly as Government expenditures themselves. But let me say this: waste and fraud in the Federal budget is exactly what I have called it before — an unrelenting national scandal — a scandal we are bound and determined to do something about.

Tax Proposals

Marching in lockstep with the whole program of reductions in spending is the equally important program of reduced tax rates. Both are essential if we are to have economic recovery. It's time to create new jobs. To build and rebuild industry, and to give the American people room to do what they do best. And that can only be done with a tax program which provides incentive to increase productivity for both workers and industry.

Our proposal is for a 10-percent across-the-board cut every year for three years in the tax rates for all individual income taxpayers, making a total cut in tax rates of 30 percent. This 3-year reduction will also apply to the tax on unearned income, leading toward an eventual elimination of the present differential between the tax on earned and unearned income.

I would have hoped that we could be retroactive with this, but as it stands the effective starting date for these 10-percent personal income tax rate reductions will be called for as of July 1st of this year.

Again, let me remind you that while this 30 percent reduction will leave the taxpayers with $500 billion more in their pockets over the next five years, it's actually only a reduction in the tax increase already built into the system.

Unlike some past "tax reforms," this is not merely a shift of wealth between different sets of taxpayers. This proposal for an equal reduction in everyone's tax rates will expand our national prosperity, enlarge national incomes, and increase opportunities for all Americans.

Some will argue, I know, that reducing tax rates now will be inflationary. A solid body of economic experts does not agree. And tax cuts adopted over the past three-fourths of a century indicate these economic experts are right. They will not be inflationary. I have had advice that in 1985 our real production of goods and services will grow by 20 percent and will be $300 billion higher than it is today. The average worker's wage will rise (in real purchasing power) 8 percent, and this is in after-tax dollars and this, of course, is predicated on a complete program of tax cuts and spending reductions being implemented.

The other part of the tax package is aimed directly at providing business and industry with the capital needed to modernize and engage in more research and development. This will involve an increase in depreciation allowances, and this part of our tax proposal will be retroactive to January 1st.

The present depreciation system is obsolete; needlessly complex, and is economically counterproductive. Very simply, it bases the depreciation of plant, machinery, vehicles, and tools on their original cost with no recognition of how inflation has increased their replacement cost. We are proposing a much shorter write-off time than is presently allowed: a 5-year write-off for machinery; 3 years for vehicles and trucks; and a 10-year write-off for plant.

In fiscal year 1982 under this plan business would acquire nearly $10 billion for investment. By 1985 the figure would be nearly $45 billion. These changes are essential to provide the new investment which is needed to create millions of new jobs between now and 1985 and to make America competitive once again in the world market.

These won't be make-work jobs, they are productive jobs, jobs with a future.

I'm well aware that there are many other desirable and needed tax changes such as indexing the income tax brackets to protect taxpayers against inflation; the unjust discrimination against married couples if both are working and earning; tuition tax credits; the unfairness of the inheritance tax, especially to the family-owned farm and the family-owned business, and a number of others. But our program for economic recovery is so urgently needed to begin to bring down inflation that I am asking you to act on this plan first and with great urgency. Then I pledge I will join with you in seeking these additional tax changes at the earliest date possible.

Overregulation

American society experienced a virtual explosion in Government regulation during the past decade. Between 1970 and 1979, expenditures for the major regulatory agencies quadrupled, the number of pages published annually in the *Federal Register* nearly tripled, and the number of pages in the *Code of Federal Regulations* increased by nearly two-thirds.

The result has been higher prices, higher unemployment, and lower productivity growth. Overregulation causes small and independent businessmen and women, as well as large businesses, to defer or terminate plans for expansion, and since they are responsible for most of our new jobs, those new jobs just aren't created.

We have no intention of dismantling the regulatory agencies — especially those necessary to protect [the] environment and to ensure the public health and safety. However, we must come to grips with inefficient and burdensome regulations — eliminate those we can and reform the others.

I have asked Vice President Bush to head a Cabinet-level Task Force on Regulatory Relief. Second, I asked each member of my Cabinet to postpone the effective dates of the hundreds of regulations which have not yet been implemented. Third, in coordination with the task force, many of the agency heads have already taken prompt action to review and rescind existing burdensome regulations. Finally, just yesterday, I signed an executive order that for the first time provides for effective and coordinated management of the regulatory process.

Much has been accomplished, but it is only a beginning. We will eliminate those regulations that are unproductive and unnecessary by executive order, where possible, and cooperate fully with you on those that require legislation.

The final aspect of our plan requires a national monetary policy which does not allow money growth to increase consistently faster than the growth of goods and services. In order to curb inflation, we need to slow the growth in our money supply.

We fully recognize the independence of the Federal Reserve System and will do nothing to interfere with or undermine that independence. We will consult regularly with the Federal Reserve Board on all aspects of our economic program and will vigorously pursue budget policies that will make their job easier in reducing monetary growth.

A successful program to achieve stable and moderate growth patterns in the money supply will keep both inflation and interest rates down and restore vigor to our financial institutions and markets.

'Economic Recovery' Proposed

This, then, is our proposal. "America's New Beginning: A Program for Economic Recovery." I don't want it to be simply the plan of my Administration — I'm here tonight to ask you to join me in making it our plan. [Applause, members rising]

I should have arranged to quit right there.

Well, together we can embark on this road, not to make things easy, but to make things better.

Our social, political and cultural as well as our economic institutions can no longer absorb the repeated shocks that have been dealt them over the past decades.

Can we do the job? The answer is yes, but we must begin now.

We are in control here. There is nothing wrong with America that we can't fix. I'm sure there will be some who will raise the familiar old cry, "Don't touch my program — cut somewhere else."

I hope I've made it plain that our approach has been evenhanded; that only the programs for the truly deserving needy remain untouched.

The question is, are we simply going to go down the same path we've gone down before — carving out one special program here, another special program there. I don't think that is what the American people expect of us. More important, I don't think that is what they want. They are ready to return to the source of our strength.

The substance and prosperity of our Nation is built by wages brought home from the factories and the mills, the farms and the shops. They are the services provided in 10,000 corners of America; the interest on the thrift of our people and the returns for their risk-taking. The production of America is the possession of those who build, serve, create and produce.

For too long now, we've removed from our people the decisions on how to dispose of what they created. We have strayed from first principles. We must alter our course.

The taxing power of government must be used to provide revenues for legitimate government purposes. It must not be used to regulate the economy or bring about social change. We've tried that and surely must be able to see it doesn't work.

Spending by Government must be limited to those functions which are the proper province of Government. We can no longer afford things simply because we think of them.

Next year we can reduce the budget by $41.4 billion, without harm to Government's legitimate purposes or to our responsibility to all who need our benevolence. This, plus the reduction in tax rates, will help bring an end to inflation.

In the health and social services area alone the plan we are proposing will substantially reduce the need for 465 pages of law, 1,400 pages of regulations, 5,000 Federal employees who presently administer 7,600 separate grants in about 25,000 separate locations. Over 7 million man and woman hours of work by State and local officials are required to fill out government forms.

I would direct a question to those who have indicated already an unwillingness to accept such a plan. Have they an alternative which offers a greater chance of balancing the budget, reducing and eliminating inflation, stimulating the creation of jobs, and reducing the tax burden? And if they haven't, are they suggesting we can continue on the present course without coming to a day of reckoning?

If we don't do this, inflation and the growing tax burden will put an end to everything we believe in and our dreams for the future. We don't have an option of living with inflation and its attendant tragedy, millions of productive people willing and able to work but unable to find a buyer for their work in the job market.

We have an alternative, and that is the program for economic recovery. True, it will take time for the favorable effects of our proposal to be felt. So we must begin now.

The people are watching and waiting. They don't demand miracles. They do expect us to act. Let us act together.

Thank you and good night.

Bibliography

Books

America's New Beginning: A Program for Economic Recovery. Washington, D.C.: The White House, 1981.

Bartlett, Bruce R. Reaganomics: Supply Side Economics In Action. Westport, Conn.: Arlington House, 1981.

Boyarsky, Bill. The Rise of Ronald Reagan. New York: Random House, 1968.

Broder, David; Cannon, Lou; Johnson, Haynes; Schram, Martin; staff, The Washington Post. The Pursuit of the Presidency 1980. Edited by Richard Harwood. New York: Berkley Books, 1980.

Brown, Edmund G. Reagan and Reality: The Two Californias. New York: Praeger, 1970.

Butler, Stuart M. Enterprise Zones: Pioneering in the Inner City. Washington, D.C.: The Heritage Foundation, 1980.

Cannon, Lou. Ronnie and Jessie: A Political Odyssey. New York: Doubleday, 1969.

Edwards, Lee. Ronald Reagan: A Political Biography. Ottawa, Ill.: Caroline House, 1981.

Heatherly, Charles L., ed. Mandate for Leadership: Policy Management in a Conservative Administration. Washington, D.C.: The Heritage Foundation, 1981.

Hobbs, Charles D. Ronald Reagan's Call to Action: Realistic Democracy. Chicago, Ill.: Nelson-Hall, 1976.

Lewis, Joseph. What Makes Reagan Run: A Political Profile. New York: McGraw-Hill, 1968.

McAllister, Eugene J., ed. Agenda for Progress: Examining Federal Spending. Washington, D.C.: The Heritage Foundation, 1981.

Reagan, Ronald. Creative Society. Old Greenwich, Conn.: Devin-Adair, 1968.

Reagan, Ronald and Hubler, Richard G. Where's the Rest of Me? New York: Duell, Sloan, Pearce, 1965.

Smith, Hedrick; Clymer, Adam; Silk, Leonard; Lindsey, Robert; Burt, Richard. Reagan the Man, the President. New York: Macmillan, 1980.

Valis, Wayne H., ed. The Future Under President Reagan. Westport, Conn.: Arlington House, 1981.

Von Damm, Helen. Sincerely Ronald Reagan. Ottawa, Ill.: Green Hill, 1976.

Articles

Anderson, Robert G. "Supply Side Economics: Miracle Cure or More of the Same?" Freeman, November 1980, pp. 673-676.

Arkes, Hadley. "Reagan's Moment: And America's?" American Spectator, July 1980, pp. 7-10.

"Behind the Campaign Rhetoric: What the Candidates Really Believe About Economic Policy." Business Week, November 3, 1980, pp. 74-78.

Beman, Lewis. "What Supply-Siders Hope to Achieve." Business Week, November 17, 1980, p. 158.

Buchanan, Patrick F. "'Super Cabinet' Destined for Collapse." Human Events, January 10, 1981, pp. 15-17.

Cameron, Juan. "Coming Cuts in Business Taxes." Fortune, November 3, 1980, pp. 71-72.

Cannon, Lou. "The Reagan Years: An Evaluation of the Governor Californians Won't Soon Forget." California Journal, November 1974, pp. 360-366.

Carleson, Robert B. "The Reagan Welfare Reforms." Institute Socioeconomic Studies Journal, Summer 1980, pp. 1-13.

Clymer, Adam. "Reagan: The 1980 Model." New York Times Magazine, July 29, 1979, pp. 22-25.

Collins, Lora S. "Electionomics 1980: Clues to a Reagan Presidency." Across the Board, October 1980, pp. 15-21.

Conaway, John. "Looking at Reagan." Atlantic, October 1980, pp. 32-36.

"The Deep Divisions on the Big Issues." Business Week, November 3, 1980, pp. 78-88.

Deutsch, Richard. "Reagan's African Perspectives." Africa Report, July/August 1980, pp. 4-7.

Dugger, Ronnie. "Ronald Reagan and the Imperial Presidency." The Nation, November 1, 1980, pp. 430-436.

"Haig: How Hawkish Is He?" Human Events, December 27, 1980, pp. 1-8.

Hobbs, C.D. "How Ronald Reagan Governed California." National Review, January 17, 1975, pp. 28-32.

Judis, J. "Battle for Ronald Reagan." Progressive, August 1980, pp. 36-39.

Kirschten, Dick. "Don't Expect Business as Usual From Reagan's Business-Like Cabinet." National Journal, December 20, 1980, pp. 2174-2179.

Kirschten, Dick. "Reagan and the Federal Machine: If It Doesn't Work, Then Fix It." National Journal, January 17, 1981, pp. 88-93.

Kondracke, Morton. "Ronnie's No Barry." New Republic, December 1, 1979, pp. 16-19.

Kramer, Michael. "Will Reagan Give Big Cities the Business?" New York, December 8, 1980, pp. 21-22.

Larson, Dale. "Reagan Rewrites the Record." American Federationist, October 1980, pp. 10-12.

Lekachman, Robert. "Reagan's Price Controls." New Republic, November 22, 1980, pp. 18-20.

Lindsey, R. "What the Record Says About Reagan." New York Times Magazine, June 29, 1980, pp. 12-16.

Louviere, Vernon. "A New Era for Business." Nation's Business, December 1980, pp. 22-28.

"The Major Issues of the 1980 Election Campaign: Pro and Con." Congressional Digest, October 1980, pp. 225-256.

Marshall, Eliot. "An Early Test of Reagan's Economics." Science, January 2, 1981, pp. 29-31.

Minnery, T. "Religious Right: How Much Credit Can It Take for Electoral Landslide?" *Christianity Today,* December 12, 1980, pp. 52-53.

Nations, Richard. "Reagan to the Rescue." *Far Eastern Economic Review,* January 23, 1981, pp. 20-22.

Neill, S. B. "Reagan's Education Record In California." *Phi Delta Kappan,* October 1980, pp. 136-138.

"The New Administration Is the Key."*Business Week,* December 29, 1980, pp. 66-71.

Novak, Robert D. "Reagan's Great Opportunity: The Test of a President Elect." *National Review,* November 28, 1980, pp. 1444-1448.

O'Banion, Kerry. "Reagan's Energy Program: A Time for Conservation." *Nation,* January 3-10, 1981, pp. 16-20.

"Reagan, Black Leaders and Black Voters," *National Review,* August 22, 1980, pp. 1000-1001.

"Reagan: Putting his Philosophy to Work Fast." *Business Week,* November 17, 1980, pp. 154-158.

"Reagan's Advisers: A Winning Team?" *The Economist,* October 25-31, 1980, pp. 58-60.

Rosen, Gerald R. "The Reagan Era." *Dun's Review,* January 1981, pp. 45-47.

Rothschild, Emma. "Reagan and the Real America." *New York Review of Books,* February 5, 1981, pp. 12-18.

Salzman, Ed. "California 'Mafia' in the Reagan White House." *California Journal,* May 1980, pp. 176-178.

Sears, John. "President Reagan." *New York,* November 17, 1980, pp. 22-25.

Smith, Hedrick."Reagan: What Kind of World Leader?" *New York Times Magazine,* November 16, 1980, p. 47.

Steel, Ronald. "War Issues." *New Republic,* November 1, 1980, pp. 16-18.

Stein, J. "Reagan's Plans for Intelligence." *Nation,* July 12, 1980, pp. 40-41.

Tucker, Robert W. "Reagan Without Tears." *New Republic,* May 17, 1980, pp. 22-25.

Walsh, John. "Reagan Years: Regrouping on Education." *Science,* November 28, 1980, pp. 991-992.

Weintraub, Sidney. "False Premises on Inflation: The Economy According to Reagan." *New Leader,* November 17, 1980, p. 6.

"Why Reagan Tapped Donovan for Labor." *Business Week,* December 29, 1980, pp. 46-47.

Wilson, John Q. "Reagan and the Republican Revival." *Commentary,* October 1980, pp. 25-32.

Index